1995

D1503344

Green Cities

Green Cities

ECOLOGICALLY SOUND APPROACHES TO URBAN SPACE

Edited by David Gordon

Montréal · New York

BLACK ROSE BOOKS No. V138
Hardcover ISBN: 1-921689-55-1
Paperback ISBN: 1-921689-54-3

Canadian Cataloguing in Publication Data

Gordon, David
Green cities: ecologically-sound approaches to urban space

Includes bibliographical references.
ISBN: 0-921689-55-1 (bound)
ISBN: 0-921689-54-3 (pbk.)

1. Urban ecology (Biology) I. Title

QH541.5.C6G73 1990   574.5'268   C90-090083-0

Cover Design: Pierre-Paul Pariseau
Editing: Tessa McWatt
Design and Photocomposition: Philip Raphals
Illustrations: Mary-Ellen Irving

Publication of *Green Cities* was made possible by the generous support of the Ontario Ministry of Natural Resources.

The completion of these proceedings was in no small part dependent on the efforts of numerous individuals who were there when needed most. Special thanks and appreciation for many hours of help to some who were always there: Bill Bradley, Tara Harrington, Wayne Heasman, Sally Lerner, Henny Markus, and Joanne Opperman.

Mailing Address

BLACK ROSE BOOKS
C.P. 1258
Succ. Place du Parc
Montréal, Québec
H2W 2R3 Canada

BLACK ROSE BOOKS
340 Nagel Drive
Cheektowaga, New York
14225 USA

A publication of the Institute of Policy Alternatives of Montréal (IPAM)

Printed in Canada

Table of Contents

INTRODUCTION:
A Green Renaissance
David Goode

Take any great city and the human creativity that produces wonder. The skyline of Manhattan, the Grand Canal in Venice, the Champs Elysees in Paris, St. Peter's Square in Rome — all have their magic. There is no doubt that some of the features of cities represent the pinnacle of human creative achievement. Yet, cities also contain conditions ranging from the squalid to the barely habitable, where millions of people survive despite their environment. Looked at as ecosystems most large cities are in a precarious state, dependent as they are on the outside world for their survival, with no built-in mechanisms for long-term sustainability. They are ecosystems in decay. Yet, most of the world's population now lives in urban areas and the growth of huge urban centres is a world-wide trend which will inevitably have profound environmental and social consequences — unless, that is, we can find ecologically sound alternatives as a basis for city life.

The problem is urgent. United Nation's figures for population growth in urban areas throughout the world demonstrate a dramatic growth in recent years. The first city of one million people was Peking

---

David Goode is Head of the London Ecology Unit. Previously he worked for fifteen years with the Nature Conservancy Council where he was Assistant Chief Scientist responsible for research in nature conservation. Since 1982 he has been devoted to bringing an ecological perspective to urban planning in London's environment and has published his personal view of this in "Wild in London." He is one of the most prominent advocates of the need for the green city in Britain and Europe.

in about 1800. By 1900, there were sixteen cities with over one million people and by 1980 the number of such cities had risen to 235. During my father's lifetime (he was born at the beginning of this century), the urban population of the world has grown to the point where it now exceeds the total world population when he was born. In many Western countries the proportion of the population living in urban areas has risen from about 50 percent in 1950 to about 80 percent today.

Future predictions seem more like science fiction, but they are realistic predictions of urban growth on a world scale. By the year 2025 the number of cities with over four million inhabitants will be about 135, which will represent a quarter of the world population. These will include cities with twenty to thirty million inhabitants. We are moving towards a colossal number of people living within built urban environments.

A fundamental consequence of urban growth is the increasing alienation between mankind and the natural world. Natural processes seem no longer relevant to a society dependent on the technological fix. Yet one only has to scratch the surface to reveal how distorted is the ecology and economy of most Western cities. Daily functions depend almost entirely on import of energy and raw materials and export of wastes outside the city limits. As an organism, the Western city is profligate in its energy use, which is exacerbated by the daily migration of commuters to and from the city centre. Viewed on a world scale, such daily travel is a form of madness which we might previously have associated only with lemmings.

But this is just one aspect of urban living that precludes an ecologically sound lifestyle. By building cities in the way we have, we are divorcing ourselves from nature. What contact is there with the seasons in a modern air-conditioned shopping mall with its built-in trees? Sadly, we have banished nature from most of our townscapes and the resulting environment reflects only too well the assumption that we can exist entirely in isolation from the natural world. It seems that urbanites are fast becoming an egocentric species thriving on human culture alone. People are not only unaware of their natural roots but are becoming divorced from all aspects of the natural world upon which they ultimately depend. And, for those who are aware, it may seem impossible for individuals to do anything about it, caught as they are in the intricate web of the modern city.

If this rift between mankind and nature is to be healed, a host of new initiatives is required in the way that we plan, design, and manage cities. We need to consider ways in which people can relate more closely to nature in cities either by protecting the surviving vestiges of the natural world, or by creating completely new opportunities for nature to exist within an urban setting. By examining the ecology of cities, there is much that we can learn about natural processes within the urban environment: which species are able to survive and what restoration is possible. By applying that knowledge we could alter the face of many cities to a dramatic extent.

Initiatives of this kind are now gaining momentum, and we are witnessing new values being established in many cities, especially in Europe and North America. Studies by Herbert Sukopp in West Berlin led the way in the development of a nature conservation program for the city which has provided a model elsewhere in Europe. Many British cities now have nature conservation strategies adopted by planning authorities whilst in the U.S. guidelines for implementing urban wildlife programs are now widely accepted. In all of these the object is to provide a framework for nature conservation in regional or local planning. This assumes that comprehensive surveys will be carried out to identify important wildlife habitats. Policies for conservation must be agreed upon by the authorities concerned, and new criteria adopted for evaluation of wildlife resources which take account of social values. Such approaches have now become well established. They provide a firm basis for the protection of wildlife habitats, few of which would have survived in the face of urban development ten years ago.

But planning only goes so far, and much of the urban environment is determined by landscape designers. Some, who see the value of working with nature, have played a key role in developing new approaches within urban areas. Notable amongst these were Ian McHarg, Nan Fairbrother, Bob Dorney, and Ian Laurie, all of whom have provided inspiration for the creation of more natural landscape. They realized that many of our townscapes are biologically sterile when they could be rich and diverse. Why should so-called landscape schemes end up as green deserts with lollipop trees? Even formal town parks offer opportunities for a richer variety of habitats, but this is rarely achieved. As Laurie says, "All too often nature is driven out of town by those who pay lip service to landscape and amenity values."

One reason is that, until recently, ecology had no place in landscape design. But times are changing and many good design teams now employ ecologists. Naturalistic planting is becoming more widely accepted. But there is still the problem of traditional park managers who regard unkempt vegetation as a blot on the landscape. Even when a flower-rich meadow has been successfully created it may still be in danger from being mowed down by an over zealous tractor driver.

Progress is, nevertheless, being made. Ecological landscapes have long been established in the Netherlands, and in Britain a variety of naturalistic landscapes have been created within new towns. Much has been achieved since a few practitioners met in the early 1970s to discuss ecological approaches to urban landscape design, and when a joint conference between ecologists and landscape designers was held in Britain in 1983, it was clear that there was no shortage of expertise. Our problem lies in overcoming the inertia of current practices and persuading clients, which generally means public authorities, that natural areas in towns are not only possible but also attractive and desirable.

One facet of the dichotomy between people and nature is that even landscape designers may be oblivious to the underlying natural elements of landscape on which a city has been superimposed. How much better it is to capitalize on the vestigial features of that landscape with all its cultural history than to cap it with a twentieth-century veneer. Appreciation of local landscape history, even within a town, can be of utmost importance in retaining a sense of place. All too often vestigial features of an earlier landscape are swept away in the course of new developments — rivers and streams put underground, ponds filled, ancient trees felled. Greening is as much about retaining these links with the past as with ecological restoration. Nor should we forget that an understanding of historical ecology may provide a vital clue to the maintenance of particular habitats, as was the case in establishing prairie habitats at the Wisconsin Arboretum where the role of burning was critical to success.

In those parts of cities where all vestiges of nature have been eradicated, habitat creation must take priority. Examples like Camley Street Natural Park in London, or Toronto's Ecology Park, currently have a vital role as demonstration areas. Others will follow as the value of such places is more widely appreciated. The potential for creation of more extensive wildlife habitats in the urban environment is already well illustrated by examples such as the Tifft Farm wetland nature preserve created on a disused hazardous waste dump on the outskirts of Buffalo, or, more strikingly, the Leslie Street Spit offshore from Toronto which, though totally artificial, has become colonized by a great variety of plant and animal species and now has considerable value as a prime wildlife resource in close proximity to this major city.

If we can create ecology parks to compensate for areas with a deficiency of nature, why should we not create more varied habitats on and around buildings. Green rooftops are becoming accepted in West Germany where the technology is now well developed, and there are clear advantages for river engineering in having reduced run-off from such rooftops during spate conditions.

It is surprising what can be done with a little imagination. On one building in London's Covent Garden, called Odham's Walk, a series of small gardens has been constructed at different levels within court-yards, creating the impression that the building is covered in trees and shrubs. The scheme was not designed to promote wildlife, but it has resulted in a variety of birds breeding in a part of London where they would not normally occur. The building provides a suitable environment for five breeding pairs of blackbirds. None of the surrounding buildings has any greenery whatsoever; nowhere else would you hear birds singing. But the people who live in Odham's walk enjoy the song of the blackbirds. If this can happen by chance how much more might be achieved if we set out to design specifically for wildlife.

What does all this add up to? Much can be achieved by all the professions involved in planning and design of cities to cater more positively for nature. But the top-down approach is only one facet of the solution. Success will not be achieved without the support of local people. I have witnessed this on countless occasions in recent years.

One example which highlights changing attitudes is a tiny fragment of woodland in west London called Gunnersbury Triangle. When developers submitted plans for warehousing, local residents argued strongly that the place was of more value for wildlife and the matter went to a public inquiry which established important precedents for nature conservation in cities. The developers argued that it had no value for nature conservation. It was too small. It had no rarities to speak of, had no significant diversity, and failed to qualify on any of the well-tested criteria used by the government agency for nature conservation. But the crucial factor was its value to local people which was well demonstrated when two hundred residents packed the town hall and argued forcibly that this was the only place where they had contact with the natural world in their neighbourhood.

The inquiry inspector decided in favour of nature conservation largely because of this strength of feeling. People clearly wanted to enjoy nature in the place where they live. The wood is now protected and used by countless children for nature studies and much enjoyed by local residents.

Not all these battles are so successful, but there is little doubt that a major element in success is the strength of feeling generated when people are dispossessed of nature. Studies have demonstrated the emotional benefit to be gained from contact with nature in cities. Freedom, peace, solitude, and harmony are some of the positive benefits, along with spiritual refreshment away from the stress of city life. Even small ecology parks can provide such oases.

There are intellectual benefits too, like learning about nature for the first time. As the young inner-city boy who, gazing into a jam jar wriggling with pond-life, said: "Blimey, there's things what live here!" And when that pond was threatened by a new development, he was one of those who asked: "What's going to happen to all my minibeasts." The emotional commitment on the part of the children was considerable. They took buckets of frogspawn away to other ponds, saving as much as they could before the pond was destroyed.

There is a very strong need for green. It may be a very deep emotion: the need for something green and wild or a place to go for sanctuary or solitude — a place to experience wilderness in the city. The need for such places is at the heart of the concept of a green city whether in the form of ecology parks, city farms, allotment gardens, or just neighbourhood wildspace.

This need is what motivates groups like the Green Guerrillas in New York, who are devoted to setting up and running local community gardens in some of the most run-down districts in the city. The need is greatest where environmental conditions are worst, and it is not surprising to find their endeavours bearing fruit and new values being cherished.

A vital aspect of this grassroots movement in cities is that people are able to take control of something for themselves. Success in establishing a green city must depend on local action and local responsibility, whether it is fish ponds in Calcutta or a paper recycling centre in downtown Detroit. Self-reliance is the key. Bureaucracies may facilitate, but at the end of the day it is local people who make things work.

Which brings us finally to the need for political support. No one can deny that awareness of environmental issues has increased dramatically in recent years. Ozone depletion and the greenhouse effect are now being taken seriously. Yet few politicians are willing to grapple with the underlying problems which go to the heart of the sustainable city. Admittedly, some public authorities have adopted environmental charters, but we have a long way to go before their implementation starts to have a real effect on city life. Acute problems of waste disposal, traffic congestion, and water supply are more likely to induce action in many of our larger cities, as has already occurred in major cities in developing countries where politicians are faced daily with crisis management. Even in Western cities, many of the problems are already becoming critical, as Ann Spirn has so ably demonstrated in her book the *Granite Garden*. Realization may dawn when the public transport system of New York or London is strikebound and people have to take bicycles.

One thing is clear. People do care about their environment and politicians are beginning to recognize that sound environmental policies attract votes. I well remember the mayor of a London borough, surprised by the massive turn-out for the opening of a nature reserve, turn to his Chief Executive and say "You know, this is the most popular thing we have ever done. We had better have another of these." There is hope for the future and I am sure that the philosophy and case histories contained in this book will do much to advance our thinking and bring the green city several steps nearer to fruition.

Part One: What is the Green City?

"Green city" is a relatively new concept, carrying the regionally unique and sometimes conflicting visions of form common to any emerging model. Partly because of this, the green city as we now conceive it is most easily defined at the local level. Biophysically, what should "green" mean other than nurturing of the local flora and fauna?

But the quest to give "green city" a meaning must go further to include an examination of how this primary form of human habitat — the city — might be structured ecologically. At its broadest, this restructuring demands that cultures deliberately choose a path of urban development which diverges radically from the model of the past many centuries. And, perhaps most challenging, it assumes a society that can exercise enough control over patterns of urbanization and individual behaviour to ensure the emergence and persistence of green cities.

The papers in this section describe the path each author has taken in developing a definition of the green city. Taken together, they articulate ideas on culture, globalism, international economics, and local initiative that provide rich food for thought to anyone interested in emerging green city models.

To begin, Michael Hough discusses what might be done to further the greening of the urban landscape. He makes the critical point that if this idea is to become normal practice, "a concerned and environmentally literate community" is required, and that we are, therefore, faced with a very real educational challenge. This insight draws attention to the fact that implementing any idea presented in these pages requires that people be convinced of its worth.

Viewing the green city as an economic entity characterized by local self-reliance, David Morris also sees a high degree of cultural and environmental literacy as a prerequisite to its realization, because only such literacy allows people to recognize that conventional economic models are fundamentally unecological and, therefore, unsustainable. He requires us to view the city as a system which must be in balance in order to endure. And because we must in some sense choose to adopt such a view, the implication is that the development of a profoundly ecological culture must precede or at least parallel the change in perspective.

The view from Latin America and Asia raises issues about urban greening that are best dealt with in a global context. Enrique Leff makes it clear that the seemingly insurmountable barriers to urban greening in Latin America are not the result of any one geographically distinct phenomenon, such as climate, and are beyond the control of any one nation. Many nations are responsible for the conditions that prevail in developing countries and the power to improve these conditions depends upon international cooperation to address such problems as inequities in existing trade practices.

From another perspective, as David Morris suggests, each nation, region, and community can develop urban greening in a locally appropriate manner that may be applicable world-wide. By focusing our energies on projects that enhance local self-reliance, we will inevitably produce models and technologies that are locally applicable in many places. Exchange of mutually respected information and experience among greening communities is seen as the key to this move from local to global.

Assuming that all of this cooperative rescaling of global society can be achieved, we are still left with a perplexing question: Why? What is it about the green city that attracts so much energy and attention? Despite regular predictions of an ecological collapse brought on by the current urban growth model ("more is always better"), it seems unlikely that our interest in the greening of cities is based solely on concerns about our biological sustainability. We have, after all, had thriving "un-green" cities for centuries. William Jordan offers an interesting answer. After several hundred years of malevolence towards wilderness and nature, we are taking the path back, or, more accurately, we are inviting nature to become an integral part of our home. Greening the city might just be our ritualized return to nature, not as a back-to-the-land movement dusted off from the 1960s, but as a process rich in cultural tradition that celebrates our dependence on the natural world by welcoming it into our habitat. Perhaps this urban ecological initiative foreshadows the emergence of an environmentally literate world.

Formed by Natural Process — A Definition of the Green City
Michael Hough

The green city concept is as much a way of thinking as it is a physical reality. It brings together the notions of urbanism and nature, ideas that most people have normally separated into water-tight compartments. There has been an overwhelming propensity to focus on the problems of the larger environment while ignoring the one where most of us live. Putting urbanism and nature together provides us with an opportunity to create cities that are healthy, civilizing, and enriching places in which to live. This may seem obvious today, but urban health has traditionally been seen from the fixed viewpoint of human health. From an environmental perspective, the history of urban growth since the nineteenth century has been one of progressive improvement in human health and progressive deterioration in environmental health. For instance, advances in sanitation to combat disease were based on the development of piped water and sewer systems. But with these clearly necessary technological advances came the seeds of attitudes that continue to plague us today: the throw-away society, misuse of resources, out-of-sight out-of-mind, and so on. Also, there is an inability to make the connection between social benefit and environmental cost. The benefits of sanitation and well drained streets are paid for by the costs of eroded and polluted

Michael Hough is a special consultant with Hough Stansbury Associates, a landscape design firm, holds teaching positions with York University and the University of Toronto, and has lectured in many universities in North America and Europe. He was the chief researcher and designer of the naturalization program undertaken by the National Capital Commission in Ottawa.

rivers and a deteriorated larger environment, which inevitably reflects back on public health. Thus, at its broadest level, the green city means an environmental perspective that begins with the city. This makes sense since all environmental decisions are made by urban people with urban attitudes in urban places. Solutions to the environment as a whole have to begin, therefore, at home.

The green city also embodies the need for environmental ideals that are firmly rooted in pragmatic reality — having your head in the clouds but your feet on the ground. It is about a concerned and environmentally literate community prepared to ensure that beautiful cities are made a reality. It involves an investment in the place, an emotional commitment that surpasses real estate and financial imperatives. On this basis, I suggest some principles that encompass some dimensions of the green city.

Economy of Means

Economy of means is the principle of least effort where one gets the greatest returns for the minimum of energy and effort invested. Current practice usually works the other way around. Traditionally, parks and open spaces have been seen as a nurtured high-maintenance horticultural landscape whose basis for form depends on high-energy inputs and horticultural technology. As a universal solution to urban landscapes, it offers little in diversity, sensory richness, or sense of place. There is a contradiction in values in the desire to nurture this "pedigree" landscape but suppress the "fortuitous" and diverse landscape of naturalizing waste spaces. But changing economic and social conditions are forcing us to reevaluate conventional views of what open space is all about. Necessity generates new solutions. The naturalization of formally manicured landscapes is increasingly becoming an accepted alternative in many places — along road rights-of-way, in some parks and institutions. We have found novel but practical means of dealing with turf maintenance, such as introducing sheep to industrial sites (such as in North York) and geese to look after sewage treatment lands (such as in Vancouver). We find that prairie farmers mow the verges of roads for hay, which provides income while keeping the verges tidy. The rehabilitation of once degraded landscapes with native forests, wetlands, and meadows minimizes costly maintenance and enriches the environment. Reintroducing natural succession to landscape management involves skills different from horticultural maintenance. It involves the transfer of biologically sound rural skills of forestry and land management to the city — namely, the concept of design over time. These processes are more economically viable, produce more useful and richer landscapes, and are environmentally more appropriate. If these benefits are the results of budget cutbacks, then we should support the concept of economy of means.

Diversity

The diversity principle deals with health. If health, in an environmental sense, can be described as the ability to withstand stress, then diversity may also imply health. In the context of the city, diversity has biological and social relevance. Quality of life implies, among other things, being able to choose between one environment and another, and between one place and another. As an experience, it implies interest, pleasure, stimulated senses, and sensory enrichment. A city that has places for foxes, owls, geese, natural woodlands, regenerating fields, and urban wilderness is more interesting and pleasant to live in than those that do not have these places. Cities also need hard urban spaces, busy plazas and markets, noisy as well as quite places, cultivated landscapes, and formal gardens. I would caution against a view of the green city that does not include the urban, or nongreen side of cities. The former is only enhanced by the latter.

Productivity and Environmental Relevance

The notion that parks are exclusively for recreation is derived from the nineteenth century origins of the parks movement and does not fit changing urban values and shifts in urban society. Among today's issues are those that concern the unemployed, aging populations, increasing ethnic immigration and movement to the suburbs. Toronto has one of the largest Chinese and Italian populations in North America and the city's ethnic population exceeds 50 percent of the total population. There are Third World issues such as poverty and hunger and deteriorating social environments. We see vast areas of urban land that overwhelm public space in area but which, for the most part, lie idle and unproductive. A major shift in emphasis is needed, signs of which are already appearing, where urban open space may be seen to perform a productive and environmental role in addition to its traditional recreation and aesthetic functions. This has long been the case in much of Europe where every square inch of open space produces food. During the Second World War in Britain, for instance, the cities produced over 10 percent of the country's total food supply. There were piggeries in Hyde Park and near Oxford Circus in London; agricultural shows took place in the basements of downtown department stores; urban apiary owners had a lot to say about the kind of trees planted in parks; and the inner city acquired a new unity with the countryside. Since the war urban food growing has declined; but we begin to see the reemergence of allotments on utility rights-of-way, market gardens on industrial lands, community gardens initiated in poorer neighbourhoods, and mini urban farms in thousands of ethnic homes — testimony to the fact that open space is seen by many to be more important as productive soil than as non-productive aesthetics. Work in the United States and Britain has shown how important the concept of community gardens and urban farms can be to depressed urban neighbourhoods, in reinstating a sense of pride and social cohesion. They also have the pragmatic and essential function of providing food for needy families where un-employment and poverty have become a major urban problem.

Environmentally, the health of the city is derived from a recogni-tion that its land base, including its parks, should function to im-pound storm water to reduce its impact on the larger environment; to modify urban climate by reforestation of large areas; to create diverse wildlife habitats by protecting and, of course, creating wetlands, forestland, and natural and man-made corridors; and to see urban land for its biological usefulness in the renovation of waste water. Many years of work by Dr. Sopper at Penn State University and the Ontario Ministry of the Environment have shown the practicality under appropriate conditions of using forests and wetlands as living filters.

Capitalizing on the Nature of the Place

Much of the design of our cities seems to have been based on the notion that we live in California or some other sand and sun-drenched utopia. Collectively we spend enormous sums of money and energy freeing ourselves from the constraints of weather indoors, while turning our backs on an outdoor environment that has become increasingly unliveable. It is only reasonable that we should be spending an equivalent amount of effort designing outdoor space for liveability, in winter and in summer.

Another crucial consequence of ignoring climate is the loss of a sense of place — of that sense of connection with a particular urban or naturally indigenous environment. The universal application of high-energy, high-upkeep horticultural landscapes that I was referring to earlier, has created to a great extent that sense of "it could be anywhere" in our open spaces — the design solution independent of place. Having discarded the traditional ways in favour of the new, we need to focus on how designed landscapes can capitalize on what is inherently there rather than falling into the trap of discarding old ideologies for new ones. I have noticed, for instance, that the current enthusiasm for replacing mown turf with native wildflowers, using seed mixes that are often not native to a local region, has the potential to create another form of universal landscape that is also high maintenance.

Environmental Education Begins at Home

Environmental literacy lies at the heart of the green city concept. The perceptions of the city as separated from the natural processes that support life has long been a central problem in environmental thinking. People do not associate nature with a city environment except as domesticated pets — poodles, tabby cats, skyrocket junipers, roses. It has been said that children know more about life in the Florida Everglades and about Bengal tigers from watching television than they do about understanding the natural events in their own back yards. The problem of understanding one's home environment is that it is so familiar. Yet this understanding is central to a larger environmental view. Decisions about water pollution, the preservation of whales, whooping cranes, energy, wilderness, and everything else are made by urban people and are coloured by urban attitudes and perceptions.

Summary

The concept of the green city is a biologically and socially relevant idea; it affords richer and more diverse environments; it is cheaper to do and is entirely practical. It is something that both government and individuals can act on. There is no doubt in my mind that perceptions of what cities are all about are shifting in the face of impending necessity, and necessity is a powerful agent for change. Increasing consciousness of the environment as a whole is modifying views on long-term versus short-term investment in nature. A long-term investment in things like soil fertility, perpetuation of forests, and environmental stability may be seen to be a better bargain than quick profits at the expense of the future. A remark by the biologist and planner Patrick Geddes sums up much of what I have been talking about. He said, "Civics as an art has to do not with imagining an impossible no-place where all is well, but making the most and the best of each and every place, especially of the city in which we live." This seems pretty good advice to follow and a good place to begin.

The Ecological City as a Self-Reliant City
David Morris

Paul Valery, the French poet and philosopher, once said the central problem with our times is that the future is not what it used to be. John Naisbitt talks about ours as the age of parentheses, the age of in-between. The old way of doing things has proven hollow and sometimes quite destructive, though we have not yet learned the rules for the new ways of doing things, so we are in the age of in-between.

Maybe it would be wise to step back a second and look at the assumptions upon which we have built our systems and our cities. I believe that the two fundamental assumptions underlying the way we have designed our communities are the assumption of cheap energy and the assumption of cheap disposal costs. In fact, a barrel of oil that cost five dollars in 1910 cost a little over a dollar a in 1965. The cost of throwing away a ton of garbage remained pretty much the same from 1900 to 1960. We could, as a result, ignore the operating efficiencies and the byproducts of the systems that we developed. The designers of machines, the designers of buildings, and the designers of cities could ignore the efficiencies of those systems and their waste products.

David Morris is a futurist, author, lecturer, and consultant living in St. Paul, Minnesota, and is also a Director and staff member of the Institute for Local Self-Reliance, based in Washington D.C. In a poll conducted by the University of Pittsburgh, his book Neighbourhood Power *was voted one of the two best books on neighbourhoods. David frequently speaks to trade associations, business organizations, and government gatherings on the decentralizing thrust of modern technology and its economic and political implications.*

The result was evident. We developed inefficient equipment and inefficient systems. For example, our cars translate about 20 percent of the energy content of the fuel that is burned in the engine into motive power, into traction going forward or backward. Our electric power plants deliver about 25 percent to 35 percent of the energy that they burn to electricity that comes into homes or businesses. We leave about 50 percent of the plant matter that we grow on the fields, and 80 percent of what we consume is eventually thrown into dumps. The lawn is a good example.

We have developed systems that are fragmented. We fragmented the three fundamental functions of any economy: production, use, and disposal. We have separated the farmer from the kitchen, the power plant from the appliance, the worker from the work place, and, eventually, the bank from the depositor and the borrower, and the government from the citizen. Today, the average commuter travels about twenty to twenty-five miles to work; the average kilowatt hour travels about two hundred miles to do its piece of useful work; and the average food molecule travels a thousand miles to do its piece of useful work. I mentioned the last fact in southern Missouri to a group of farmers, and one of them came up afterward and said to me that I was wrong. He raised chickens. The previous year he had tracked a chicken and discovered that it had travelled 2,500 miles between the time that it was raised and the time that it was eaten.

Cities have become very dependent entities. A city of a hundred thousand people imports two hundred tons of food a day, a thousand tons of fuel a day, and sixty-two thousand tons of water a day. That is one side of the equation. The other side of the equation is that it dumps a hundred thousand tons of garbage a year and forty thousand tons of human waste a year. We have accepted mobility and fragmentation, and we have accepted long distribution systems as the price we pay for progress and development. Indeed, we have elevated separation and long distribution systems to the status of virtues. We have internalized those principles in our way of thinking about our local economies so that if you asked a planner how to promote development in Toronto, he or she would say to look for outside investments to invest in our city and to promote distant markets to buy our goods. Moreover, we need to dump our wastes farther and farther away. That import-export paradigm permeates our way of thinking and a way of planning.

The import-export paradigm is the way our economy runs. It is also the way our waste economy runs. Today, the city of Philadelphia is sending its incinerator ash to Ohio, but that is just a temporary situation. In June, it will be sending it to Panama. That, as I say, is how we internalize the paradigm. We do not think there is anything unusual about it until we put it together and play it back to ourselves, and then something inside us says that it is crazy.

The integrated planetary economy was supposed to make us more secure, but has it? Global trade expands and so do planetary tensions. For example, developing countries are now exporting more and more food to the developed countries. They are doing that to earn the hard currency necessary to repay debts that they incurred primarily to help to build up their export industries. They are exporting more wheat and more commodities to developed countries, but diverting resources means growing less and less food for domestic consumption. An increased export industry has increased malnutrition in developing countries.

The developed countries are in an interesting protectionist/free trade dance, a kind of *pas de deux* of late planetary economics in which each country tries desperately to preserve at least some amount of its sovereignty and its productive assets, while not interfering with free trade and the mobility of resources. We see in each of our countries this idea being played back by our political leaders, and that form of planetary economics has already begun to change our cultures. The argument over metrification has already been resolved in Canada. It is still an ongoing controversy in the United States. Why are we moving toward metrification? Because it is easier? Because God told us to? We move toward metrification because we assume that in a planetary economy it is better to have all parts sized the same in the same form of measurement so it is easier to send them everywhere. We changed our educational system and the way we think, and we had to re-educate an entire population and change our culture so that those parts could be in metric measurement rather than in English measurement.

Today, the major controversy between Canada and the United States around free trade tends to be focused on what we call a subsidy to industry. In the U.S., the White House has argued that Canadian national health insurance is a barrier to free trade because Canadian corporations do not have to pay for health insurance. Therefore, they can price their products noncompetitively against the rest of the world. About nine months ago, the Reagan White House recommended that Canada get rid of its national health insurance in order to promote free and open trade.

This is what happens when we buy into a paradigm and it begins to ricochet back on us. The lubricant for the planetary economy has been the mobility of capital. We believe fervently that capital should be at least as mobile as raw materials and products. Today, we do that with a vengeance. Last year there was twenty times more currency traded than was necessary to underwrite world trade. In fact, if you are in a city and you look at your local productive assets, you will see that the assets will disappear or reappear depending on what is happening with exchange rates throughout the world. Those exchange rates are in turn responsive to rumours, gossip, and today's news, as financial electrons are moved around the world.

We are more reluctant to embrace the unimpeded mobility of the third factor of production, labour, but we are inching up to it. Once again, the White House in the United States, through the Council of Economic Advisors, recommended six months ago that we abolish all barriers to migration, the reason being that we would improve the economy. Obviously, what has happened here is that we have lost sight of a very important tenet of any society: the principal of community. Community, a sense of the place you call your home, becomes unimportant.

An indication of how fragmented our thinking has been and how little we understand the nature of community was demonstrated this week when I, along with seventy million other Americans, watched "Amerika," that very controversial television series which portrays the United States ten years in the future, after the Russians have taken over without a shot being fired because of the apathy and demoralization of Americans who no longer loved or protected their community. Interestingly enough, Chrysler, which was to invest $7 million in advertising during the series, decided to withdraw its advertising. Chrysler is the American automobile company that imports most of its cars, but its commercials have a strong patriotic twist: "The pride is back, back in America." They felt it inappropriate to be underwriting a show which showed America being taken over without a shot. They withdrew that $7 million of advertising, but they did not put that $7 million into local production systems in the United States. Meanwhile, ABC decided to film 50 percent of the show in Toronto. In the mini-series, the Russians burned down the capital, but, in the production of the series, ABC rebuilt the capital in Toronto. The other interesting aspect of "Amerika" is that the Russians weakened America by dismembering us into bioregions. In other words, they made ours an ecological economy and, as a result, devastated us.

We've ignored Benjamin Franklin's advice: the man who would trade independence for security, usually deserves to wind up with neither. We made that trade and have become an increasingly insecure people. And then the rules changed. They changed almost overnight. Cheap energy and cheap disposal were no longer assumptions that we could embrace. Energy prices rose more than 1,000 percent. They have declined in the last five years, but can be expected to reach former levels by the early to mid 1990s. Even more important, disposal costs have risen dramatically in the last few years. In fact, disposal costs have risen more rapidly than have energy prices. In 1975 it typically cost three to five dollars to dispose of a ton of garbage. Today in the United States, it costs between thirty and fifty dollars. In 1970, to dispose of a barrel of hazardous waste cost between five and ten dollars, and most companies just spilled it on the side of the road. Today, it costs about three hundred dollars a barrel, and for many companies the disposal of hazardous waste now has a legal liability attached to it that is infinite. The corporation can dispose of its hazardous waste today, and twenty years from now it might face a lawsuit for more than the total net worth of the company.

Because the underpinnings of the system have changed does not necessarily mean that we have changed. What is important to note about these price changes is that they occurred not because of a real world exhaustion of supply, but because of a change in political attitude. *We* changed the rules. The rising price of oil did not occur

because oil began running out, but because OPEC artificially limited
the supply. The cost of waste disposal did not rise because we suddenly ran out of dump space. It rose because communities, by establishing new disposal rules, artificially limited the supply. We
consciously and willfully changed the cost of doing things the traditional way.

One of the enduring legacies of the environmental movement is
that it has begun to move the price of doing things closer to the cost
of doing things. The price is what we, as individuals, pay. The cost is
what the community, as a whole, pays. What the environmental
movement has begun to do is to internalize the external costs of doing
things into the price. That is what OPEC did as well. It raised the price
of oil to its long-term cost. The environmental regulations have raised
the price of disposal to its long-term cost. These price signals, in turn,
have spurred new technologies and a new sense of entre-
preneurialism.

At the same time that we changed the price structure of the way
we have been doing things, there has been a political revolt against
long distribution systems. I think it began in the early 1970s in northern Minnesota, where the farmers began to notice these gigantic
structures being imposed on their land. High-voltage transmission
lines with 745,000 volts of electricity were being sent through them.
When one of the farmers took a long fluorescent bulb and stood two
hundred feet away from one of these transmission lines and it lit up,
he knew something was wrong. The farmer turned around and began
shooting out the insulators on those electric poles. What ensued was
a war between the farmers and the electric utility companies in which
helicopters were running shotgun as they put the new transmission
lines up. It was the farmers against the FBI in northern Minnesota.
Communities have tried to stop the transport of radioactive waste
through their boundaries, unsuccessfully for the most part. However,
communities have become much more sensitive about being places of
transit for goods and services.

The rules have changed. Political protest is emerging. There is a
sensitivity to it, but so far we have not created a new paradigm, a new
way of organizing our knowledge and our information. A new
paradigm is vital. Marcel Proust once said that the voyage of dis-

covery consists not in seeking new lands but in seeing with new eyes. We must see our communities and our cities with new eyes. It is in pursuing a globe of villages and not a global village that we begin to create that new paradigm. The objective of that new paradigm is to extract the maximum amount of useful work from the local resource base. That may sound like a very modest proposal, but it is a modest proposal with profound repercussions, because the more useful work we extract, the more self-reliant and self-contained we become.

What is meant by useful work? One of the best examples occurred in the early part of the century with Thomas Edison. Thomas Edison was a friend of Henry Ford and one of the great inventors and entrepreneurs. He developed electricity systems and Henry Ford developed a transportation system. They would visit each other frequently. One day Henry Ford came to visit. In that period, everyone had a white picket fence around the single-family detached homes. As Ford entered the gate, he found it hard to push, and he thought it peculiar since Edison was not only a mechanical genius but also a perfectionist. Ford could not understand why such a perfectionist would have such a faulty mechanism in his front yard. After dinner, Ford raised the question to the great inventor and Edison, with a twinkle in his eye, said that the gate was attached to a pump and that as you swung the gate open, you pumped a little water into the home water tank. Every one of Edison's guests did a little useful work. All the other houses in that neighbourhood had gates, and their gates were a little easier to push, but all the guests left behind them at most was just good cheer and no useful work. Edison extracted useful work out of an overlooked resource — muscle power.

The modern day Edison may be a man named Ted Taylor, who is extracting more and more useful work from one of our most abundant resources, the water molecule. Ted Taylor is a physicist who worked in Los Alamos on the design of nuclear bombs in the early 1950s, and he has since moved on to bigger and better things and become infatuated with the characteristics of the water molecule. In the early and middle 1970s, he began to use water to replace electricity. He took a garden variety water hose and he sprayed the water in a fine mist into the winter night air where it froze, not into ice but into a slush, and then dropped into an excavated pit in the ground. He put an insulated cover over that pit, and what he had was stored energy, which could then be used for space conditioning or air conditioning at some later time. He was using the night air and the winter air to replace the need for electricity. In fact, near Buffalo, New York, there is now a cheese factory, the Cutters cheese factory, that operates a Taylor ice pond to cool its food. It would otherwise have to use electricity to run compressors year round. The payback for the ice pond is less than three years.

Ted Taylor then went one step further and began using sea water on the Long Island Sound between New York City and Connecticut. He found that the interesting characteristic of the water molecule is that, as it freezes, it pushes out all impurities and contaminants. As you freeze salt water in the presence of excess water, what results is pure ice and a briny coating. He has found that this desalinization process is half the cost of traditional desalinization using electricity. In the next step, he postulated that if it pushes out contaminants, maybe it can push out chemical contaminants and biological contaminants as well. He began to test it with a polluted aquifer on Long Island. When he was spraying it into the air, he was freezing it into a slush, and the contaminants were pushed out as a way of cleaning up the aquifer.

This year on the northern shore of Long Island, they are building an iceberg. The iceberg will be about two square city blocks long and about a hundred feet high. It will not melt completely during the year, but its peak melting rate is in August which, interestingly enough, turns out to be the point of maximum demand for electricity for cooling and for fresh water. We find, then, that the cycles of nature are compatible with our needs. Ted is now dreaming of the next step, which is to take solar cells, or photovoltaic devices, and electrolyze the water, dividing it into hydrogen and oxygen, and use the hydrogen to speed up the production of methanol from plant matter. Water can displace power plants and oil wells, with the assistance of nature's "ceorl." What did Ted do? He put his mind to it. He applied his genius to the paradigm of local self-reliance.

How far can we carry that particular principle? Estimates that have been done indicate we can reduce by between 50 percent and 60 percent the amount of fuel that is needed for the useful work we produce.

We can extract from the air, the water, and the soil most of what we need. To do that, we need to emphasize production. It is noticeable that the environmental community tends to be split between those who want to extract the maximum amount of productive wealth from a given piece of land, and those who want the land to remain fallow. In fact, the environmentalists have a reputation in the country of being predominantly those who want something just to remain as it is, while what we need to do is to begin to realize that the natural world, in some cases, can be made even more efficient. Although there is an argument between the utilitarians and the deep ecologists, the fact remains that an interaction with the environment can be made more efficient. For example, we convert solar energy into plant matter at about 1 percent conversion efficiency, not including all the fertilizer that we dump into the agricultural products of our society. We can, however, use different forms of plant matter, like single cell algae, that do not have to expend a great deal of energy maintaining their own system, raising the efficiency to 5, 6, and even 7 percent. Up to 7 percent of the solar energy can be converted by photosynthetic processes to cellulose and other raw materials. We can get fifty dry tons per acre of algae, and plant matter can be converted into not only food or fuel, but also chemicals and plastics.

Fifty years ago, a movement of scientists and engineers, called the Chemurgy movement, arose throughout the world. These people looked at their countries and realized that their agricultural sectors, which were major parts of our economies at that time, were in a deep depression because they were producing too much. They had become enormously productive while their markets, the human appetite, had become stable. The Chemurgy movement then said we need to begin to use plant matter as an industrial product and not only as a food supply. That should be our demand. People like Thomas Edison, people like Henry Ford, people like George Washington Carver, and people in other parts of the world, came together and began experimenting with their agricultural surplus as an industrial product. In 1932, the Italian ambassador to Great Britain arrived at the court of St. James dressed in a suit made of milk. Italy had discovered how to weave the casein of protein in milk into clothes. In Germany, the major product was wood and they learned to take trees and make them into plastics and fuel. They drove their cars on wood gasified into fuel.

In 1941, Henry Ford, at the fifteenth annual homecoming day parade in Dearborn, Michigan, unveiled his biological car. It was a car made of soybeans. The body was made of soybeans. The fuel and the tank came from corn and the wheels were made of goldenrods. (Interestingly, the goldenrods had come from Thomas Edison's experiments during the last years of his life.) This was the biological car, and it had some interesting characteristics. Because the soybean plastic weighed half that of a steel-bodied car, the car was lighter and was, therefore, more efficient in terms of fuel consumption. The car, if dented modestly, could easily have the dents knocked back out. If in a serious accident, you did not have to worry about the cuts that you would ordinarily get from steel shards. The inside of the car, because it was an organic material, was warmer in the winter and cooler in the summer, and it was also less noisy.

Henry Ford had hoped that, after World War II, the automobile industry would be a huge market for agricultural products. As we know, after the war, the price of oil collapsed and the Marshall plan from the United States created export markets for the agricultural system, so Henry Ford's dream was postponed. It was postponed for thirty or forty years. Interestingly enough, the term Chemurgy hit its peak in the 1940s. After 1951, at least in the United States, the term was no longer in existence. In 1978, the term was revived. As the assumptions began to change, as we began to confront an agricultural system that had too much plant matter, and as energy and disposal costs changed, we began to change the way we think of our agricultural system.

Self-reliance is, I think, technically feasible, but is it economic? As mentioned previously, the everlasting legacy of the environmental movement will be the discussion of price and cost. If we can shift from a partial cost accounting system to a full cost accounting system, then local self-reliance is economical. What is the cost of driving a truck? What is the cost of driving a car? We should ask not what is the price, but what is the cost. Studies which ask this question have been done and are beginning to become much more sophisticated.

A specific example of price versus cost is the price of rocksalt, which is used a great deal more in the U.S. than it is in Canada. Rocksalt is, of course, a de-icing agent, and it is very cheap (at one to two cents a pound). There is, however, an alternative to rocksalt that can be made out of plant matter. It is called calcium-magnesium acetate and can be produced at present for about twenty cents a pound. That is a price ten to twenty times more than rocksalt.

Rocksalt, however, has some problems. It corrodes the underbody of cars and it corrodes bridges. Consolidated Edison, which is the electrical utility in New York City, found out that rocksalt causes a great deal of problems in their electric supply sewer systems. To test where an electric cable is viable, a needle is placed through the outside cable sheath in order to make contact with the wire. Those little tiny pinholes then become a conduit for water to seep into the wire, bringing salt with it which then begins to corrode the inside of the wire. This can cause an electrical short circuit allowing the current to surge, which then begins to produce a flammable gas. If there is a spark, it explodes. Last year, Consolidated Edison spent $75 million because of exploding manhole covers in New York City. That is a cost of rocksalt.

New York State informally estimated the actual cost of rocksalt at eighty cents a pound, once all the external costs were internalized. Which do we buy? If you tell the public works department that it is going to save everybody a lot of money if they spend twenty cents a pound for calcium magnesium acetate, they will respond that we might save everybody else a lot of money, but we are going to go broke and we have other things to spend our money on. What we need to do as a society is to set up rules that bring price and cost together. As it is right now, for every hundred pounds of rocksalt that is purchased by an individual, the individual pays two dollars and the community is taxed seventy-eight dollars.

When I discuss the global economy and trade as the underpinnings for our economic development, invariably people come up and talk to me about comparative advantage and, invariably, the argument of "bananas" comes up. The argument is that perhaps we should be locally self-reliant, but surely Canada should not, because of the climate, be raising its own bananas. Surely it is cheaper to import those bananas. Perhaps, but, once again, what is the price and the cost? Bananas that come from Central America come from countries which do not permit unions, through companies that do not pay any taxes, and by production methods that have no environmental regulations. I have not done the study, but propose to you if you calculated the amount of dollars that have been spent by the United States in military intervention in Central America and divided that by the number of bananas that are imported into the United States, you would find that it is very costly to import bananas rather than to grow them by yourself.

When looking at economic signals, we need to think holistically. Self-reliance has many economic benefits. System failure becomes a modest risk, and one thing that we are learning as our systems get larger is that the risks also get larger. Twenty years ago a catastrophe meant that there was a flood or an earthquake. Today a catastrophe means the end of the ozone layer. The downside risks of the systems that we have developed often involve the end of the human species.

Local self-reliance also has a downside risk, but the risk is modest. You could try something and it may not work, but the loss is modest. Second, local self-reliance leads to a diversity of experimentation. As communities experiment with different technologies, we accelerate that learning curve. Third, local self-reliance, by definition, reduces pollution because it improves efficiency. Efficiency reduces waste, which means reducing pollution. Fourth, local self-reliance is economical because it recycles money internally for more productive purposes that would otherwise have to be spent on maintaining the system. A crude estimate done a few months ago indicated that fifteen years ago in the United States we were spending between 1 and 3 percent of our overall income for cleaning up after ourselves. Today we are spending almost 15 percent for the same purpose. Finally, an advantage of local self-reliance is that we begin to channel our ingenuity into developing new bodies of knowledge that may be appropriate to a world that has very different conditions. The technologies that we are developing in North America, for example, are technologies appropriate to nations that are resource rich and people poor, while 80 percent of the world's population lives in countries that are resource poor and people rich.

The technologies developed to make Canada self-sufficient or self-reliant will not be appropriate or compatible with the needs of developing countries. But the knowledge developed to make Toronto self-reliant will be of interest to the rest of the world and will become a major export.

The primary benefit of local self-reliance is not economic, it is psychological and social. It improves decision making because the costs of the decision and the benefits from the decision begin to fall on the same community. We do not separate the productive process over long distances. Psychologically, we improve the self-confidence and the security of our communities by miniaturizing the economy.

Local self-reliance means miniaturizing the economy. It means achieving what Fritz Schumacher, the author of *Small is Beautiful* and one of the great British economists of our time, dreamed of, which was local production for local markets from local resources. Is that utopian? It turns out that the scrap-based manufacturing industry can be much smaller than the virgin material based industry. When you recycle materials back to a factory, the factory can convert those into new products competitively at much lower levels of output.

The best available example is the steel industry, where the new technologies are called mini-mills. Mini-mills use electric furnaces and 100 percent scrap. They are very small. A virgin ore based vertically integrated steel mill produces between two and three million tons a year. A mini-mill produces on average 200,000 tons a year. The healthy fast growing part of our steel industry is based on scrap that comes regionally and markets that may also be regional.

In my work with Saint Paul, Minnesota, on developing a home-grown economy, one of the first tasks was a search for locally owned unassigned patents, patents not assigned to the corporation for which they work. We sifted through that patented knowledge to see what would be useful for a home-grown economy. One of the bits of knowledge had come from somebody who had worked at 3M. He was a retired scientist, and he had the task of improving Scotch tape. It appears that 3M is forever trying to improve Scotch tape, and every time they try, they fail and out comes, for example, audio tape or post-it notes. They do not seem able to improve Scotch tape, but each time they fail, they become richer. It is a wonderful process of discovery.

This gentleman's task was to get Scotch tape to stick while wet, which he failed to do. What he succeeded in doing was to develop a glue that, when put in a waste water treatment system, aggregates, or pulls together, all the wastes including the virus wastes and chemical pollutants within that sewage system. They then developed a process which is now in its second year of pilot plant testing in southern California, whereby they dump this glue into the waste water plant with clay, and the glue causes everything to adhere to the clay which then drops to the bottom. They filter it out and then fire up the clay in kilns to about 2,000 degrees Fahrenheit, ending with a lightweight concrete aggregate material that is very competitive for construction purposes.

Interestingly enough, this process, called CCBA, is a chemical process and not a biological process that cleans up the water. Sewage systems do not clean up water right now; they only clean up the biological organisms that are considered contaminants. They do not clean up the heavy metals because that is not yet required. This process does. One of the most interesting aspects of the process is that its scale economies, or its lowest unit costs, peak at the neighbourhood level. Between twenty or thirty thousand user households of that system is the lowest unit cost.

A final example of scale issues relates, once again, to the agricultural sector. Russell Buchanan, a scientist in Maryland, envisions the rise of botanochemical complexes, rather than petrochemical complexes, as we learn to extract from cellulose the same things that we can extract from petrochemicals. One is a hydrocarbon, and one is a carbohydrate. If you put one word on top of the other you will see that they are basically the same. The difference, however, between a botanochemical complex and a petrochemical complex is that it is easy to transport oil over long distances, while it is not easy to transport plant matter over long distances. Botanochemical complexes will then tend to be locally and rurally based, near their source of raw materials and supplies.

I think that local self-reliance can become an economic development strategy, and cities are the best place to try them out for a number of reasons. Most of us live in cities. Cities tend to be large enough to have an internal market to incubate new knowledge. They have a market large enough to initiate businesses and products. Cities are concentrated areas of science and technology. Cities have the ingenuity, the expertise, and the machine tool shops to build the prototypes and to try them out. Toronto's research and development budget is, however, probably zero. Almost no city has a research and development budget. We do not define the issues that need to be solved, and we do not provide our own resources to solve those issues. We could, but we don't.

Economic development must be seen as a means to an end and not an end in and of itself. Albert Einstein once said that perfection of means and confusion of ends characterize our age. We are so mesmerized with technology and development that we forget to ask: Technology for what and development for whom? We have become consumers of change, but we do not know the difference between progress and change. Bertrand Russell once defined the difference in this way. He said that progress was ethical and change was scientific, that change was inevitable and that progress was problematic. In other words, progress is value-laden. As we change, we need to ask ourselves if we are progressing. We can have a green city within a brown world by moving all of our production and disposal systems very far away from our city. However, to truly embrace the ecological motivation behind a green city, we must become responsible for the wastes that are generated for our own convenience. The only way to do that is to begin to move that loop of production and use and disposal back together and back locally.

Vision and Joy of Green Cities
Rashmi Mayur

The demands of civilization are unquenchable. Never before in its long history has this spacious, materially rich and ecologically balanced planet been so ruthlessly exploited and dismembered as now. As the population increases, its tentacles reach the farthest corners of the world, resulting in ecological imbalances and threatening the very survival of life.

Some problems of civilization go back many millennia, but many of them are of the recent past — since the origin of the industrial-urban centres during the last three hundred years. Already, 40 percent of five billion people live in these centres, and 52 percent of 6.1 billion will live in cities and towns at the dawn of the next millennium.

There is a monolithic development in cities around the world. They are asphalted, human-dominated, exploitative, polluted, unhealthy habitats. In short, they are agglomerations — continuously expanding — containing people, machines, and stores with unqualified dominion over humans. Our cities are supremely dominated by people, and they are overgrown monstrosities with gluttonous appetites for material goods and fast declining carrying capacities. Laws

Dr. Rashmi Mayur is the Director of the Urban Environment Institute in Bombay, India. He has advised the United Nations Environment Program and the U.N. Fund for Population Activities, and is President of the Global Futures Network. He is a member of the Environment Committees of six state governments in India; Advisor, Bio-Energy, Office of Technology Assessment, U.S. Congress; Chairman, U.N. Conference on Waste Recycling; and advisor, Governments of Surinam and Costa Rica.

of nature are immutable. Only catastrophe awaits such a system of disharmony.

Green Cities

"Greening cities" is a natural response to the unliveable, entropic, and monstrous cities we have so far created. A green city is a living city by definition. It is an existing city, where the full potentials of all the intricately interconnected forces of nature are realized. In a sense, a green city is complete in its survival capacity. Input and output of energies are well-balanced; or even better, output of energy results in a surplus of value.

Such a city is an agglomeration of biological material and cultural resources with a maximum byproduct of harmoniously nested relationships. Specifically, such a city is designed on the following concepts:

- It is not dominated by humans.
- It is self-sustaining.
- Material and biological constituents are well-balanced and integrated.
- It is a recycling city in which waste is a resource for utilitarian purposes.
- Relationships among all the elements are supportive, cooperative, and not exploitive.
- Such a city contains vast open spaces, gardens, parks, farms, rivulets or streams, coastlines, and wilderness, and is inhabited by humans as well as other species, such as birds, animals, and fish.
- A green city is a conserving city. It is based on the minimal needs principle in order to eliminate or reduce waste. In case any waste is inevitable, it is recycled into useful products.
- It is a clean and healthy city, with minimal or no pollution.
- In a green city, health is paramount. Since diseases and sickness are entropic, emphasis is on natural living, recreation, sports, yoga, exercises, and organic, unprocessed, nonchemicalized, not over-cooked food.

- The city would be planned so that all the elements — humans, nature, material byproducts, technologies — will be harmonized in aesthetic relationships. Houses, schools, roads, parks, trees, skylines, and shopping centres will provide beautiful and rhythmic habitats. Designs, colours, shapes, sizes, and proximity will be based on imagination, innovation, and natural relationships.
- The city will provide for a full range of cultural developments. Theatres, water sports, beaches, public concert halls, friendship gardens, science and history museums, and public plazas will provide opportunities for human interactions, love, friendship, kindness, sharing, and joy. In other words, the city will be an Agora, a festival for joy and full development.

The green city is the ultimate in urban and human planning. It is a challenge to the monstrous, ugly, diseased, corrupt, and exploitative urban centres we have created. It provides human existence and a new dimension to the future course of civilization.

Green City Experiments

There are innumerable experiments around the world for constructing living green cities. In Ogaki, Japan, agriculture is integrated with industries. In Kuala Lumpar, Malaysia, human waste is used for growing fish, and in Rio de Janeiro, Brazil, waste paper, bottles, and cans are picked and separated for recycling. These and other examples are a trickle compared to the avalanche or onslaught of bulldozers, neon lights, dehumanized high consumption, and the greedy, technologically overpowering, violent monstrosities overtaking cities around the globe. Yet these examples give a hope and a challenge.

Greening Bombay

With 9.5 million people, Bombay is a bustling metropolis in a developing country. Like Jakarta, Karachi, Sao Paulo, or Cairo, it is a city run amok in a race with time and has all the pathologies of large Third World cities plus more. It is a city where dreams have become

nightmares and death waits around the corner. The green city movement is an alternative path to development. Here are two examples:

Culture at Traffic Islands

During the last two years, efforts have been made to convert traffic
islands into gardens and cultural centres. At the Haji Ali traffic circle,
a sculpture of eternity is surrounded by a garden. Just nearby, in
another traffic circle, a rural scene within a garden is designed to give
an aesthetic look with a cultural ensemble. Plants process pollution
and the rural stone carvings enliven the urban milieu near a sea shore.
At night a colourful fountain gives the area a visual delight.

Two kilometers to the east, another garden at a traffic circle gives
the area, dominated by people and buildings, a soothing and mellow
effect. In the central business district, near the State Secretariat, the
industrialist, Mr. Kesar Mahendre, has converted an open space near
a paved area into a creeper garden. Dead stones are converted into a
living green garden.

Urban Agriculture

Beyond, as one leaves the city, open spaces near the railway tracks
are vegetable farms, where poor people earn a living supplying
vegetables to the city and assisting in pollution control. As land in the
cities continues to shrink desperately, such creative uses of land offer
many economic and environmental benefits.

The significance of the experiments above can be understood only
if we realize how urbanites are responsible for the miserable plight of
villagers, whose economies are held at ransom by the metro cities.
Bombay, like most cities in Asia and Latin America, receives its food
essentials from villages as far away as eight hundred miles, thereby
preventing villagers from buying them at a price they can afford, and
wasting the large amounts of energy required to transport food items.

Two other programs need special attention for greening cities. In
Poona, a city of two million people, ninety miles east of Bombay,
farmers collect vegetable and fruit waste, feed their cows, and thus
recycle waste in order to supply milk to the city. In Ahmedabad, a
city of three million people three hundred miles north of Bombay,

urban sewage, after primary treatment, is used to grow grass to feed cows and goats to supply milk to the city.

In Bombay a few years ago, an experiment to compost twelve out of 3,500 tons of garbage was initiated. Despite its economic limitations, the project has proved that the solid waste in cities of poor countries is rich in biological materials to provide, after enrichment, excellent organic fertilizer for farmers in the nearby villages. In another successful project in Mexico City in 1983, we transformed an open dilapidated place into a vegetable garden, using urban biological waste, after separating recyclable materials. The project served the same economic and environmental objective as the one in Bombay.

There are many such programs for conservation in cities, but unfortunately their impact is limited. However, it is not the success or failure of these experiments which is debated here. We recognize their limited impact due to the onslaught of the irrelevant and expensive Western techno-economic models, but the purpose cannot be questioned.

Conclusion

The greening cities movement represents a fundamental revolution in our approach to the future of urban civilization. It is not that we are against technologies and development. Our fundamental challenge is to the kind of exploitive, alienated, ecologically ruined and socio-economically disintegrated urban civilization that we have created. We need green and living cities which use sustainable technologies, which are well-integrated, which are small and human, and which are based on planning for conservation and total human development. The present sick and slummy cities of the Third World are an insult to civilization. Hope lies in involving people at every level to work toward redesigning these cities to the dream of mankind, where visions of the future can be realized and the joy of living can be experienced.

Incidental Greening — Saving Resources in Asian Cities
Christine Furedy

Most of the presentations at this conference relate to what cities or governmental and voluntary organizations can do in terms of conscious planning for better ecological balance in the city. We have, however, heard from David Goode about unintended wild places that survive in big metropolises such as London. Asian cities also pursue planned greening, as Rashmi Mayur has mentioned, largely through tree-planting. You can find some wild places in any city, but in Asian cities, which are subject to great pressures as people seek living space, refugees or migrants from rural areas invade spaces that are not normally built up, spreading into the wetlands and steep valleys that might otherwise remain wild.

Against these handicaps to greening in crowded Asian cities, we have to set another type of greening: perhaps it should be called "incidental" or "informal" greening. It is the greening that occurs as a result of what people do, usually very poor people, in very resource-scarce places, in their daily lives, for their own survival, without explicitly thinking of the ecology of the city as a whole. Here, I am referring to "greening" in the broad sense in which it was defined for us in the opening session of this conference — activities that enhance diversity in the relations between the built environment and the natural, that are resource-conserving and ecologically sound.

This includes the growing of plants, even in congested slums, the keeping of animals, and the use of animal and human wastes for food production. These practices have a role in conservation and in main-

Christine Furedy is a Professor of Environmental Studies and Sociology at York University in Toronto.

taining aspects of ecological diversity and conservation in otherwise desperately pressured cities, but they are not without their problematic aspects.

I will draw most of my examples from Calcutta, which to most people is the symbol of urban breakdown, a city that seems to have reached the point of nonsustainability. Ironically, although it is a problem-ridden city of great struggle and great poverty, it is also a city that for those very reasons makes the most efficient use of its wastes of any city that I know of in the world. I will not start, however, with Calcutta, but with an urban gardener in another very different Asian city — Tokyo.

Organic farming in suburban Tokyo

Mr. Ohira's family has farmed in the vicinity of Tokyo for three hundred years. He is the eleventh generation of farmer in the family, and as Tokyo's city has grown up and swallowed its surrounding area, the family has determinedly kept a large part of the family farmland for growing vegetables. Compost-making is, of course, the linchpin of the farm. He uses no artificial fertilizer or pesticides of any kind.

The seeds of the beans seen in the background of Figure 1, have been passed down in his family since they began farming here. He draws upon local materials from beyond the farm for his compost pile. He has an arrangement with all the gardeners who service the neighbourhood, cutting those wonderful hedges that the Japanese green their cities with. All the tree clippings and hedge clippings go into his compost pile.

But even more delightful, he gets all the used chopsticks from the suburban restaurants and grinds them up and adds them into his compost. It takes ingenuity and determination to practise organic farming in a city like Tokyo. Another point that I want to emphasize is the principle of continuity. This nurturing of tradition by an individual family is contributing to seed diversity and sound ecological practice.

Figure 1. An organic farmer whose family has farmed the same land for three hundred years turns the compost pile that receives the household's wastes, hedge clippings and used chopsticks from neighbourhood restaurants.

Human waste use in a Chinese city

The recycling of human wastes is an ancient tradition in China. In Guangzhou, South China, nurseries incorporate fish ponds as well. Large ceramic pots placed by the side of the pond are euphemistically called "honey pots"; they hold human faeces. The wastes are dished out to both the ponds and the shrubs. In China today, modernization is rapidly eroding rural traditions in cities, and organic recycling survives in the urban fringes only in competition with chemical fertilizers, the use of which is subsidized by the Ministry of Agriculture.

Vine over squatter's shack, Calcutta

Even in very impoverished and congested conditions, as in Calcutta, you can find a little urban agriculture. Besides the squash it bears, the vine makes a hot and unaired shack a little more tolerable (Figure 2). And this is something you can see all over urban India and in other congested cities, although not perhaps as much as one would hope. There has to be an almost constant watcher as the squash ripens to protect it from theft. These, and other plants, are watered with waste water, since fresh waste is a precious commodity here.

Buddhist shrine in squatter colony, Bangkok

Sometimes the purpose of the greening is religious. A small corner of a crowded colony in Klong Toey, the large port slum of Bangkok,

Figure 2. A squatter has planted a squash vine to grow over the hut in a crowded Calcutta settlement. The vine leaves help cool the hut and the squash gives some extra nutrient to a poor family.

is preserved for a shrine. The potted plants and statue of Buddha mark it as a sacred spot.

Poultry feeding from kitchen wastes, Bandung, Indonesia

Another aspect of urban agriculture is raising animals that can feed off the garbage. It's very common to see all kinds of animals — goats, pigs, cows, buffalo, poultry — in squatter areas and this is one reason why squatters may resist rehousing in highrise apartments where they lose the chance to keep animals. These practices may create health problems, and they are usually anathema to city officials.

Milk delivery, in viva, in Calcutta suburb

In a city like Calcutta any available piece of spare land is used to graze cattle, buffalo, and goats. The goats that are brought into the city for slaughter are first fattened on the city's one large park. The élite households can ensure that they get pure milk by having it delivered to their door, still in the udder.

Cow and buffalo dung patties on wall, Calcutta

Animal dung is used extensively as fuel in the cities of India. Poor people gather the fresh droppings and plaster handfuls on walls to dry. One consequence is that there is much less of a waste disposal problem. But the city health officers see only the health problems of the cattle in the city. From the point of view of the poor, they represent a source of desperately needed fuel and employment.

Here is a paradox, a dilemma, in green practices. What is perhaps ecologically good at one level, for some people, may be seen as environmentally harmful from another perspective. For these, and other reasons of urban growth, urban agriculture is everywhere threatened.

Pavement dweller burning dung cakes in bucket stove

There are several ramifications to the use of dung as fuel in Indian cities. Undoubtedly, it has saved many, many trees, and yet, it is one source of Calcutta's serious air pollution.

**Figure 3. A grasscutter carries his load from the edge of Calcutta back
to the city to feed the cows and buffalo kept within the city boundaries.**

Grass Cutter carrying grass from urban fringe for city cattle, Calcutta

I believe that Michael Hough mentioned farmers cutting the grass
verges for fodder. It's a very old tradition in India. This grass-cutter
(Figure 3) goes out to the urban fringe, where a new road has been
built to the airport, and cuts the grass along the sides. In Asian cities,
the poor have asserted social rights to the fruits of public property
and urban wastes.

These examples have illustrated some of the important, but not
strictly intended, ecological relationships that are created as poor
people live out their lives in the city. Now, I'll move on to the systems
of "food-from-waste" that are of great significance to Calcutta.

View of East Calcutta wetlands

To the east of the city there is a very large wetland area, in fact the largest remaining wetlands adjacent to a major city in the world. Calcutta, indeed, was built in a swamp that constricted its eastward expansion. The city has gradually eaten into the wetlands, but there are still about twenty-one square miles remaining.

The main garbage dump of Calcutta

The city administration set up a garbage dump in the swamp in 1864 (that was the only use they saw for the wetlands then). They subcontracted out the management of the dump. From the very beginning, it was thought that a manager would be attracted to the task if he could also undertake land creation and "sewage farming." This he did, and even designed the landfilling so that bodies of water remained between strips of dumped refuse, and these ponds were used as fish ponds.

The garbage farms

So, from the late nineteenth century, Calcutta has been growing vegetables directly on its garbage. No elaborate or scientific methods of composting are used. Garbage is simply dumped, and after a few months the land is parcelled into plots for vegetable farmers. Nowadays this is organized by the municipal corporation, not by a subcontractor. One even occasionally sees squatter farmers who have sneaked into fresh dumping areas.

It is estimated that there are about eight hundred hectares of garbage farms on old dumping land there today. These plots grow about twenty-five varieties of vegetables throughout the year. They have no problem of water in the dry season as they draw upon the remaining ponds around the dump. Calcuttans believe they have the best tasting and freshest vegetables of any large Indian city, and I agree with that judgment.

Coconut shells removed from garbage plots

Figure 4 is of a pile of old coconut shells that have been removed by the farmers as they tilled the compost. (Green coconut milk is an important street food in the city.) The shells, a nuisance for the

Figure 4. All that the farmers need mainly to remove from the refuse brought to Calcutta's dump is old coconut shells and bits of rubble. Synthetic items are largely picked out by poor people within the city.

farmers, will not be wasted. People will come and gather them, strip them and use the outer husk or even the broken hard shell itself as fuel.

Close-up of garbage

The reason that Calcutta's garbage can grow such wonderful vegetables is that it is made almost entirely of organic matter with dirt and ashes. It is some of the most remarkable garbage that you would ever wish to see in the world. You simply do not find in the garbage dump very much in the way of any nondecomposable material. All the synthetic, manufactured materials — the metals, glass, rubber, plastics — have been meticulously picked out at various points along the way. And, to date, there is little in the form of contaminants such as heavy metals or solvents in the refuse. The residue breaks down naturally and very readily in the tropical climate. It forms a very rich growing medium — the farmers use no artificial fertilizers.

Calcutta has thus solved the problem encountered by so many other cities which have set up mechanical compost plants: the problem of accessible markets. Most cities have not been able to transport compost to farmers at an affordable price. Calcutta does not have to worry about getting its compost to the farmers because the farmers come to the compost.

Main sewage canal

The other component of Calcutta's food-from-waste system is the city waste water and sewage. The exploitation of this resource has been much more informal than the setting up of the garbage farms.

Fish ponds and bamboo sluice-gates

The wetlands originally formed the tidal backwash for the many tributaries of the Ganges that run through the delta to the Bay of Bengal. Until the late nineteenth century the water was salty and brackish, then the rivers and streams began to silt up (perhaps partly from deforestation in the mountains) and the area no longer received tidal flows. The fishermen divided up the land into embanked fish ponds, and they turned to the sewage canals for water. They began to siphon off the waste waters, letting in controlled amounts through bamboo gates. Their sources of water remain the waste water and rainwater. There are four to five thousand hectares of fish ponds left of a once much larger system.

Polyculture fish farming in shallow ponds

These are shallow ponds, from two to three metres deep. This shallowness allows them to act as natural oxidation ponds in which the action of bacteria, sun, and wind purifies the waste water. This is the only form of treatment that Calcutta's sewage receives since, incidentally, the city has no sewage treatment facility.

The fish farmers net the fish — different kinds of carp and tilapia — by driving them into nets. They are auctioned in nearby villages and quickly sold in the Calcutta markets. No health problems have been associated with this fish farming. Properly managed waste water fish ponds have been shown to be safe in other countries, such as Israel and Hungary.

The productivity of these ponds could be enhanced if the fisher-folk had better seeding methods and more controlled fishing. But these pond systems have developed as folk traditions, without expert advice. The city regarded the use of the waste waters as illegal (the fisher-folk breached the canals to let out their contents). Recently, however, these practices have received world-wide attention and waste water aquaculture has been proposed as a component of the Ganga Action Plan to clean up the Ganges River.

Agriculture on pond embankments — integrated farming

Integrated farming is also practised in this area. The embankments between the ponds are planted with vegetables; the pond water is used to irrigate the vegetables, and cattle are grazed on the embankments. Of course, the farmers do not call it "integrated farming" — that is for development manuals. It simply represents for them the sensible use of scarce resources.

This, then, is the remarkable food-from-city-wastes system that arose partly by design and partly from the search for new resources, and survives on the fringes of Calcutta.

All of the examples of "greening" I have referred to in this presentation are now under threat. For instance, the Calcutta Metropolitan Urban Development Plan calls for the filling in of the wetlands, that living filter system that served food production, waste disposal, and, incidentally, air quality. Much land reclamation has already taken place and further new towns are to be built to the east of the city.

Even the very small scale activities of keeping a few chickens or planting vegetables and medicinal herbs have no assured future in crowded, modernizing cities of developing countries. Almost all cities have bylaws against raising animals, and population pressures are forcing the poor into highrise buildings, often lacking balconies where plants can be grown.

The developing cities, like Toronto, need a new approach to urban planning based on fresh thinking about the "ecological city." The road to this new approach could be shorter if we first look at what people, mostly poor people, are actually doing already, not with the intention of creating ecosystems that are sustainable, but simply because they have certain needs in their own households that they try to meet with accessible resources. Sustainable cities will be cities that care about social equity and whose administrations seek to enable poor people to improve their lifestyles while improving the natural environment of the city.

Let us, then, look at those activities and assess which ones contribute to a wider purpose and which do not. And let us look at the constraints upon such activities that inhibit them, make them illegal, or, in the case of a very broad development plan, would create massive change in the ecology of a region. Let's remember the importance of continuity and diversity and find the way to conserve and support all kinds of incidental greening in world cities.

REFERENCES

Furedy, C. 1988. "Natural Recycling in Asian Cities." *Raise the Stakes (Planet Drum Review)* no.13:6-7.

Furedy, C. and D. Ghosh. 1984. "Resource-conserving Urbanism and Waste Disposal — the Garbage Farms and Sewage-fed Fisheries of Calcutta." *Conservation and Recycling* 7, nos. 2-4:159-65.

Ghosh, D. and S. Sen. 1987. "Ecological History of Calcutta's Wetland Conversion." *Environmental Conservation* 14, no. 3:219-26.

Hough, M. 1984. *City Form and Natural Process.* New York: Van Nostrand Rhinehold.

The Global Context of the Greening of Cities
Dr. Enrique Leff

The intention of my paper is to present a conceptual clarification of the urbanization process in Latin American cities which arises from recent studies that describe the process in an environmental perspective. It will not elaborate on the more immediate possible technical solutions to the urban problems. Rather, a global view is taken to analyze some of the social and environmental considerations that must orient urban planning policies.

Greening the city in the context of the urban explosion of Third World cities implies a reconstruction process that goes beyond anti-pollution measures, conservation of green areas, and reforestation of the surrounding environment of the city. As well, it goes way beyond better transportation systems, public services, and waste recycling technologies to rationalize the use of resources and energy within the urban ecosystem.

Urban agglomeration, together with its environmental negative effects, is the result of a number of historical and economic processes, including the over-concentration of industry due to the dependent patterns of development, combined with an inadequate land tenure structure, inappropriate agricultural techniques, and rural population growth. This leads to an increasing flow of immigrants to the

Dr. Enrique Leff is currently the Coordinator of the United Nations Environment Program's (UNEP) Environmental Training Network for Latin America and the Caribbean, and is also the Coordinator for the Project on Environment and Development, Centro de Investigaciones Interdisciplinarias en Humanidades Universidad Nacional Autonoma de Mexico.

metropolises in demand of jobs and services, at rates the city can no longer afford.

The centripetal forces of urban concentration have already trespassed the physical and social absorbing capacities of the mega-cities. This process has externalized social and ecological costs in the form of saturation levels of air, water, and noise pollution. It has also generated acute regional imbalances and social inequalities. Ultimately, it has degraded the basic ecological mechanisms that assure sustained productivity of natural resources and the social basis for a democratic management of the productive processes by communities. The metropolization process has generated a growing deficit in public services and the reversal of *economies of agglomeration.* This is leading to the degradation of the quality of life for people, to pressing social inequalities and increasing ecological cost, and to the rising prices of inputs from the regional environment.

Greening the cities cannot be thus attained through traditional urban planning approaches only. It implies a new concept of the city in which it is not assumed to be a centre for consumption of the surplus produced in the countryside through the over- exploitation of natural and human resources. Greening the city implies the articulation of urban functions in an overall sustainable development process. It implies new functions for the city and its reintegration into the overall productive process through a more balanced spatial distribution of agri-ecological, industrial, and urban activities.

This cannot be attained through centralized decision-making processes. It demands the participation of grassroots organizations in rural and urban communities to manage their natural resources, transformation processes, commerce of goods, and public services. It promotes more autonomous and decentralized processes for the construction of new rural productive rationalities.

This global approach helps define a specific concept of what greening the cities would imply for these so-called underdeveloped regions, and this will in turn generate normative guidelines to give new orientations to innovative efforts in the field of appropriate technologies, landscape design, and urban planning, by integrating architects, urban planners, rural developers, and community promoters.

The Growth of Latin American Cities

In an issue paper prepared for the World Commission on Environment and Development, Sachs (1985) characterized the urban explosion as "the most radical and most rapid social transformation ever to have occurred. The urban population of the Third World will almost double between now and the year 2001. Approximately half of humankind will be living in towns, many among them in megacities. The urban poor will soon become the majority."

Yet, until very recently, the urbanization process was an unquestionable sign of progress and economic development. The building of cities was part of the construction of a transformed environment whose purpose was not only to produce wealth, but well-being as well. The city became the natural locus for the transformation of raw materials to obtain commodities. Agricultural outputs and raw labour force were transferred to the cities and industrial centres where economies of scale and of agglomeration combined to optimize technological efficiency and economic productivity. Traditional lifestyles and local values were traded for a higher urban culture, and the trade-off seemed be a smooth transition toward a post-industrial civilization.

The environmental and social problems arising from the urban explosion have put forward the question of its actual costs and benefits. Not only noise, air, and water pollution are becoming acute problems, but the city is also giving birth to new types of social movements which are more threatening because of their explosive potential due to the concentration of active forces. The confluence of the urban structure, economic context, and political processes has called for new approaches in urban sociology and in the political economies of urbanization as well (Procter 1982). Yet, a study carried out to assess whether economies of scale exist in urban production, based upon a "chemically pure" marginal productivity theory and having been empirically justified, found, for example, that in fifty-eight urban areas of the U.S. there was an agglomeration effect for areas of more than two million people (Segal 1972). These findings on the economic behaviour of the cities in the industrialized countries has a striking contrast with the quality of life and the economic performance of the mega-cities in the Third World.

Not surprisingly, the urban sociologies have characterized the price of progress in the metropolization process as one of "urban exploitation, social exclusion, and environmental degradation" (Kovarick 1979). It has been stressed that in "predominantly rural countries the cities could rely to a considerable extent on the economic surplus extracted from the countryside. But when the ratio of the urban to rural dweller is two or even three to one, even the strongest urban bias would prove insufficient in mobilizing the necessary *per capita quantum of resources to make the city go*" (Sachs 1985).

The urbanization process and its metropolitan concentration in Latin America and the Third World is becoming larger in magnitude than the more stabilizing trends of the cities in the industrialized countries. In 1900, London was the only city to have over five million people. In 1925 there were three, New York being the largest. In 1980, 60 percent (or eighteen of the twenty-nine) of cities having more than five million people were cities in the Third World regions. Five of them were Latin American cities. If those tendencies continue, in the year 2000 the world will have fifty-seven metropolises of over five million inhabitants, of which forty-four would be Third World cities, twelve of them in Latin America. They would include, besides the existing two larger cities of Mexico City and Sao Paulo, cities like Rio de Janeiro, Buenos Aires, Bogota, Lima, Belo Horizonte, Guadalajara, Caracas, Santiago, Curitiba, and Porto Alegre.

The rates of population growth and urban concentration in Latin America are among the highest in today's world. Some estimations show that its local population might be of 625 million people in the year 2000, with 75 percent settled in the urban environments. Forty-eight cities will hold a population greater than that which existed in 1970 in the whole region, and the ten largest cities will have more than 135 million people. Rural migration to the cities is still the main contributor to the urban population growth in many cases. During the 1960s, 72 percent of the population growth of Sao Paulo, 54 percent of Caracas, and 33 percent of Bogota, was due to immigration into the cities. This growing urban population is settling in increasing precarious conditions, showing the incapacity of this urbanization process to provide basic infrastructure and public services to the people. During the 1970s, the annual growth of precarious urban settlements in Mexico was 12 percent, while the average annual urban population growth was only about 2.3 percent (Gutman 1982).

Urban Expansion in the Context of Dependent Economies

Even though these figures showing the Third World taking the lead in urban growth rates are sufficient to criticize the simplistic idea that the urbanization process is an unquestionable sign of cultural and economic progress, we have yet to characterize the complexity of this phenomena in the context of dependency and underdevelopment. The configuration of the cities in the Third World must be explained through the changing functions they have performed through the integration of dependent economies into the international order. The colonial cities were the centres of political and economic power link- ing the colonies to the imperial metropolis. Once political inde- pendence was obtained, this bureaucratic centralism followed a certain inertia in the centralizing organization of the emerging Latin American nations. This tendency was reinforced by the role played by their exporting economies in the world order. Actually, it was not exporting activity itself which was the cause of the urban industrial concentration, but its importing counterpart. Importing enterprises became established in the urban centres, where buying power was concentrated. As the industrialization process based on import sub- stitution advanced, more sophisticated capital intensive technologies were introduced to the productive process and to the already central- ized systems of distribution.

The role played by the State in many countries has taken the urbanization process beyond any economic rationality. The in- dustrialization process was stimulated by import barriers, special credit, tax receptions, and subsidized inputs. Besides these measures, the state established a basic infrastructure for production bearing the social cost of the general conditions necessary for the industrializa- tion process, which means establishing transport systems, basic collective services, energy and water supplies, schooling, and housing. This has certainly encouraged business and industry to get established and to be profitable, externalizing its real cost to society and to the environment. The concentration of the more dynamic industries in a few cities, the modernization of rural areas, and the dissolution of the traditional role of societies, have led to an increasing flow of immigrants to the central cities, reinforcing their process of metropolization.

To confirm the degree of industrial concentration in the main Latin American metropolises, the following data for 1970 will be significant. The federal capital of Argentina concentrated 80 percent of Argentina's industrial product. Rio de Janeiro and Sao Paulo accounted for 75 percent of the Brazilian industrial production. The federal district and its larger metropolitan areas spreading to the state of Mexico, together with Monterrey and Monclova in the state of Nuevo Leon, represented 65 percent of Mexican industry. This complex process of urban industrialization clearly contrasts with the differentiated roles of cities emerging from the Industrial Revolution, where political capitals were not the seat of this process, as exemplified by London, Rome, Paris, or Madrid compared with Manchester, Milan, Alsace-Lorain, the Ruhr, or Barcelona (di Filippo 1979).

The lack of homogeneity in the construction of the urban environment can be characterized as a very unequal organization of the urban space and of the distribution of pollution costs among different sectors of society. Although one can find social differences in every city, the social division of the urban space and services is much more polarized in Third World cities. The unequal appropriation of the benefits of economies of agglomeration has no correlation to the distribution of its costs (Ibarra et al. 1984). The social and environmental costs of urbanization are not only evident in the external environment, the distribution of space (green areas and public services), and in different neighbourhoods of the cities, but it is also closely correlated to the internal labour environments where the working classes are employed and where pollution standards, to prevent the ill effects of substances being used or produced in the

production processes from affecting the health of workers, are loose
or nonexistent.

Urban Decentralization: Greening from the Ground

Any proposal for the greening of Latin American cities will have
to be assessed, taking into consideration the historical conditions of
its overall urbanization process, which is ongoing, and, in many
cases, reinforced through the actual policies of the urban development. Despite the apparent value of remodelling efforts establishing
pollution norms for industry and mobile sources, or of trying to
return to the cities a part of the green areas that they once had, the
overall increase of pollutants cannot be reduced without stopping the
growth of the industrial activity in one city or the number of cars
circulating through its streets. Population control measures will also
be ineffective by themselves in diminishing the demands of employment in public services in the short and medium term. The population
that will reach an active age at the turn of the century is already born,
so a measure applied today cannot reverse the tendencies for enlarg-
ing the urban population to up to two-thirds of the total population.

The real issue does not lie in trying to deurbanize our future
civilization, and certainly does not lie in reproducing and spreading
the actual patterns through the promotion of what have been called
poles of development. The very strong social and ecological impact
on the industrialization and the urbanization processes in use by
conjunctural international market opportunities (in the construction
of oil cities, for example) is eloquent in the irrationalities that have
been arising in cases like in the southeastern region of Mexico with
an oil boom in the last few years (Legorreta 1983). Other efforts in
housing and basic public services, directed through centralized
government actions, have relative success in spite of increases in
public investments in these sectors, and important international
financial contributions.

It is possible to demonstrate that such policies have not been able
to reverse regressive tendencies in housing and to improve water and

sewage services, for example. This is due to a lack of a spatial strategy coordinated with the overall development process and, above all, to the fact that such decentralized and bureaucratic policies are based on the principle that the management capacities of a central government are the only means to overcome the problems of urban and rural development (Neira 1981).

Urban decentralization would have to focus on the development of a somewhat new urban system through the promotion of small and intermediate cities integrated to the distribution of productive activities. The territory should be viewed as supporting diversified agri-industrial processes where urban structure and functions are balanced with the ecological and social forces of each region and its communities. Beyond the considerations of the impact of traditional productive practices in the urban life patterns on the environment, an environmental perspective for urban and industrial development implies the mobilization of an environmental potential drawn from the ecotechnological productivity of social, cultural, ecological, and technical processes which can be mobilized as active forces for a more balanced, equitable, and sustainable development (Leff 1986).

Urban Development in the Tropics

One of the main causes that has affected the metropolization process of Latin American countries, and that will certainly condition the urban relationships for the spatial distribution of human settlements, is the tropical environment in which these countries are mostly located. Without due consideration of the characteristics of this environment, it will be difficult to explain the current patterns of metropolization as well as to devise new policies for some human settlements and agri-industrial integration. Over 60 percent of the territory in Latin America is lowlands, humid mountains, tropical rain forests, and the semi-arid Chaco (Nelson 1977). This vast area represents the most important agricultural reserve where the agricultural frontier is actually pressing to expand and to establish new human settlements and productive activities. Any coming efforts to relocate such activities and to redistribute the population must consider new approaches for the sound management of resources in this environment, new criteria for the construction of the urban infrastructure and public services for these human settlements, and for the incorporation of these marginal spaces into national economies.

Tropical ecosystems show the highest natural productivity of any ecosystem, which is associated with their complex organization and diversity. They also happen to be the most fragile ecosystems on earth. Because of these characteristics of the productive environment, the overall process of production has to be planned to enhance the ecological potential and not to collapse it because of any inappropriate technological models imposed. From this perspective, the overall technological system has to be devised so as to blend with a natural resource system viewed as an ecological, sustained productive system. The urban systems should be viewed through this perspective, not as centres consuming surplus matter and energy from surrounding environments, but as articulated infrastructures that contribute to enhance the environmental, productive forces of society (Leff 1986).

The urbanization process affects the overall environmental potential through the growing demands of matter and energy. Urban growth does not only generate increasing costs to supply such materials, but also induces rates and patterns of extraction that severely affect the natural resources' ecological system. For example, the rising cost of water supplies to Mexico City, which is established at over six thousand feet and is drawing increasing demands of water from the environment, is not only a matter of the rising cost of water to supply the needs of Mexico City. It implies, as well, an overall process of deterioration of the regional environment where water is extracted to make possible the increasing urban growth of Mexico City. The construction of any city built up on a tropical ecosystem requires an ecological design so the flows of material coming in and out, its transportation, sewage, and waste disposal systems, do not disrupt the overall ecological equilibrium of the environment. One should not disregard the tremendous potential of solar energy available in the tropical regions to derive more ecologically sound and self-sufficient urban energy supply systems as well.

Environmental Urbanism With the People

The recommendations arising from the first international congress on the planning of big cities, held in Mexico City in 1987, stated that "in order to continue the process of development it was required to incorporate the natural resources and the human capacities insufficiently used by the actual model of concentration. The intervention of the state is thus required, but in such a way as to maintain the innovative capacities of the centre and to stimulate the creative capacities of the populations not yet incorporated. For this purpose it is mandatory to maintain cultural diversity and to broaden the collective participation of the people."

"In synthesis, the decentralization process would require policies to install in selective areas the infrastructure and necessary services to support the development of new regions, policies for the relocation of economic activities so as to be able to use underutilized and new resources, policies to encourage collective participation of the people in the decision making and in innovative processes, and cultural policies aiming at the modernization of society but protecting at the same time regional cultural differences. Three lines of immediate action should characterize the decentralization of the Mexican metropolis. The first consists in establishing a new industrial capacity outside of the metropolitan area through different state policies. The second consists in eliminating past artificial advantages in favour of industrial and urban concentration. The third would be to avoid new industrial activities or to expand the already existing ones while eliminating those that generate high social and environmental costs."

The importance of new approaches to people's participation in urban planning has already gone beyond academic considerations, to practical actions for municipal administration and for decentralization processes within several countries. "The experiences of Medellin, and more recently in Curitiba, show the possibilities of improving actual systems of urban management without undergoing structural changes. Cuba created with its popular power a political formula to transfer the decision and administrative power to local instances. Panama has also adopted some kind of popular participation to induce decentralization through municipal administration. Chile has promoted the decentralization of the urban services. Peru has adopted, in its political constitution of 1980, a law for the municipalities, and, in 1981, decentralizing measures for the local management of urban development. In Mexico, amendments to the 115th constitutional article provide for the strengthening of municipalities to encourage a process of decentralization (Neira 1981).

Greening the cities should require the agreement of different flourishing forces, the innovative capacity of the urban designers and city planners, ecological architecture and landscape planning, and the creative participation of the people to develop their own solutions to their own urban problems. Greening of cities cannot be accomplished unless new approaches and actions can counteract current tendencies that "un-green" our environment. This is a task that cannot be achieved without international cooperation. The professional and technical capacities of the developed countries could be of invaluable potential as long as they are not used to impose urban patterns that are inappropriate to the physical and social environments of Third World countries. Architects, planners, and social scientists might find this challenge of building green cities in the environmental context stimulating to their creative capacities, and one from which both worlds would certainly benefit.

REFERENCES

Di Filippo, Armando. 1979. "Distribucion Espacial de la Actividad Económica, Migraciones y Concentración Poblacional en América Latina." In ECLAC/UNEP, *Estilos de Desarrollo y Medio Ambiente en América Latina*, Santiago de Chile.

FUNAP. 1986. *Conferencia sobre Población y Ciudades Pequeñas y Medianas en América Latina y el Caribe*. Ciudad de Mexico, febrero 24–28, 1986.

Geisse, Guillermo. 1979. "Renta de la Tierra, Heterogeneidad Urbana y Medio Ambiente." In ECLAC/UNEP, *Estilos de Desarrollo...*

Gutman, Pablo. 1982. "Problemas y Perspectivas Ambientales de la Urbanización en América Latina." *Comercio Exterior* 32, no. 12:1304–14.

Ibarra, V., S. Puente, and M. Schteingart. 1984. "La Ciudad y el Medio Ambiente." *Economía y Demografía*, Mexico.

Kovarick, Lucio. 1979. "El Precio del progreso: Crecimiento Económico, Expoliación Urbana y la Cuestión del Medio Ambiente." In ECLAC/UNEP, *Estilos de Desarrollo...*

Leff, Enrique. 1986. "Ecotechnological Productivity: a Conceptual Basis for the Integrated Management of Natural Resources." *Social Science Information* 25 (3).

—. 1986. *Ecología y Capital: Hacia un Proyecto de Ecodesarrollo.* Mexico: UNAM.

—. (Coordinator) 1986. *Los Problemas del Conocimiento y la Perspectiva Ambiental del Desarrollo.* Mexico: Siglo XXI Editores.

Legorreta, Jorge. 1983. *El Proceso de Urbanización en Ciudades Petroleras.* Mexico: Centro de Ecodesarrollo.

Neira, Eduardo. 1981. "Las Políticas Metropolitanas en un Contexto de Experiencia Global." CEPAL.

Nelson, Michael. 1977. *El Aprovechamiento de las Tierras Tropicales en América Latina.* Mexico: Siglo XXI Editores.

Pinto, Anibal. 1984. "Metropolización y Terciarización: Malformaciones Estructurales en el Desarrollo Latinoamericano." *Revista de la CEPAL* no. 24.

Procter, Ian. 1982. "Some Political Economies of Urbanization and Suggestions for a Research Framework." *International Journal of Urban and Regional Research* 6, no. 1:83-87.

Sachs, Ignacy. 1980. "Cities and Resources." *Social Sciences Information* 19, no. 4/5:673–84.

—. 1985. "Human Settlements: Resource and Environmental Management." Issue Paper for the World Commission on Environment and Development (WCED/85/Info. 16), Paris.

Segal, David. 1976. "Are There Returns to Scale in City Size?" *The Review of Economics and Statistics* LVIII, no. 3:339-50.

Tokman, V.E. 1980. "Pobreza Urbana y Empleo: Líneas de Acción. Se Puede Superar la Pobraza? Realidad y Perspectivas en América Latina." (E/CEPAL/G. 1139), Santiago de Chile.

Vuskovic, Pedro. 1981. "Opciones Actuales del Desarrollo Latinoamericano." Mexico: CIDE.

Making an Urban Wilderness: Reflections on the First Fifty Years of the University of Wisconsin Arboretum
Dr. William Jordan

One of the unusual things about what I have to say is its very strong historic emphasis. For the last ten years, I have been working as an editor and public outreach and development staff member at the University of Wisconsin Arboretum, in Madison, Wisconsin. The University of Wisconsin Arboretum has an unusual history and, for the last several years in particular, we have spent a great deal of time reflecting on this history. We have now reached our fiftieth anniversary, and we have been doing this reflecting partly in order to do some planning for our own future, and also because it has begun to occur to us that what happened at the Arboretum during the 1930s and 1940s was an event of signal importance for the conservation movement of that time and perhaps even for the environmental movement that we have seen in the 1960s and 1970s and which we are carrying on into the 1980s and 1990s.

I thought I would begin by simply pointing to two fundamental ecological tenets that everyone is aware of and, to some extent, lives by. First is the primacy of relationships between living things and their environment; and second is the ongoing and inevitable process

William Jordan is the editor in charge of publications and public relations at the University of Wisconsin-Madison Arboretum. He is the founder and editor of the twice-yearly journal Restoration and Management Notes, *and a founder, member of the Board of Directors and Supervisor of Administration for the recently formed International Society for Ecological Restoration and Management.*

of change, whether ecological change or evolutionary change. As a result of these two fundamental tenets, any kind of environmentalism that is ecological in tone and character will be concerned primarily not with objects in the landscape but with relationships with and between creatures and the landscape. It will see the landscape not as a collection of objects in a museum to be preserved, hung on to, or kept. It will see the landscape not even as an environment (a term that has always seemed to me to be somewhat alienated, an environment being that part of the landscape that is out there), but rather as a habitat for plants and animals — including ourselves. In short, we would, as environmentalists, ultimately seek to break down a false distinction that tends to arise between our species and the rest of nature.

I suppose this happens precisely because we are a peculiar species, and although Aldo Leopold argued for functioning as a "plain citizen" of the biotic community, I myself would be inclined to remove the "plain." I think I can understand why Leopold felt he had to emphasize the "plainness" of it, and at one level, of course, he was right. But if you think about it, one of the most obvious things about our species is that we are rather peculiar, and particularly adept at rearranging our habitat and carving out niche spaces in the biosphere in highly creative and imaginative ways. This, then, I take to be the fundamental concern of the kind of environmentalism that appeals to me. Oddly, as I reflect on it now, it seems that some of these things do not become most evident when we reflect on and concern oursel-ves with the wilderness, although this has been a major preoccupa-tion of a large wing of the environmental movement at least since early in this century and probably since the time of Thoreau, Emer-son, Muir, and Theodore Roosevelt in the latter part of the nineteenth century and in the early twentieth century.

This becomes clearest when we look at our immediate habitat, including the areas that are devastated by activities like surface min-ing, which I mention as a particularly dramatic example of how people rearrange the landscape in more or less arbitrary or creative ways. It is interesting that in the course of his very impressive attempt to break down the distinction between our species and the rest of nature, Frederick Turner, a professor of art and humanities at the

University of Dallas, has pointed specifically to mined areas in Great Britain as having appealed particularly to certain of the Romantic poets. Turner also points out that the Grand Canyon could be regarded as the same sort of thing. What, he says, if the Grand Canyon were man made? It might have been, and in fact we have things rather like the Grand Canyon in places where we have been mining copper, lead, iron, and coal for the last fifty or hundred years. It is in these places, where we actually live, that we have to think about the kind of habitat that we are creating for ourselves, and of exactly how we fit into this habitat. Since we have a great deal of authority over shaping that habitat, ultimately we will be deciding how to shape it. I think at the mine sites in particular, and in cities, what we really have is a chance to practise environmentalism at its greatest intensity.

This, then, brings me to the thing that I want to talk about, the thing which emerged from a little group of people at the University of Wisconsin Arboretum some fifty years ago in the midst of the depression and the dust bowl of the 1930s, and this is the process of ecological restoration. Not just the imitation, but the literal copying of nature — but copying meticulously in a completely self-effacing way, carrying out a kind of agriculture, but an agriculture designed to counteract and directly reverse the effects of traditional agriculture, in order to to create gardens modelled precisely and meticulously on natural models.

In the last ten or twenty years, the process of ecological restoration has received a rapidly growing amount of attention from environmentalists. A signal event in the United States was the passage, just ten years ago in 1977, of the Surface Mining Control and Reclamation Act, which mandated a certain kind of reclamation which in some instances at least approaches genuine ecological restoration on sites recently or newly disturbed by surface mining. At the same time, the idea of ecological restoration is remarkably modern. No one has written a history of it because so far it simply has not achieved enough coherence, identity, or visibility to have attracted that kind of attention.

On the basis of informal reading and talking, however, the earliest example I am aware of was the restoration of brackish wetlands in Boston by Frederick Law Olmsted, just about a century ago. Of course, people have been going out into the landscape and into deforested areas to plant trees since the Middle Ages. But we are not just talking about planting trees, remember. We are talking about the restoration, the actual recreation — or at least the attempt to recreate — an entire historic landscape or ecological community.

As far as we know, however, the first attempt to do restoration systematically, on a large scale, and in a scientific setting, was carried out at the University of Wisconsin Arboretum and began about half a century ago. The Arboretum was founded in 1934, and committed itself to an ambitious program of ecological restoration on the property, a patchwork of derelict farms just beyond the edge of the city. This project turned out to be what we now think of as a classic attempt at ecological restoration in the purest sense. What I would like to do here is briefly to describe how this project progressed over the years, and along the way, to offer some comments on its significance, its implications both for the landscape and for our own relationship with it.

The Arboretum exists on the shores of a small lake called Lake Wingra, which retained a semi-wilderness atmosphere despite a

Figure 1. The Curtis Prairie of the University of Wisconsin-Madison Arboretum.

series of serious ecological disturbances between the 1880s and about 1920. The lake itself had been separated from much of the bordering wetlands. The wetlands themselves had been dredged and diked in the course of an ambitious attempt to create a model suburban community. The project eventually failed, but it left the lowlands scarred by canals and dredge spoils and, less obviously, by lowered and no longer fluctuating water levels. In the meantime, the surrounding uplands had been transformed, as Leopold said, beyond recognition by the familiar combination of plowing, grazing, logging, construction, and protection from fire.

The point is simply that the Arboretum was by no means a "natural area" when it was acquired. Like virtually every part of our area it had been profoundly altered during a century of European occupation. The ecological communities, notably the prairies, native to the site were virtually gone; the forests and wetlands were profoundly changed. Many of the native species of plants and animals were gone, and numerous exotic invaders were present. Hence the plan Leopold proposed — to develop a collection of native ecological communities on the site — meant that a great many of these would have to be rebuilt, recreated, and restored — in some cases virtually from scratch.

It is interesting, in the context of this symposium, to take a look at the social, political, and environmental circumstances in which the project developed. It was rooted, first of all, in a civic interest in creating open space or parkland for the city. It was, I think, only because this effort was unsuccessful in its original form that its proponents carried it to the university to see if they could sell the project in the form of a laboratory and a classroom. It is also important to keep in mind that the whole project was very much a product of the dustbowl and the depression. First of all, it was the depressed land prices of the 1930s that made it possible for the university to acquire land on a very generous scale. By 1941, when the major phase of land acquisition was over, they had acquired 480 hectares on the outskirts of the city. This would be inconceivable now anywhere within an hour's drive of the city. They were buying 80 hectare parcels of land for prices like $13,500 and $15,000. In addition to this, the depression had generated federal programs like the Civilian Conser-

vation Corps (CCC) which created a camp on the Arboretum site and
provided a plentiful supply of free labour — upwards of two hundred
young men — working under the auspices of the National Park
Service. And it was this that allowed Leopold and his colleagues to
try some things that might in any other context have seemed wildly
impractical. And it is clear, too, that the project itself and the novel
idea behind it were in many ways a response to the dustbowl conditions of the 1930s, and to the deforestation, which were nearing
completion in the upper Great Lakes at the time.

**Figure 2. The Civilian Conservation Corps collecting prairie plants,
September 1936. Photo by Ted Sperry.**

It is important to keep all this in mind because it gives some insight
into how this idea developed and was carried out, and also because
it helps explain why it had so little influence elsewhere during the
subsequent three or four decades. It was a difficult model, I think,
precisely because it had been carried out under such peculiar conditions — or rather conditions that did not prevail in the midwest
during the 1940s, 1950s, and 1960s.

Now let me tell you a bit about how the project was actually carried out. Leopold had pointed to the pre-settlement vegetation of Wisconsin as a model for the Arboretum project, and at the centre of the plan was a commitment to restore tall-grass prairie. This is the community which has been most severely reduced in scale since the time of

Figure 3. One of six photographs in sequence of the Civilian Conservation Corps digging and planting Prairie Dock into the University of Wisconsin-Madison Arboretum prairie, June 1939.

settlement in the upper midwest. Right from the beginning it seems everyone wanted to restore prairie. As a matter of fact, today, prairie in the central part of the country is at the very forefront of what one might call the ecological restoration movement, and it is interesting to see that this was true at Wisconsin right from the beginning. If you get interested in the pre-settlement landscape, you immediately discover these prairies, and if you get this bright idea to restore the landscape, right away you will want to make it a prairie. So graduate students were sent out into the field to collect seed for the prairie restoration, and the CCC boys were sent out with trucks to do the heavier work of bringing in sod from relic prairies scattered around the southwestern part of the state.

All this was done in a very makeshift fashion. The developers had very little equipment, and they knew very little about the different plants, so they did the obvious thing. They went out and they took pieces of prairie in chunks and brought them back and planted them in the ground. They did bring back some seed to establish prairie nurseries, and a certain amount of planting went on from small nurseries. Since this was the drought period, they found themselves doing a lot of watering, and they lost lots of plantings simply because they really could not water a twenty-four hectare prairie with only water carried in buckets. They also started some of the early experimental plots to find out what kind of factors influence the development of prairies. This, you have to remember, was a university project, and three or four very distinguished ecologists were involved, notably John Curtis, Norman Fassett, and Aldo Leopold.

They began learning a lot about the plants that make up prairies, their requirements, how to propagate them, and so forth. And they carried out some of the classic experiments on prairie fires. This is especially interesting because it illustrates how, by trying to restore the system, we find ourselves really coming to grips with how the system works. We find ourselves having to know what makes the system work and which ingredients have to be put into it to make it work. So right from the beginning we see restoration leading directly to a deeper understanding of the role of fire as an ecological force in the community, and so to a clearer understanding of the role the Indians had played in shaping the prairie, and so finally to a profound insight into our own relationship to prairie. And that, I think, gets to the heart of what restoration is all about. By doing it, we discover who we are ecologically, who we are in relationship to a particular landscape, a particular kind of ecological community. This is a key point, and I will return to it later.

Though the prairies have always been more or less the centrepiece of the restoration effort, the Arboretum has also undertaken restoration of other communities over the years. These include two types of maple forest, pine forests, and even a small amount — a total of about five hectares — of boreal forest. An early attempt was made under Leopold's supervision to rearrange the Arboretum's troubled marshes. Most of this is work we would now undo if we could, but it was an honest attempt to create waterfowl habitat, although not exactly restoration, because restoration, at least as we have been defining it in Wisconsin, would mean putting the marsh back the way it was in about 1830.

Today, taking our successes, our partial successes, and our failures all together, we do have representatives of all the major ecological communities native to Wisconsin — over thirty if you count the various types of prairie and so forth separately. Most of them are to some extent artificial — that is, restored or partly restored — and some of these really are evocative of pre-settlement Wisconsin — the landscape John Muir describes, for example, in *Story of My Boyhood and Youth*. Leopold, in a 1940s reflection on that landscape, had written of "1,000 acres of silphiums" and suggested that no one would ever see such a sight again. Yet at the very time he he wrote those poignant lines, Leopold was involved in an attempt to recreate a piece of prairie at the Arboretum. Now, some forty years later, we do not have a thousand acres of prairie, but we do have sixty. And we do not have buffalo, though buffalo are being included in large-scale restoration projects elsewhere. In any event, it seems the partial success of this effort suggests the possibility at least of a positive answer to Leopold's purely rhetorical question.

And that raises the question of just what we are to make of this project. What good is a place like the Arboretum? Of what importance is this business of ecological restoration? Well, to begin with, of course the official business of the Arboretum is to provide a facility for research, especially research on ecological restoration and management. I mentioned the rediscovery of the technology of ecological prescribed burning in the course of restoring Curtis Prairie, and today the burning of these prairies is one of our rites of spring at the Arboretum. We are also doing extensive research on the control of exotic species, and seem to have completely defeated the sweet clover that had been a major pest, and are making headway with other troublesome invaders such as wild parsnip and Tatarian honeysuckle.

Figure 4. Guided Walk at the Curtis Prairie, 1980.

Lots of teaching is done in the Arboretum, both at the university and at the lower grade levels, and we have many groups such as scouts, schools, churches, and civic groups involved in the process of restoration, beginning with simple things like seed collecting on the prairies in the fall. In fact, I have come to think of this as one of the major things that the Arboretum is all about — it is a place where people can come out and actually get involved in putting a piece of the landscape back together.

Indeed, a great deal has been done to develop a comfortable relationship between the Arboretum and the surrounding city. A major problem is input of storm water, and we have constructed a series of six desilting ponds which intercept water coming down from storm drains, purifying it to some extent before it moves into our lowlands and into the lake. And, of course, the Arboretum provides a park-like area in which all the atavistic things that people like to do when they are on vacation or when they have time for recreation can be done. You usually find people doing things like racing, running, bicycling, fishing on the lake, looking at trees, and so on.

That brings us to the part of this story that has come to interest me the most, which is the broader question about ecological restoration and its implications both for the landscape and for our relationship with it. What can we say about this? Well, first of all, the moderate mixed success of projects like ours at the Arboretum, and other similar projects that have been undertaken since, does suggest that it is possible in some cases, and under certain conditions, to recreate *more or less* authentic representations of natural communities. It is important to stress the "more or less." These communities are seldom, if ever, fully authentic. But in some cases, if we work hard enough at it, we may come reasonably close. And this is encouraging if you are concerned about the role — or even the presence — of the classic ecological communities in future landscapes dominated by human beings.

But there is something else going on here as well, and it is, if anything, even more important than the ability of the restorationist to create — to manufacture — replica natural communities. We see this if we turn our attention away from the *product* of restoration — the restored community as an object in the landscape — toward the *process* of restoration itself. It is in doing this that I have come to think of restoration not merely as a marginal sort of environmental technology, but as a process, an act, a *deed,* of critical importance for our relationship with the rest of nature, and so, one might argue, for the conservation of "nature" in a landscape dominated by human beings.

I said at the start that as environmentalists, our primary concern should be about relationships. I would like to suggest that this is what ecological restoration is all about, and that it is through this process of restoration that we dramatize the falseness of the distinction between ourselves and the rest of nature. Consider this: the product of restoration is an *artificial natural* community. And when you use those two words together they cancel each other out and you begin to realize that they mean nothing when used in opposition to each other. We do this in a very literal way when we set out to "restore" a "natural" system. We break down this distinction by literally reentering nature and reenacting our historic relationships with nature. In fact, I have to come to think of restoration as a kind of ritual by which we reenact the three great periods in the relationship between our species and the rest of nature, beginning, very literally, with hunting and gathering, going on to a whole panoply of agricultural practices, and then concluding with some very sophisticated science, especially ecological science.

This is a kind of ritual, even a sacrament, and even a public liturgy of reentry of nature, of the repossession of nature, and of the creation of a habitat for ourselves and a place for ourselves in the historic landscape. It is an art, then, as Frederick Turner has pointed out, but it is also a performing art, a matter of very great importance to our society. As a result, we have begun to think of the Arboretum in recent years not as a preserve, but as a theatre or an arena in which we can carry out this ritual reentry of nature and to go back to the idea that Leopold proposed originally: "This, in a nutshell, is the function of the Arboretum, a reconstructed sample of old Wisconsin to serve as a benchmark, a starting point, in the long and laborious job of building a permanent and mutually beneficial relationship between civilized men and a civilized landscape."

REFERENCES

"Cultivating the American Gardener." *Harpers Magazine.* August 1985.

Part Two: Naturalization at Work

If we are going to have green cities we must learn how to make them green. The authors in this section focus on existing strategies and technologies that can contribute to the greening of cities. They also examine some of the dilemmas inherent in pursuing such change. For example, the design of any naturalization project raises the hard question of what is "natural." In many areas of the world the "natural" landscape includes imported, hybridized, exotic, or alien species which countless generations have come to regard as their natural environment. Additionally, most people have ingrained attitudes about the separation of rural and urban to dispense with before ecological urban design can become general practice. Perhaps we can learn from the Dutch in this regard. By choosing to naturalize land reclaimed from the sea, they faced the question of what is "natural" decades ago and their experience is a valuable first reference for anyone embarking on a green city planning process.

When considered together, the examples of specific naturalization techniques presented in this section suggest two things. First, the techniques of ecological landscape design are available, have been successfully implemented, and produce outcomes that can be maintained. Second, ecologically designed urban areas will inherently serve multiple functions. Naturalized rights-of-way become human recreation corridors that also facilitate the ecologically important movement of wildlife between the urban area and its fringe. Managed forests can safely dispose of municipal sewage effluent and, at the same time, replenish groundwater tables. Keeping the highway verges of Texas in wildflowers actually saves money. It is clear that such ecological retrofits pay their way by providing a variety of benefits.

Restoration is a theme common to many of the techniques discussed in this section. Returning nature to the city is seen as both physically and socially restorative because these projects build community cohesiveness and offer opportunities for people to take more control of their lives. The benefits of creating ecology parks, that turn derelict urban lots into green oases, are clearly both physical and social. Pursuit of a common goal becomes a process of social restoration. By means of such greening experiments, the city can become a place where new natural diversity augments or even creates healthy social vibrancy.

This section offers a look at an ecological planning framework, a series of naturalization techniques, and the restorative roles these can play in urban areas. All of the projects described have been implemented, and many of their elements have become a part of regular planning and business practice. The usefulness of these examples suggests that we need to search out and document successful urban ecological projects wherever they are. These will be our texts — and we have a great deal to learn.

The Productive City:
Urban Forestry in the Netherlands
Tjeerd Deelstra

Currently in the Netherlands there is little forest and even less "urban" forest. It is useful, then, to have an impression of the history of the formation of and changes in the Dutch landscape in order to understand why we are now working on urban forests. The total population of the Netherlands, by the way, is about fourteen million, with two-thirds of the people living in the western urban section — the "Randstad" or rim-city — which is all below sea level.

The Netherlands has a very special position in the biosphere of Europe. The western part is intensely built up, but it also has a variety of wetlands and big open spaces managed as agricultural land. There is an inherent ecological conflict between the unique wetland position of the Netherlands and the heavy degree of urbanization. This, together with other forms of land use such as transportation, mining, and agriculture, gave rise to a planning process out of necessity, as well as to programs in environmental studies and urban ecology.

Two thousand years ago there were few people living in the country. In the Middle Ages, when elsewhere in Europe an urban

Tjeerd Deelstra is Director of the International Institute for the Urban Environment at Delft, in the Netherlands. He is an advisor to the Dutch Government on environmental protection and participates in the UNESCO research program on the Ecology of Human Settlements. As an advisor to the U.N.'s World Health Organization office for Europe, he is engaged in the development of "healthy city" plans in about twenty major European towns.

system was already established, Holland was mostly an unpopulated area of tidal land at the mouth of the rivers Rhine and Maas. This was a wild bush landscape of creeks and marshes covered sparsely with small "wet" woods. During the middle ages, a ridge of dunes was formed, separating the tidal landscapes from the sea. Sweet water began to form behind the dunes, creating large areas of forested peat marsh landscape. When people first arrived, they began to harvest this peat and to slash and burn it for agricultural purposes. These first settlers settled down along the rivers on little sandy hills, and developed the open land behind the farms where the peat areas once were. They "ate up" the landscape.

Later, this peat area was drained in many places. It became so low and empty that it filled with water. Milling became necessary to pump the water out, but while pumping out the water the spongy peat would sink, forcing the pumping out of water even more quickly and the invention of bigger mills. It really became a sort of competition with nature. This required the close cooperation of settlers in the form of Water Boards (which still exist and are essential for the actual water management system of Holland). The first type of settlement development had a type of local recycling economy in a close relationship with the environment, with peat heating the ovens, grain growing on the land, and harvested meat and fish served with natural drinking water. The land in the developed low-lying wetlands was, because of the high groundwater table, best suited for cattle breeding and dairy production, and it developed an open economy based on exchange. It produced more dairy products than the cities needed, and the surplus was sold on foreign markets, while grains were imported from places like the Baltics. Also, wood was imported for house and ship building from the southern and eastern uplands regions of the Netherlands, Belgium, and Germany.

Out of the open economy, around the year 1300, a pattern of harbour and market cities began to grow in the western low-lying areas outside of where the largest part of the population now lives. Around the beginning of this century, this resulted in an infrastructural network off the coast of the Netherlands going all the way to the Ruhr area in Germany — a place where there are real wooded hills. So what did the Dutch do when cities began to establish there? They made little windscreens in the open land for protection, and gardens to produce food within these cities. It worked very well, looked very nice, and, taken all together, there is a lot of green space in cities in the Netherlands. This was an urban forest, at least until a century ago, of green roves providing a nice atmosphere in all seasons, and windscreens along roads and beside farm houses outside the towns.

The scale of nature in the Netherlands is not as dramatic as that of North America, having no wild and open countryside. We have to make do with little things and are now in the process of mapping all the values in our old built structures, such as whatever might be growing on the walls. Nature observers, youth clubs, and old people are gathering this information. Also, land uses change, for example, as when one military works was no longer needed and the bastions were transformed into promenades, areas to walk around.

After the Second World War a population explosion occurred in the Netherlands, and with our very complex, artificial and open urban system, a lot of pollution was created. The whole landscape is an artificial system, reorganized to be used as a means of production for the cities. The area of Rotterdam harbour, for example, was completely transformed with artificial canals; nice natural reserves were given up. Dunes are needed to filter drinking water pumped out of the polluted rivers, especially because we are below the end of the Rhine into which all kinds of dangerous wastes from Switzerland, Germany, and France are dumped. Since we have to build on soils that are not very stable, we dig out sand from deep areas to use as artificial foundations, thus forming lakes around cities in combination with the building process. We also have a lot of waste being dumped, and as a tradition since the 1930s most cities cooperate to make compost from household waste through a common system of compost plants. A recent problem, however, is the toxification of this compost, but there are programs to control this and to make healthy compost once again. Our city planning is what we call in Dutch "making work with work," because since, for example, we have to dig out sand and make a pond or a lake in order to build, it can be combined with the making of a park.

This country, with its open economy and its spoiling system of management for cities, produces a lot of solid waste that is dumped into various systems, such as controlled landfills and open flat landscaping areas where there is now a new type of landscape — hills. The last type of landscape is an example of a system built around the cities to allow people to stay in contact with the city and to have a type of nature accessible and not too far away.

Amsterdam, in the seventeenth century, was a little city with a big lake. This "Haarlemmer Lake" was the result of using peat for heating houses, and of storms making it bigger and bigger. There is a history of land reclamation and land protection — Haarlemmer Lake was reclaimed about one hundred years ago. The "Y," an open inland sea connecting Amsterdam eastward through a sort of loop with the North Sea and the Atlantic, was closed off by a storm-dam in the 1930s. New canals facilitate shipping. The new "Y-Lake," first brackish, now sweet, became important as a natural resource, with many fish and fowl. The most recent reclaimed "Polder" was taken into use in the 1960s. A major recent decision was not to develop this last planned polder, or reclaimed area, in Y-Lake. This is a monumental success for the environmental movement because an open water area that is now very important for the migration of birds from Scandinavia south to Africa will be preserved.

There is now a very recent tradition to first plant trees, and to then create settlements: trees grow slower than houses can be built. There are all sorts of interesting management techniques for these woods, lanes, avenues, and windscreens, such as selective harvesting. It is interesting that, when settlements in the polders were begun, there was a narrow row of trees that once grown older were alternately cut down instead of clear cut. The replanting of trees is also done this way, providing a continuous process of management and design. In the design approach as developed in the 1930s, therefore, there was an idea of how to manage the system and also to produce a little bit of timber.

In the 1930s there was a famous group of urban planners in Amsterdam who together with the local government developed research methods for urban parks. The existing urban green areas were only decoratively green. The group prepared a plan for the future development of the city that was not executed until the 1950s because of the Second World War. The plan produced a park as a result of the production of sand. As a forerunner of the plan, the first urban forest was made by the same group of planners in the thirties. It is an example of a bigger area artificially created for a combination of functions. In the plan for this "Amsterdam Wood" there is an interesting zoning system of more intensively used areas and very limited use areas where, for example, birds breed. During the past fifty years interesting ecosystems have developed in the park. In the thirties there was also the beginning of physical planning in the Netherlands on a regional scale. A recent regional plan for Amsterdam, Haarlem, and other urban areas connected these centres with each other within a large framework that incorporates the making of green woods.

Every city in the Netherlands has a slightly different tradition of how to deal with forest. In The Hague, for instance, the interesting thing is that in the layout of the town, existing green areas, which in this case are situated mostly on dunes or sand ridges, were incorporated. It was not so much the making of new forests, as in the case of Amsterdam, but of trying to use existing areas because The Hague has a spotted or mixed urban pattern. Former country houses in these dunes were incorporated and opened as public parks. This, of course, required special management techniques, because they are a combination of a very artificial and more natural woods. In places such as the public parks of The Hague, very artificial, sometimes very beautiful, flower shows go on while other areas are more natural, and there is a tradition of having demonstrations of what the original wild areas in the Netherlands looked like.

Regional planning requires a balanced growth of cities. Since the Second World War there has been a national program for "buffer-zones" — areas between cities that have to be kept "open." Based on this post-war planning option, several projects were executed in the 1950s, 1960s, and 1970s, and others will follow. The idea is to prevent cities from "gluing together," a process where many miles of urban area is formed, and to plan for a good urban pattern with a well thought-out combination of open space (including forest) and more built-up areas. In buffer zones there are public gardens where one can pick up spices for cooking, and there are programs in schools for children to learn how to grow and observe nature. To walk into the urban wood next to the city is to just walk out of one's living quarters.

In some areas the public has a role in management. The landscape in these areas is completely artificial, but the subject is in a sense related because the choice of species depends upon what the soil makes possible. But also it is a sort of mirror of nature, a reflection of the Dutch idea of what a natural landscape is. We cannot learn from tradition, because the tidal landscape is no longer present, so we have to think of how to make a new landscape. That is the continuous debate: What is nature in our country? What is artificial? Can we imitate things? Can we make little Switzerland? Can we make it all Dutch when we do not know what that is?

There is an effort to combine agriculture in buffer zones by re-organizing it to make more woods and special places for intensive recreation. It will be an amenity for urbanites to walk and to bicycle through all types of landscapes thus created. Sometimes there will be hills out of waste (landfill). Once executed, urban dwellers will have a "walk arounder." Walking on the landfill suddenly gives one a surprising view of the urban area which was never before possible in such a flat country. It is very strange because there is a dune, the only type of hill we know, in a landscape that was never hilly. One does not feel as if one were living in a big metropolis. With all these people living together in the fringe of cities, it is still possible to have a sense of being in a small green town while still profiting from the economy and culture of a world city.

Physical planning in the Netherlands has long been engaged with ecology and landscape design. The first map of the ecological infrastructure of the Netherlands was made by the National Physical Planning Agency in the 1960s. The elements consisted of homogenous areas and gradients, where one environment is changing to another type of environment. A plan was made to develop, out of possibilities and potentials, a wider network of ecosystems along the rivers.

As a follow-up, in relation with the urbanized areas, a development scheme for an ecological infrastructure in urban fringes became possible. This was followed by habitat studies of, for example, fish shelter in existing areas and measures to make natural areas of bushes for shelter and clean water for food. Urban forests are now also viewed as a means to reinforce the ecological infrastructure of the country.

Later, a general ecological model of the Netherlands was made that put together, through a mapping exercise, existing and potential natural ecosystems. The model depicts the various possible functions of ecosystems. Factors considered were carrier functions, storage functions, the vast assimilation functions, protection functions, information functions, and regulation functions. It was a model of how nature functions and serves society, not only in producing things but also in regulating life and giving people information. This type of modelling was needed to balance ongoing development pressures.

Another approach to planning introduced in the 1980s is the development of scenarios — a trend scenario, where we expect a growth in population, economy, or a need of space could, for example, lead to a completely built-up area, either concentrated or in a type of motor-car oriented society with a deconcentrated pattern of living.

Planning means coordination of financing from the private sector and from the various public sectors. It means harmonizing public opinion and private action. Research has shown that the ideal situation of how people would like to live is quite opposite to the recent tradition of the 1960s, where highrise buildings were normal. Moreover, urban planners in the Netherlands have learned how to deal with these matters. An example is the incorporation of old farm functions in urban extensions. In a former orchard where willows were traditionally used for production of sticks, for example, there are now biology programs for schools. This shows how education in nature programs can go along with the preservation of relics of the old landscape in cities. Other examples could follow. A whole range of former farm elements are useful in cities. Urban farms can show city dwellers, especially children, how bread and cheese are made. They learn that this comes from nature, not from industry. This strengthens environmental awareness and commitment.

The physical arrangement of cities in their surrounding landscapes, as a result of ecological modelling, can be characterized as follows. In more intensely used parts, there are monocultural green areas for sports and the like. Further out, there is a zoning to nature reserves linking the town with other monofunctional areas for agriculture and related uses. The in-between areas are multifunctional and mixed.

In multifunctional areas a special technique of working with waste material from buildings, with the assistance of local inhabitants, is applicable to nature development. Other approaches look more for original wild flowers: there are a lot of seeds produced in the Netherlands to have on our roadsides and in public parks. Design methods are now used in planning based on an integrative approach to landscape, movements of people (traffic), and housing planning. There is a choice for a so-called organic approach, because the Dutch feel that they must have something other than a rectangular seventeenth century developed or reclaimed landscape. Sometimes, this "organic" style of design implies returning to that earlier tidal landscape which is taken up as a motive for organizing an urban area. Research on soil types and possible vegetation goes along with this.

Some of the projects mentioned earlier are self-funding, because over time they will produce wood. The national urban forest program, designed to increase the production of wood, incorporates a tradition of social research. Apart from ecology, this type of socially oriented and practised approach is essential in the planning process.

For instance, as a result of socio-economic research, it was proposed to the Senate that farmers over a certain age who would like to forest their lands should have subsidies. There is also research on consumer behaviour that leads to special designs. For the Dutch, any tree is valuable wood, and with careful detailing, for example by having little metal bands to prevent tree damage when bicycles are present, many uses can be accommodated.

Part of the project for urban forestry is a program to inform the public, such as a series of posters addressing the fact that there are always conflicting views on the environment and that it is necessary to negotiate. Many people bring many ideas or wishes, and we should be in a continuous debate for harmonization, which is really typical for Dutch planning. Also typical is an awareness that at many times a new item on the political agenda arises, including the recognition of a problem such as the ecology of cities. Then, as a society, you gain control over it. You will find technical solutions, then manpower, and then come to a maintaining phase to keep the environment healthy, sustainable, and fit to live in for a long period of time.

Naturalizing Parks and Nonpark Open Spaces
Michael Hough

What I want to consider is the question of what naturalization means in terms of habitat creation. It is very easy to say that we must naturalize landscapes, but much more difficult to actually do it. One thing about naturalization is that it creates diverse habitats, and the greater the diversity of habitat, the fewer "unhealthy" species, such as rats and pigeons, there will be. This is a very important factor for urban areas, and there is a lot of work being done on precisely these aspects of habitat creation.

I also want to consider the question of preservation, and I will do so from a new point of view, along with considering what is meant by wildflowers, because I have great concern about the wildflower movement in Canada. Unlike in Texas, where the wildflowers are all native, here the movement seems to be leaning towards another form of universal horticulture. I also want to suggest that perceptions are important, and to show what one can do in design to offset some problems associated with naturalization.

The first important thing about naturalization is that not all parks should be naturalized. There are many areas where that is the last thing one wants to do. We often wonder about what should be done with areas that have traditionally (for the last forty or fifty years) been mown by machines.

We need to think about the idea of diversity, of different places for different people. Sometimes the universality of turf begins to create problems such as in low flat areas where there are water ponds. Obviously, something must be done in situations like this, because it is difficult to get the mower through and expensive to keep the place looking as if it did not have ponding.

The exact opposite happens where we create a series of habitats completely from scratch. At a refinery in Mississauga, Ontario, where there was absolutely nothing there to start except for some fill, a series of habitats have been built up over the last ten to fifteen years. A pond, a wetland, and different kinds of woodlands have evolved. This kind of diversity is very important, because it is one answer to unwanted rats and pigeons. When we started, there were only pigeons present, and although I did not see any rats, I am sure they were also there. Today, ten years later, you can see foxes in the bush and muskrats in the pond. A tremendous increase in the diversity of species comes about, in effect, by creating habitats, or alternatively by leaving them alone.

The problem is not only *public* perception, but also the perceptions of the maintenance men who are actually doing the work. A good example of where one should *not* be mowing is along steep slopes. But this is a problem of assumptions because the operators of the mowers are really proud to be able to successfully mow steep slopes. They look at it with pride. But the steeper the slope, the more they risk their lives. Another good example of where you do not mow is underneath dense woodlands. Again, with mowing under dense woodlands, there is a question of pride. Getting a mower underneath impossible canopies and around every single tree gives a very great sense of satisfaction to those people who enjoy mowing.

This example of the universal mowing problem leads me into the other issue, that of a sense of place. There are many places in Canada that look like places in the United States. We are talking about regional diversity here. What makes one place different from another? One of the problems of the horticulture movement gone wild is the fact that it tends to obliterate much of the sense of a place. The intrinsic quality of Ottawa's environment, for example, is so easy to create, but with much of its landscaping one feels that one could be almost anywhere. It is this universality of approach to the way we manage land that is fundamentally at issue here.

We have begun to look at alternatives to leaving many of these places alone. Those places that are intrinsically difficult, like draws, slopes, and little streams, would, if just left alone, decrease overall mowing and increase diversity and the sense of being somewhere different. It gives a sense of identity. The whole aspect of diversity in what are now traditionally mown parks begins to give us a wonderful set of options for different kinds of needs. Some people like simply sitting out and painting; some like to look for frogs in a stream; others like playing football. Each of these sorts of places needs a different kind of environment.

Returning to perceptions again, one of the problems we always face when wanting to naturalize an area is, for example, what to do about hay fever and other undesired effects from specific species. Naturalization also tends to create the sense that a place is not safe. In the Delft area of Holland, the Dutch went in and simply reforested entire courtyards. It is safe there, but somehow here it is thought not to be. Why is that? There are negative aspects other than the perception of crime, such as the difficulty of cleaning up these places. But if people knew a little bit more about plant succession, I think they would arrive at more positive conclusions. For instance, one of the real problem plants is ragweed, but ragweed occurs at the very earliest stage of the successional process only. For a lot of problems we must depend on education, so that people will understanding the basis of their environment.

The aim is to create different forms of habitat through a process of managed succession. The concept of managed succession is that rather than planting an area with the trees that you want fifty years down the road, you plant trees that are at the early stage of the successional process. In this area, plants like alder, poplar, and aspen create, in the first five years, an environment that is more conducive to the longer lived species such as maple and oak. In an ideal world one plants the early successional species to first create the proper habitat, and then the longer lived species at a later date. Over a period of 150 years or so, a mature forest will evolve. It can be achieved much sooner, however, by the process of managed succession.

In one naturalization experiment we began with poplars and aspens. After those had been in for about three years they were about fifteen feet high. The plants that we introduced underneath, in fact, are now taking off very well. There are a whole series of alternatives that we have been looking at to try and define the easiest and least complicated method of regenerating this kind of habitat, because over

time it is by far the cheapest kind of landscape that you can create. It
is also the most complex.

What we saw in the Texas wildflower program was the consequence of natural succession. It is the kind of thing we would love to
see in Canada. We have a different kind of succession here, and trying
to recreate something from somewhere else is really part of the problem rather than part of the solution. One finds many seed catalogues,
for instance, where many of the seed mixes are from many different
regions of the country. After the second year of growth the more
aggressive local native weeds begin to come in and eventually the
wildflower mix that is not native to the area completely disappears,
because it does not have the same stability as the local weeds. It is
very pleasant while it lasts, but it also means very high maintenance,
and I do not believe that it does very much for identifying the sense
of place, to which I referred earlier. What is native in this area though,
is old field succession that has an enormous diversity of plants that
provide the best cover at the time of year when it is most needed —
autumn.

Now a few words on design alternatives. One of the problems of
naturalization, in terms of its public acceptance, is the fact that it is
not seen in design terms. It is always seen as the kind of biological
approach of leaving things alone without any basic design structure.
I think that many municipalities have this problem with naturalization, because the best way of naturalizing is to leave a place alone in
many cases, and it looks as if you have abandoned your responsibilities to the public. I have been working to develop a sense of
design structure that makes naturalizing look purposeful, rather than
simply abandoned.

I suggest some alternatives. One of the key things for naturalizing
some areas is to ensure that there is some lawn left. In a project we
did at a refinery that is associated with a housing community, we
made a point of creating lawns that were associated with the housing
and the roads, and of creating very strong forms and patterns. That
is, we made sure to design the edges in a way that looked purposeful
and beautiful. Another example is at York University, where the
edges are not mown but have been created in a very definite purposeful pattern. They were not just left; they were designed into the

landscape. Again, the idea of having a pattern of mown and unmown areas gives a sense of complexity and purpose that is much more acceptable in design terms than it would be if you simply left the place alone.

Another idea relates to high-use areas, which people use for picnicking and so require mowing everywhere. At one of the great gardens in Britain, Heva Castle, it is so expensive to mow all the vast lawns that they have left many of them alone, particularly at the edges, and simply make pockets of mown lawn for people to lie around in. Similarly, an approach attempted in Britain which is more difficult to do here, except in some conservation areas which do not take a lot of people, is to mow pathways which then become the structured landscape through the naturalized area. Both examples demonstrate a sense of purpose in thinking of the design and use implications of naturalization programs.

Finally, another factor that is critical to consider is that when areas are being naturalized the public must be told what is being done or is about to be done. In addition to things like designed edges and developing some sort of design structure into the landscape, you need to tell the public what is going on, either in the form of community meetings, signs, or both. It is critical to the success of any naturalization program.

Naturalizing Existing Parklands
William Granger

Although ornamental horticulture certainly has a place in urban parkland design, construction, and maintenance, it does not have the only place, and that is the feeling behind the North York parks and recreation naturalization program. "All too often urban open space designers react to small but eager pressure groups concerned with one particular sporting activity or with the view from their own backyard. The single most important design criteria becomes political expediency and not long-term community serviceability. A curious phenomenon takes place, and we find that it has been so long since most people have seen undisturbed nature that people forget what nature really looks like. In come the mowers to trim up the weeds. In come the pruners to trim up the trees. Picnic tables, swings, tennis courts, swimming pools, ball diamonds are all introduced to fill what is obviously a void, often an embarrassing nothingness" (Jones 1982).

In Ontario, the history of deliberate and wanton natural destruction is a long but a fairly simple one. The earliest European settlers to Upper Canada around the year 1800 were largely United Empire Loyalists from Pennsylvania and New York State who came north for political reasons, and they had already established an agrarian society. Prior to 1800, most of Upper Canada supported a rich, very diverse hardwood forest, and what happened to that forest almost certainly laid the foundations for the present day disregard for natural areas in Ontario.

William Granger is Arborist Supervisor for the City of North York, in Metro Toronto, where he has been conducting naturalization work in city parks for several years.

Timber was seen first and foremost as a commodity. *A Statistical Account of Upper Canada,* complied in 1822, lists the types of good hardwood timber available simply "for the cutting" in each of Upper Canada's townships at the time (Gourlay 1974). Gourlay States in his General Introduction to *Statistical Account* that "God instituted property, and clearly tells us that, by the proper use of it, we can rise to excellence; but without property, or the chance of acquiring it, no good can be expected of us."

Many obviously accepted Gourlay's interpretation of the proper use of property, because by 1854 the Province of Upper Canada (now Ontario) supported 1,618 sawmills, as compared to 610 grist mills (Lizars 1913). Clearing the land was a prudent and profitable industry to become involved with during the developing stages of Upper Canada. One man who made both a fortune and a political career from lumbering was William Pearse Howland, who came north from the States with his brothers in the late 1830s and began buying and developing sawmills throughout Upper Canada. W.P. Howland was named Lieutenant-Governor of Ontario (July 1868-November 1873) and was eventually knighted by the British Crown for his efforts in the development of Upper Canada and the Dominion of Canada.

The lumbering operations for profit took a severe toll on the natural forested lands. As an example, the *Halton Atlas* in 1877 stated that the good hardwood timber had all but disappeared since the lumbermen commenced their operations (Halton 1877).

In spite of the lumbermen's pillage, or perhaps in concert with it, massive timber-stripping and burning operations were undertaken by settlers to clear off the croplands. A 1905 account of the "early days," as told in *Early Pioneer Life in Upper Canada,* describes the deforestation as follows:

> Considerable time was spent in the winter by the pioneer in felling the trees, preparatory to clearing the land. The sound of chopping and the crashing noise made by the falling trees, as they yielded to the woodsman's axe, could be heard in all directions. In the fall of the year, previous to this, "underbrushing" was done. This consisted of cutting down the small trees and bushes and throwing them together into piles, so that they would not be in the way of the chopper. The trees were chopped so that they fell into a pile or

"winrow." During a dry spell in summer, a day was set for the "burn," when the piles in the "fallow" were set on fire. After this, what remained was cut into logging lengths, a logging bee made, and these lengths drawn together by oxen, and again made into piles and burnt. The chucks that remained after this second burning were collected by the farmer and his men (the women folks and the children often assisting at the "chucking") into little pieces, and once more set fire to and kept burning by heaping up the burning fragments and pieces of logs until they were all reduced to ashes. The brush, consisting of the limbs and branches, was collected into separate piles and burnt.

The net result of all the lumbering and land stripping was that water tables were irrevocably lowered to the point at which many sawmills went out of business. More important, any notion that natural areas were important was, in many cases, irretrievably lost to successive generations of farmers and their children. The problem is not unique in our country. Indeed, the denuding of the natural environment which took place in almost all new agrarian-based societies continues to take place across the world today in the name of progress, or profit, or both.

With the end of the primarily agrarian society and the advent of industrialized society in North America early in this century, people began to move in large numbers from rural communities to towns and cities. With them, young people brought to the city an honestly gained belief that nature was something to be looked at outside of town, if at all. The automobile made travel from town accessible to the masses, and not much thought was given in North America to provision of natural green space within urbanizing areas prior to World War II. Exceptions to this only seem to have been provided deliberately in the large cities of New York (Central Park), Philadelphia (Fairmont Park), and Toronto (High Park). The major interests of each of these public open spaces was to provide areas for entertainment and public sporting events. That natural areas were left untouched in each of these sizeable tracts is because the city fathers did not have sufficient funds to develop all areas of each park at one time. Although Frederick Law Olmsted, principle landscape architect of Central Park in 1858, discussed "a constant suggestion to the imagination of an unlimited range of rural conditions," he drew on the traditions of British landscape art. Olmsted and Calvert Vaux, his assistant and an English-born architect, removed and reposited hundreds of thousands of cartloads of rock; brought in hundreds of thousands of cubic yards of topsoil; created lakes and ponds by rerouting streams and laying 114 miles of pipe; and planted four to five million trees, shrubs, and vines. Central Park includes baseball diamonds, tennis courts, playgrounds, wading pools, artificial skating rinks, Loeb Boathouse, and Delacorte Theatre, most of which were not completed until Olmsted had retired and Robert Moses took over as parks commissioner from 1934 to 1960 (Davis 1981).

Moses, in the first quarter of 1934, proposed that Olmsted's original plans be augmented by the addition of a zoo, a Great Lawn, and the entire North Meadow area carved into playing fields. He turned Olmsted's sheepfold into an English Inn called Tavern-on-the-Green. He continued to build and revise the park asphalting cinder walks, lining paths with sentry-like London Plane trees, and displacing any vestige of untouched nature in the 840 acre park.

The City of North York, Ontario, never really got started in the parks and recreation field until nearly a century later. Typical of many small North American towns and villages on the outskirts of larger, established cities, North York was a sleepy township of 25,000 persons at the end of World War II (North York 1978). Ninety-five percent of the present-day population moved to North York after 1951; their homes are built on what was formerly farmland.

Not until 1950, in a city like North York which began as a largely rural municipality and then began to develop subdivision-type housing after World War II, was any kind of a recreation program or recreation facility thought of for outlying suburban municipalities. A number of larger cities provided pieces of parkland, sometimes common green-type parklands, and sometimes larger parks, such as High Park in Toronto. In New York, there was obviously Central Park, and in Philadelphia, Fairmont Park, but in outlying municipalities parkland was not thought of until well after World War II.

The first budget in North York was $5,500 in 1950 to provide all of the parkland and all of the parkland facilities that the citizens of North York needed in order to live full and happy lives. Often school board properties were used, often ornamental horticulture was the order of the day, and certainly things that were provided by the local municipality were swing sets, baseball diamonds, backstops, and general active recreation facilities. Typical of many municipal parks and recreations departments, local park land was manicured to short, mown grass standards. The generally perceived notion was that un-manicured landscapes were messy, collected garbage, provided shelter for rodents and wild animals and encouraged antisocial behaviour, and led to much of the natural parkland being built on, or if adjacent to residential development, to be filled and turned to mowed manicured grassland.

This sort of development took place through the 1950s, 1960s, and early 1970s, but I do not want to mislead you into thinking that all people have been served badly by this kind of parkland. That is not the intent of naturalizing parklands in the 1980s. What we tried to do in presenting a report to our park's recreation committee and council, and what other municipalities now are beginning to talk about doing, is to redress some of the imbalance that occurred in outlying municipalities particularly, but also in some of our larger cities.

The reasons we felt that there was something of an imbalance are that we have heard from many residents that they need somewhere natural to go within Metropolitan Toronto and North York. Certainly the kinds of parkland management that we practised, even if we tried to preserve woodlots, clearly did not leave much of nature in place. The understory was removed completely, the large, often mature to over-mature maple beech forests that are indigenous to North York were left with no understory and with very severe competition from lawnmower and herbicide damage, and often even attempts to be kind to the trees were not terribly successful.

We began to hear as well from the professional recreationists that different kinds of recreation potentials were needed in the city, because people could not leave the city as often as they once had, due to changing demographics in our city and in every municipality. Certainly the availability of recreation land for what used to be called passive recreation, but what people generally refer to now as spontaneous unorganized recreation, does not exist in most urban centres.

The first study that we relied on in our report to council was the federal *Canada Fitness Survey,* released in 1981, which focused on ten to nineteen year-olds and involved the interviewing of eleven thousand Canadians. It found the five most common activities enjoyed by Canadian youth were walking, jogging and running, home exercises, bicycling, and ice hockey. A second study, published by the Ontario Ministry of Culture and Recreation, listed the five most popular year-round activities in Ontario as walking, general exercise, jogging/running, swimming, and bicycling. It pointed out that availability and accessibility of facilities is one of the most important sources of encouragement to begin or to continue participation in spontaneous activity. The third study came from a Metropolitan Toronto planning process which was completed in 1977. It released figures indicating that 60 percent of the individuals surveyed within Metropolitan Toronto enjoyed recreational walking. This meant that more than 300, 000 North York residents are potential users of natural areas within our park system.

The link between these survey statistics and the naturalization of urban parklands is that the most popular recreation activities can best be accommodated in a natural environment. Walking, jogging, bicycling, and picnicking are certainly possible in highly maintained areas, but the maintenance dollars spent may be misdirected. As well as these studies, we had been hearing from residents. I think that staff of all municipalities hear from residents, on a fairly regular basis, that remnant woodlot areas and areas where woodlots had been removed completely during the initial development of North York were unsatisfactory as parkland next to their homes.

One example was Havenbrook park, which has a slope that was entirely regraded since a mature remnant maple beech forest was removed from the slope when initial regrading took place in the late 1950s. Some of the residents had lived there from the original time, and they remembered the woodlot and wondered if something might not be done to replace it. The answer that our design and construction landscape architecture people initially came up with was to take the turf grass away and replace it with one of Aimers' wildflower seed mixes as an interim step. The seed mix was a great success, and in its first year, 1985, the seed took. There are still a lot of weedy species in there that either blew in or came along with the seed mix, but the overall effect was very colourful and certainly well received.

We have very high hopes for this area in future years, and on the far slope a number of woody tree species have been planted, although we really are not sure how to manage this piece of land in the future. We may not manage it at all. The only management that has been required so far is to go in and take out thistles where they appeared, upon objections from the neighbours. We would also be obliged, as would any parks department in Ontario, to remove any noxious weeds listed on the Ontario noxious weeds list. To remove them we went in and hand scythed each weed, which does not really take much more effort than spraying, so we will continue the hand method.

The major change in the way that we deal with remnant woodlots, steep hillsides, and wet areas in our existing local park systems stems from an April 1985 decision by North York City Council to adopt a thirty page report from the Commissioner of Parks and Recreation entitled *Naturalized Areas in North York.* This study represented the culmination of two years research and fieldwork begun by students working on an Experience 1982 grant and completed by our own parks services staff. The adoption of the report gave the parks and recreation staff the political endorsement of the Parks and Recreation Committee and members of council to proceed with the naturalization program in twenty specified local park areas in consultation with and through cooperation with local community groups.

When we began our initial naturalization programs at Driftwood Community Centre in Edgeley Park in April 1982, we invited the assistance of a local group known as the Black Creek Venture Group, and they responded wonderfully. I think there is an interesting connection between Arbor day programs and the naturalization of parkland, where the two go hand in hand very well. Anyone involved in local communities may want to consider calling their spring seedling plantings Arbor day programs, because people normally think that Arbor day is a wonderful idea while they may not be keen about seedling plantings and turf grass.

On the Friday of our first Arbor day, we invited the Mayor, local members of council, and local separate school and public school trustees to attend and to help students from eighteen surrounding elementary schools to plant seedlings. They all attended and they all helped plant. On the Saturday, the Black Creek Venture Group hosted a pancake breakfast to finish off the initial planting of one thousand woody native seedlings into the understory of the former remnant forest. The price of admission to the pancake breakfast became a pair of dirty hands. If people at the community centre could show that they had been planting trees, the community group fed them. That is really tremendous community support, and it left everybody with a good feeling about the initial Arbor day planting.

At the end of the two day planting the former manicured front lawn was completely changed. The turf was turned over and left on top of the ground or used as a dish around the planting pit to hold any rainwater that fell. We supplied woodchips that we generate from our own forest trimming operations to place on top of every seedling planting pit. At the end of the first growing season, the grass had grown up tall around the seedlings, but each seedling had survived because of the woodchips. The grass was drawn back in the fall, and each seedling was painted with a rodent repellent that does not kill the rodents; they just do not like the taste and so generally leave after one nibble. We have had, in the end, very little loss through either vandalism, trampling, or rodent damage.

We also used another small piece of natural parkland in North York as a model for the kinds of species that we should be planting in our woodlot regeneration programs. It was really a fortuitous natural park, beginning as a former bridge abutment that had been allowed to grow on its own for about fifteen years. We found that nature readily provides plants and grows species like sumac, Manitoba maple, dogwood, white ash, and other species, such as nannyberry, serviceberry, and dogwood, that we have used on a large scale in other park locations. We were very pleased to find that those species also worked well at Driftwood Park.

We have other remnant forests that have not been disturbed, and part of our initial report to committee and council contained a very strong recommendation that those areas be preserved in perpetuity. I think this should be the cornerstone of anyone's naturalization program: to identify what you already have that is natural and then to preserve it. It is very difficult in some areas to preserve woodlots because of encroaching development pressures, or encroaching neighbourhood pressures, or even encroaching neighbours. In some of our parks, for example, we have fenced to the property line. This has been necessary to stop neighbours from throwing garbage over the steep sided ravines and slowly killing off the trees. In other parks this has not been necessary, and certainly that is the ideal if you have the option. Also, sometimes even well-intentioned storm water management schemes, or bicycle trail construction, requires review by the local parks and recreation people because there may be a way to have less an impact on the natural area. Storm water in the downstream municipalities is certainly one of the most difficult areas to deal with in terms of preserving what is there, and also for preserving the safety of the people who live alongside of what is there.

In another one of our relatively natural parks, a nut forest called Caledonia Park, the understory had also been removed. It is very small in size, only about an acre and a quarter, but it has been allowed to return, through seedling underplanting and not mowing the grass, and it is now a very popular picnic park at lunch. People come and use the benches. The grass is still mowed to the benches, especially during July and August, and this generally does not conflict with the users. We no longer mow into the woods, and we are now getting very healthy regeneration of native herbaceous species underneath the seedlings and underneath the tall overstory that existed previously.

There is a long-range practicality to the naturalization process for several reasons. The first is that forests take a long time to grow. With ever increasing transportation costs and increasingly closed-option lifestyles, these natural areas will be *in situ* when the need becomes the greatest. Urban wildlife will multiply and small ecosystems within city boundaries are quite possible.

More important than this practicality, however, is the notion that we all need relief from the hustle and bustle of urban life. Those of us lucky enough to own a garden might find this relief in our own backyards. For many, however, as fleeting as their appearances may be, the spring carpet of hepatica and dogtooth violet at Driftwood, glowing rough-leaved goldenrod in the east Don Valley, or the joy of Jerusalem artichoke in fall bloom beside Black Creek, are each singular reminders that we live in a complex and often very beautiful world.

Finally, the cost effectiveness of our natural park lands is of interest to all municipalities. The first Arbor day program held in 1982 included two kinds of landscaping. The first was traditional landscaping with large specimen size trees and shrubs planted alongside the second kind of treatment, which was seedling planting. To be really objective about the cost comparison, we considered the initial planting material costs, equipment, and labour costs for planting and maintenance costs (including mowing along the pathways and annual rodent repellent application in the natural area) for a three year establishment period following planting.

An acre of manicured, formalized parkland, complete with shrub beds and weekly seasonal maintenance for three years, costs $44, 028. In contrast, an acre of reforested parkland using volunteer labour, including three years follow-up maintenance, costs $4, 800. Clearly, the cost differential between these two types of park landscape treatment is so substantial as to warrant serious consideration by any municipal parks and recreation provider or by any large landowner. Private and institutional landowners would do well to look at the real and ongoing costs of turf grass maintenance, and especially shrub and specimen tree maintenance, if they are dealing with their shrubs and trees as individual specimens. Many thousands of acres of manicured turfgrass could easily be returned to a reforested state and demonstrate substantial cost savings to the landowners. If hand scything for weed control is required under the Noxious Weeds Act, for example, then the labour costs for maintenance will rise nominally. No other maintenance costs are foreseen in the initial ten years of reforested woodland establishment, and the cost savings are self-evident. Quite aside from these cost benefits, the environmental considerations of less noise, exhaust fumes, and energy consumption in labour, equipment, and fuel should be seen as desirable attributes of reforested urban areas.

We also find in our natural parks that we have an abundant natural seed source. It should not be a surprise, but it seems to be in some cases. Seeds fall to the ground in our natural parks and often they will grow, and perhaps only one in a million will make it to maturity, but it is part of that great natural process of regeneration. We even found that in a couple of our locations the residents are taking very well to the natural parklands next to their houses and are even coming out and protecting the seedlings that grow on their own, to make sure that someone does not get over-zealous and trim them off.

Different types of paths have been tried by different jurisdictions. At Bruce's Mill Conservation Area there is a very cheap and effective way to elevate a walkway over a damp area, saving on compaction of the forest floor and a lot of muddy feet. At the Civic Garden centre, there is another type of asphalt pathway. In the local parks we will not get into the asphalted pathway very often, unless in a flood prone area where gravel or woodchips wash away constantly. In Metro Toronto Parks there is a need, or a perceived need, for surveillance of large park areas, and the Metro police have often suggested to Metro parks that they asphalt their pathways to make them easily driveable. From a bicyclist's point of view, an asphalt pathway is a lot better than screenings or a dirt pathway, so there are advantages and disadvantages to different sorts of management.

The eventual appearance of naturalized park areas would be attractive hardwood forest settings. Once the desired line pathways are established through these forest settings, more formalized gravel or woodchipped path surfaces will be established for joggers, bicyclists, and people who hike. As well, low-maintenance rustic benches and educational signs indicating natural features and tree species are proposed. In fact, we have already begun to label some of our trees at the Banbury community centre. It is popular with a number of neighbours and neighbourhood children because they finally know exactly what it is they are looking at; it is not just another tree, a bigger tree, or a different kind of tree.

For decades we have been loosing sight of the forest for the trees. Many of us, personally and professionally, have been involved in countless battles to save individual trees or small landscaped areas. The notion of saving vast expanses of natural lands was lost to our society almost two hundred years ago and to Western civilization long before that. The forested area of North America is down to some 3.5 percent of our land mass; deforestation and desertification of

Third World countries is incrementally stripping the remaining forest from the earth's surface.

We should elevate our goals past the planting, protection, and preservation of individual trees. If we each begin to encourage and assist with community-based awareness programs, we should soon (collectively) leave behind the static landscape notions of our ancestors. With each passing day, the forest resources at the edge of our cities and our rural areas are being squandered, and it is we who should be trying to turn this untenable situation around. Some small progress has been made in revegetation programs *en mass* in urban areas and this could be a key feature of our new methods. Every municipality has vacant rights-of-way or hilly or wet areas of parkland, old dump sites, or institutional grounds in need of revegetation. Through community awareness and neighbourhood involvement, we can and must begin to re-green these areas. From there, our community forests may be able to link together on a regional basis to provide recreation, watershed management, agricultural land, fuelwood, and construction materials right in the city and on a sustained yield basis. We also will find in our natural areas, as time goes by, that we are getting a great return of very beautiful natural herbaceous understory, along with a very beautiful middle-story and overstory. There is a great deal of diversity that exists in our landscapes. All we must do is allow it to grow.

REFERENCES

Canada. 1981. Fitness and Amateur Sport. *Canada Fitness Survey*. Ottawa: Supply and Services Canada.

Davis, Gordon J. 1981. *Report and Determination in the Matter of Christo: The Gates*. New York: Department of Parks and Recreation.

Gourlay, Robert. 1974. *A Statistical Account of Upper Canada*. 1822 abridged by S.R. Mealing. Toronto: McClelland and Stewart Ltd.

Halton County. 1877. *Halton Atlas of 1877*. Halton County: Province of Ontario.

Jones, W.A. 1982. "The Once and Future Park." *Parks and Recreation Magazine* (March).

Lizars, K.M. 1913. *The Valley of Humber, 1615-1913*. Toronto: William Briggs.

North York. 1963. *Master Plan for Parks and Facilities*. North York: Township of North York, Parks and Recreation Department.

—. 1973. *Historical Outline of the Administration of the Borough of North York.* North York: Borough of North York, 1978.

Ontario. Ministry of Culture and Recreation: Sports and Fitness Branch. 1980. *Physical Activity Patterns in Ontario.* Toronto: Government of Ontario Printing House.

Pen Pictures of Early Pioneer Life in Upper Canada. William Briggs, 1905. Reprint. Toronto: Coles Publishing Co., 1972.

Shabecoff, Philip. 1987. "Earth's Natural Limits at Risk, Report Warns." *Globe and Mail*, 16 February 1987.

Toronto. 1976. *Metropolitan: Public Open Space.* Background Studies in the Metropolitan Plan Preparation Programme. Toronto: Metropolitan Toronto Planning Department.

Naturalizing Existing Parklands
A Case Study: The National Capital Commission
Edward Holubowich

The National Capital Commission, with its antecedents, is one of the oldest crown corporations in Canada. It was established under the National Capital Act of 1958 with a mandate to ensure that the shape and character of Canada's Capital is in accordance with its national significance. The commission works to create a national capital representative of the country's highest ideals and of which all Canadians may be proud.

To do this, the act states that the NCC may acquire property, construct and maintain parks, parkways, bridges, and other structures; maintain and improve property owned by the federal government; cooperate with local municipalities and others in joint projects; preserve and maintain historic places; and carry out planning related to the proper development of the national capital region. Operating within the 4,662 square kilometre region, the thousand-person commission administers approximately 150,000 acres (68,181 hectares) of federal land. The bulk of this land was acquired in the 1950s and the 1960s in the implementation of the Jacques Greber Master Plan. Land was bought and/or expropriated for the realization of the greenbelt, Gatineau Park, parkways, driveways, parks, river-front corridors, employment centres, and industrial zones.

Edward Holubowich is the Chief Landscape Architect of the National Capital Commission (NCC) in Ottawa, the Canadian capital. He provides design advice to the NCC and reviews all landscape design projects intended to be built on federal land in the national capital region.

The result of the land assembly program and subsequent design and development has created the principal open space network in the nation's capital. This network is unrivaled in quality, scale, and continuity anywhere in North America and perhaps Europe. Beauty and recreation go hand in hand, and, for example, since 1972 more than one hundred miles of safe, scenic, recreational pathways have been constructed for enjoyment by all.

For the past twenty-five years, many of the pathways, urban linear open spaces, and parks have been designed, developed, and maintained along traditional lines using horticultural techniques. The clean, highly manicured landscapes, while popular with the public, have in recent years become increasingly expensive to maintain due to increasing costs of energy and manpower.

To further complicate the picture, the NCC has embraced a new vision and mandate of making the capital a showcase for Canadian cultural events. New, exciting, large-scale festivals have become the "flagship" events for the NCC (Spring Festival, Winterlude, Canada Day, Summer Festival, and others). These labour-intensive events have begun competing with regular maintenance for our scarce labour resources.

Approximately five years ago the NCC became interested in the concept of the urban amenity forest. This concept reflects the more natural, lower-maintenance, less tailored, self-sustaining, and ecologically evolving vegetation and treed landscape. The ultimate decrease in such functions as frequent mowing, pruning, watering, and leaf raking, to name a few, would help solve some of our own resource shortages. It was therefore an economic necessity combined with the many other potential longer-term benefits that made us become more interested in the urban amenity forest concept.

In 1981, Michael Hough, of Hough Stansbury Associates, was retained to help the NCC set up an experimental plot involving urban reforestation techniques based upon experiences elsewhere and responding to our peculiar conditions and objectives. Thus was born the naturalization experiment in the southwest transitway corridor.

Purpose

The urban forest naturalization experiment was undertaken to establish a reliable body of information and practical experience in the application of managed succession forestry. The project was devised to help us evaluate, for future purposes, techniques, design criteria, minimal acceptable management requirements, and costs for urban woodland establishment over time.

The Site

Based upon predetermined criteria, a twelve-acre test plot site was established adjacent to a highly travelled recreational pathway, visible from a major highway, and next to residential housing. Varying topography, soil conditions, ease of watering, and access were also important. The proximity to the public was important in order to test public reaction and to provide information for future marketing strategies.

Objectives

The specifications for each of the seven test plots were designed to establish on a relative basis the following information:

1. The effectiveness and growth rate of different species and associations under the climatic and soil conditions peculiar to Ottawa

2. To determine the effectiveness and cost/benefit of different spacings and planting arrangements with particular emphasis on time required for canopy closure (1 m O.C. vs. 1.5 m O.C.)

3. The relative success of ground plane treatments for weed and grass control, rodent damage control, establishment of woodland litter accumulation, and canopy closure (Included were hand mechanical cultivation, various mulches including use of polyethylene ground sheets, wood chips, white dutch clover, and leaf mold mulch.)

4. Relative mortality of different species and the probable causes

5. In this experiment the decision was taken to mix 60 to 70 percent pioneer fast growing species with a 30 to 40 percent slower growing climax species

Observations

1. The NCC is not a scientific research agency. As a consequence, deviations and compromises have already been made from the original specifications for the experiment. These adjustments were necessary due to the lack of financial or labour resources at the time of implementation or during the subsequent growing season.

2. Four plots, totalling 23, 307 square metres were completed in 1982 at a cost of $2.56 per square metre. The work was done by NCC work crews. Three plots were completed in 1985. Their total area was roughly 17,000 square metres and the unit cost for implementation was $7.50 per square metre. This work was carried out by contract after public tender.

3. There has been insufficient resource or time available to gather much statistical information on growth, costs, and other specific problems. It appears that installation costs may be as much or more than standard landscape installations. It is, however, anticipated that future unit maintenance costs will be considerably less.

Preliminary Conclusions

1. With the exception of *Populus tremuloides* and *Acer saccharum,* all other species had acceptable percentage losses and could remain in the managed succession plantation list.

2. Of the mulched experiments, the use of a plastic liner covered with two inches of wood chip mulch produced the best results to date with respect to survival ratio, growth rate, weed and grass control.

3. Hand machine cultivated areas proved to produce the best overall growth rate for all species. It is, however, too expensive for large areas.

4. Timely and sufficient watering during drought periods is essential to keep mortality rates down to an acceptable level.

5. Sources for both pioneer and climax species for large plantations are hard to find. Few nurseries currently produce the types and sizes of materials required for urban reforestation.

6. Contractors who are knowledgeable in urban reforestation are not plentiful. Tender prices tend to be high and often based on the idea that substitutions are permissible.

7. The question of public acceptance and implications of large-scale new urban forests is yet to be conclusively tested. The Ottawa experiment has, to date, only met with minimal negative reaction. The traditions of the cosmetic landscape are what people normally expect.

Naturalized landscapes are often unkempt and imply abandonment of ongoing maintenance responsibilities. To gain wider acceptance will likely require a carefully planned public information and participation program. Our visual examples will likely be accepted if the edges are aesthetically designed and carefully maintained as well as reasonably far removed from pathways and private residents.

In conclusion, urban amenity forests technically appear to be a definite possibility. Long-term commitment by government as well as acceptance by the general public will likely be the two most critical factors in the acceptance of this reforestation and land management procedure.

The Ecological Restoration and Utilization of Urban Rights-of-Way
Dr. Robert Dorney

Introduction

The utilization of land under powerline rights-of-way (ROW) or above pipelines may include the shoulders of roads, since some utility rights-of-way follow roads as part of a joint corridor use. In addition, corridor use jointly by pipeline and hydro-electric lines may occur. The engineering requirements of twenty-four hour access to the corridor for safety (downed lines, explosions, etc.), periodic maintenance, environmental protection (spills, etc.), extensive rebuilding (requalification) every decade or two, and looping (additional facilities) have precedence over other potential open space uses. Rehabilitation, then, under or over gas, oil, or electric facilities precludes landscaping the ROW to large trees, that is, to reforestation, or to the building of recreational structures. Sewer lines, on the other hand, can be returned to a permanent forest cover under some conditions, and abandoned rail lines are interesting sites. Hence, each ROW has qualities which affect its after-use potential.

The late Dr. Robert Dorney, an ecologist and a professor in the School of Urban and Regional Planning, University of Waterloo, Waterloo, Ontario, was first president and chair of the Board of Ecoplans Ltd., a consulting company. He was a leader both in the development of computer mapping systems to display biophysical and cultural information, and in the field of ecological restoration. This paper was prepared from tapes made of his presentations at the International Symposium on Greening the City in Toronto.

Some after-uses which can be considered are grazing, active commercial farming, gardening, natural prairie or meadows for wildlife, shrub communities for aesthetics and wildlife, natural gardening for preservation of rare and endangered plant/animal species, and linear recreation activities (jogging, hiking, skiing). After-uses which use motorized vehicles or encourage campfires usually are not feasible. Thus, some controls on landscape uses and users are to be expected.

Since utility corridors fall under the jurisdiction of the national or provincial boards, environmental assessments prepared for these boards (for example, NEB, OEB, etc.) deal not only with construction, but also with landscape rehabilitation procedures which should be acceptable to all parties. On occasion, these procedures may be very detailed and expensive when a utility crosses sensitive landscape features, such as the Niagara Escarpment, a city park, or a natural stream valley of scenic beauty. Conditions of approval, then, for new ROW offer selective opportunities for incorporating natural meadows, shrub plantings, tree screens, or gardening activities planned in concert with the company or municipality operating the facility. Where joint utility companies occupy the same ROW, opportunities are lessened by concurrent maintenance needs (such as for parts of the Parkway Belt West near Mississauga, Ontario).

Since environmental assessments usually have public participation and public hearings, this is the time for community groups to examine the adequacy of the technical studies, and to consider what role they may play in approved after-uses for the ROW. A community gardening project, for example, could be part of the environmental submission. During the hearings, proposed community after-use can be put before the hearing board for consideration. As well, whenever municipal official plans are being reviewed, public-interest groups should examine the utility and open space section of such plans. Any suggestions incorporated at this stage make it easier to justify action later before city councils or before hearing boards.

Retrofitting a ROW to natural plant communities or to gardening uses would depend on individual circumstances. However, I believe landowners would be in a strong position to use the ROW for these uses if the utility were operating on an easement over which the parties had some control. For example, if the land were owned by the utility in fee simple, then the utility bargains from a stronger position. Generally, utilities do not make waves; they move energy or waste. Reasonable requests from responsible groups, in my experience, would be dealt with sympathetically.

Given these constraints then, what are the potentials for utilizing ROW in urban settings for greening the city? First, some planning and design considerations will be discussed. Then, examples, drawn for illustrative purposes from four situations in Toronto, Oakville, London, and Kitchener, include a sewer easement, two natural gas lines, one petroleum line, and hydro-electric corridors. These examples represent natural valley land or visually sensitive area considerations, community gardening, hiking trails, and woodland rehabilitation.

Planning Considerations

The proportion of an urban surface physically occupied by major electric utility corridors on separate ROW may be small, but its visual effect may be overwhelming. Electric, gas, and sewer lines under or alongside streets are excluded from this discussion as they do not have a separate ROW with landscaping potential. Natural gas and petroleum pipelines, as opposed to major hydro lines, are buried; hence, they have less visual effect — out-of-site, out-of-mind, so to speak.

Natural valley land corridors, now preserved as open space in newer sections of Ontario cities, often contain sewer line ROW, as sewage must move downhill by gravity. The valley is a "convenient" corridor for construction. Often these valleys are public lands as well, and sewage is a municipal responsibility.

If these public and private utilities above ground, below ground, and in a valley land of a ROW are mapped, a grid or network pattern is not unusual. Thus, any increase in natural plant cover along these ROW corridors can allow for natural plant and animal movement, often in many directions — a positive ecological benefit.

Since infrequent maintenance and twenty-four hour access are required for a ROW (except for abandoned rail lines), any natural planting or recreational use of it must recognize the primacy of these requirements. Also, utility corridors, for example the CN rail line between Toronto and Hamilton, also may carry buried telecommunications, buried gasoline lines, and overhead 250 kW electric lines. This joint occupancy of what is essentially one ROW may further restrict landscaping and recreational use, depending on which utility or operator owns the ROW, and which utility has easements for its use.

In older city areas, ROW vegetation can be mapped, and any existing recreational uses described. Then, specific proposals for new ROW landscaping and for new ROW uses would have a physical basis for discussion. Generally, restrictions due to past legal agreements, nuisances because of vandalism, and trespassing require consideration.

In urban fringe areas on new ROW being planned, greater flexibility from stipulating innovative natural landscaping and outdoor recreational uses is possible because the proponent is trying to reduce public opposition so as to facilitate approval. This means reasonable concessions at this stage are easier to obtain. Any organized community group, parks department, or city planning department with specific ideas will have a good chance of achieving implementation. Although this paper focuses on new ROW opportunities, retrofitting old ROW, some on joint electric pipeline and rail line corridors, is equally important and needs further attention.

If an Official Plan (OP) review is being considered for a municipality, the public hearing stage is the time to discuss recreational uses and landscaping policies for a utility ROW. If the public works and electric utility(ies) are requested in the OP to consider ecological and recreational concerns, the official door is partly open. For example, the Kitchener OP identifies linear hiking, biking, and jogging trails, some along electric ROW. New subdivisions being approved can be designed to fit these linkages. ROW, then, are considered as part of a multiple-use design enriching the urban fabric.

Design Considerations

Beyond the urban planning and these macro-scale issues there are some specific conceptual design issues which need to be touched on. If a ROW will destroy a wooded valley land slope, the narrow valley crossing can be made at right angles to the slope to minimize the disturbed area, and in the final design can be naturally landscaped. In Toronto, the ravine land protection policies are a case in point; these policies require landscaping restoration (replacement of pre-development vegetation) following ROW disturbances. Thus, aesthetics can be an important component in the ROW design.

Since valley land slopes may be unstable and always subject to surface erosion, any ROW rehabilitation has to stabilize the surface and the soil mass. Grasses and legumes do a better job of quick growth. Grass seed is cheap, while native herbs and shrubs are much slower, requiring years to cover a slope, and are more expensive than grass planting. Hence, ROW tend to be seeded (hydro-seeded if accessible by truck), and are decidedly "unnatural." However, to plant shrubs or trees into grasses is to "sentence" them to death or to a long struggle for survival. If this form of rehabilitation is used, a natural grass-woody vegetation "tension" ensues. Designing these *tension ecosystems* is an intriguing problem, as they are ecologically unstable, biophysical systems. Further, little experimental work has been done to provide guidance.

ROW rehabilitation designed for gardening purposes poses the problem that many older ROW were constructed when topsoil and subsoil were mixed. In addition, stones and compaction may be constraints to vegetable production. These constraints can be overcome with patience and good gardening skills, as demonstrated in the case study section which follows.

Case Studies

In this section, four cases will be presented from Ontario cities and their environs.

Rosedale Valley Road Ravine, Toronto

The first example is a buried storm sewer and water main connecting to Rosedale Valley Rd. from a large property located on the table land at Bloor and Jarvis. The sewer line also acted as a construction access road, requiring considerable slope removal. This sewer line and access road was planned to cut through a 2:1 north-facing, wedge-shaped, wooded ravine (500 m^2) dominated by old Manitoba maple (*Acer negundo*) which had colonized onto fill and rubble, forming a "natural" appearing forest. The City of Toronto, in its ravine protection policy, was reluctant to approve the access road and sewer line unless the slope could be restored to its "natural" condition. The alternative was to connect the services to Bloor St. and access via Bloor St. Thus, the cost of disrupting the ravine slope would be offset by any additional costs needed to design and to replant a natural forest node. This would be over and above the lower cost of just seeding the slope to grass, which the city would not approve.

The design concept adopted by the city (see Figure 1) included no Manitoba maple, but called for, instead, a mixture of native trees, shrubs, and herbs (Table 1) to form a self-propagating node. It was hoped that this "nodal" ecosystem eventually would recolonize the adjacent slope, restoring the slope to its former ecological diversity. The heavy shrub plantings at the top of the slope are designed to screen the slope from above, while the narrow opening at the bottom of the slope screens the "cut" for passing motorists "distracted" by the large Manitoba maples on either side.

Erosion control was obtained by check dams, by sowing grass seed, and then by placing an erosion control blanket (Hold-Gro #2) over the seed. The grass is an ecological "trade-off." Although it slows erosion, the grass competes — or creates "tension" — with the trees and shrubs for moisture, nutrients, possible allelopathic (toxic) effects, and encourages field mice (*Microtus pennsylvanicus*) and rabbits (*Syl-*

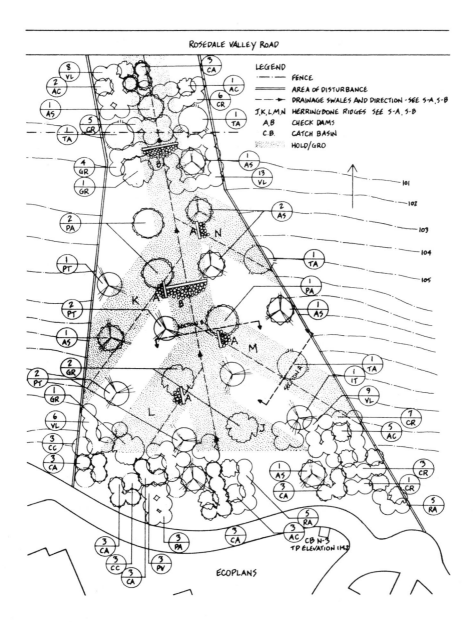

Figure 1. Design for Rosedale Valley Road slope reforestation using a "nodal-tension" ecosystem plant community concept.

Key	No.	Botanical Name	Common Name	Root	Size
AS	8	*Acer saccharum*	Sugar Maple	B&B	80 mm CAL
AC	11	*Amelanchier canadensis*	Serviceberry	B&B	250 cm
FA	3	*Fraxinus americana*	White Ash	B&B	60 mm CAL
PT	6	*Populus tremuloides*	Trembling Aspen	B&B	250 cm
QB	4	*Quercus borealis*	Red Oak	B&B	80 mm CAL
TA	4	*Tilia americana*	Basswood	B&B	80 mm CAL
CC	6	*Cercis canadensis*	Eastern Redbud	B&B	200 cm
CA	21	*Cornus alternifolia*	Alternate Leaved Dogwood	B&B	150 cm
CR	28	*Cornus racemosa*	Grey Dogwood	Potted	100 cm
PV	3	*Prunus virginia*	Choke Cherry	Potted	100 cm
RA	13	*Rhus aromatica*	Fragrant Sumac	Potted	80 cm
VL	41	*Virburnum lentago*	Nannyberry	Potted	100 cm
AN	47	*Anemone canadensis*	Canadian Anemone	Potted	100 mm pot
FV	230	*Fragaria virginiana*	Wild Strawberry	Potted	100 mm pot
GM	82	*Geranium maculatum*	Wild Geranium	Potted	100 mm pot
MS	25	*Matteuccia struthiopteris*	Ostrich Fern	Potted	150 mm pot
PQ	230	*Parthenocissus quinquifolia*	Virginia creeper	Potted	1 Gallon
PS	230	*Potentilla simplex*	Common cinquefoil	Potted	100 mm
MF	—	*Monarda fistulosa*	Wild Bergamont	—	—

Table 1. Plant list to accompany Figure 1.

(*Sylvilagus floridanus*) which girdle the trees and shrubs. Such a design is called a *nodal-tension ecosystem.*

Planted in late summer, 1983, the upper section later was replanted due to bank instability. Now, through the fourth growing season, the site looks like a viable ecosystem. The strawberry (*Frageria virginiana*) and Virginia creeper (*Parthenocissus quinquefolia*) are invading the grass and beginning to replace it on the lower, more shaded slope. Thus, the grass acts as a medium-term (10 years) ground cover where it is hoped the trees, shrubs, and herbs will eventually dominate, with no loss in erosion control. So far at least, this restoration ecosystem is on track. The planting cost in 1983 was $27, 239, including the erosion control structures.

Oakville and Bronte Creek Pipeline Crossings at CN Rail Line under Ontario Hydro Lines

The second example is a rehabilitation of two stream crossings. The intent was not to restore the site to an original forest condition but to rehabilitate it as a new grass-shrub, natural plant community. The plan was to cross these environmentally sensitive valleys with an eighteen inch pipeline with minimum disruption, and to replace the woody vegetation with grass-shrubs, first, to control erosion, second, to slow invasion of trees under the electrical lines, and, third, to blend the site with the surrounding treed slopes. Ontario Hydro also requested screen plantings at the upper and lower sections of each cut, as the pipeline was on their ROW. The valleys are generally oriented north-south, so the east-facing valley slopes are cool, and the west-facing banks hot. No topsoil was added; the existing shale-clay soils were compacted, and a 1.7-2:1 grade was achieved on three slopes, while a very steep 1.2:1 was present on the west side of Bronte Creek.

All shrub stock was potted and 30-50 cm in size. Bone meal and sphagnum moss were added to each planting hole. No subsequent watering was done. Planting was done in spring-summer 1980. Results as of fall 1986 (seven growing seasons later) appear in Table 2. Shrubs were planted at 1-1.5 m centre intervals.

From an erosion control point of view, all slopes are tight, and all initially had a good catch of grass legumes. This sod has persisted into the seventh year on west-facing slopes; on east-facing slopes the leaf fall of shrubs (especially silky dogwood) is smothering the grass. Little colonization of native tree species onto any of the ROW is apparent. In fact, tree cutting by Hydro under the power lines at Oakville Creek (fall 1987) may allow the shrubs to spread onto the cut area. Such a spreading would provide a long-time maintenance benefit to Hydro. Visually, all slopes appear "natural" and blend well with adjacent woody sections. The planting cost in 1980 dollars was $26, 000 for all four slopes.

Survival Assessment			
Species Planted	East-Facing (cool)	West-Facing (hot)	Floodplain
Hawthorn (*Craetagus crus-galli*)	P-G	P	—
Grey Dogwood (*Cornus racemosa*)	P	P-G	—
Red-Osier Dogwood (*C. stolonifera*)	P-G	P-G	—
High-bush Cranberry (*V. opulus var. americanum*)	P	P	P
Raspberries (*Rubus sp.*)	Ex	—	—
Grass/Legume Mix*	Ex	—	—

* Creeping red fescue (50 %), Kentucky bluegrass (20%), Perennial ryegrass (12%), red top (5%), alfalfa (5%), white clover (3%), birds foot trefoil (5%) at 20#/ac. (22.4 kg/ha).

[Ex=Excellent Survival, 60-100%; G=Good, 30-60%; P=Poor, 0-30%; Cl=Cloning]

Table 2. Species success for rehabilitation on east-facing and west-facing slopes of Bronte and Oakville Creek and floodplain at Bronte Creek, spring-summer 1980 and evaluated at end of seventh growing season, fall 1987.

Thames River North of London

This case study is in a rural appearing area within the community zone of London (urban shadow). The site is a forty-two inch natural gas line built in 1981 and planted late that fall. It is a wide cut: the slope is 2:1 and west facing, 1.15 acres (.46 ha.) in size, and roughly square in shape. Adjacent landowners requested a natural rehabilitation approach. Stock sizes, plantings, and planting techniques were as described for Bronte and Oakville Creeks. Species planted varied somewhat from the earlier case study (Table 3). Success after the fifth growing season (fall 1987) appears in Table 3.

One interesting result here is that the reed canary grass seeded initially on the floodplain is aggressively invading the slope, following the herringbone drains installed for erosion control which run from north to south diagonal to the slope. This grass, as well as the other grass-legume mix, has suppressed the shrubs on the south slope except for a strip up the slope along the south edge — an edge

Survival Assessment

Species Planted	
Balsam poplar cuttings (*Populus grandidentata*)	Ex
Fringed Sumac (*Rhus copallina*)	P
Grey Dogwood (*Cornus racemosa*)	G
Silky dogwood (*C. obliqua*)	G
Red-osier dogwood (*C. stolonifera*)	P–G
Nannyberry (*Virbunum lentago*)	P
High-bush cranberry (*V. opulus* var. *americanum*)	P–G
Elderberry (*Sambucus canadensus*)	P–G
Virginia Creeper (*Parthenocissus quinquefolia*)	Ex
Ninebark (*Physocarpus opulifolius*)	Ex
Virgin's bower (*Clematis virginianum*)	Ex
Grass legume mix*	Ex
Red canary grass (floodplain)**	Ex

* Seed mix as bottom of Table 2, seeded at 80#/ac (87.7 kg/ha), used on slope.
** Seeded on floodplain at 30#/ac (33.6 kg/ha).

[Ex=Excellent, 60-100%; G=Good, 30-60%; P=Poor, 0-30% survival]

partially shaded and benefitted by moisture draining across the slope. The planting is still far from reaching equilibrium. However, erosion and scouring is being controlled on both the slope and on the floodplain. It appears the reed canary grass is "too successful" and may eventually invade the entire slope except for the partially shaded south edge alongside the existing woods.

To control a small unstable 1:1 slope on the north edge of the ROW, 60 cm balsam poplar (*Populus balsamifera*) rooted cuttings were packed in sphagnum and 10-10-10 fertilizer, rolled in newspaper, and slid horizontally into holes bored by auger into wet seams in the bank. After the fifth growing season, they are now 1.5 m high (vertical height) and well rooted. Virgin's bower (*Clematis virginiana*) and Virginia creeper (*Parthenocissus quinquefolia*), planted on this wet slope with the poplars, have spread well. The cost of this planting (6,072 shrubs at 1 m centres) was $42,000 in 1981 dollars.

Ontario Hydro ROW, Toronto and Kitchener

Gardening (as well as commercial agriculture) is allowed by Ontario Hydro on some urban ROW. In Kitchener, hiking, skiing, jogging, and biking are encouraged on officially designated trails. There are many other examples which illustrate the potential for the single or joint utility ROW to become part of a linked open-space system achieving natural and cultural benefits.

Conclusions

The case studies on sewer line and pipelines presented illustrate the potential to establish naturalistic plant communities as part of a restoration-rehabilitation approach to meet specific design criteria. Three questions can be asked: 1) if we were to do these designs again, would we use fewer species; 2) if so, which species would be preferred; and 3) could lower costs be realized without sacrificing erosion and visual effects by altering the species or planting design?

As to the first and second questions, it is apparent from Tables 2 and 3 that there are seven shrub species of the thirteen which seem to overcome slope constraints in a "tension" situation with grass: staghorn sumac, ninebark, silky dogwood, Virginia creeper, raspberry, virgin's bower (wet seam), and willow. These species are likely to be winners; the others are less likely to succeed. All grass-legume mixes worked well, with reed canary grass demonstrating great invasiveness. Although reed canary grass protected the floodplain from scouring, I do not recommend this grass again if shrubs are also being planted.

As to the third question of cost, it might be preferable on pipeline rehabilitation using naturalistic plantings to plant clusters or nodes of sumac and/or silky dogwood, and to use wood chips — not grass seed — within the nodes to control erosion. Only the nonshrub areas only would be seeded. For example, a 25 percent shrub coverage at

1.5 m centre with the use of 4–5 row screen plantings could achieve visual-cost trade off: costs could be reduced by half to two-thirds. The species not tried, such as red cedar (for screens) and blackberry (to control trespass), deserve experimental trials. White cedar for screens did better in cool-moist situations at the base of slopes and moderately well to poor on exposed bank tops, but it might not be attempted again on the top of banks, unless mulch were placed to control grass competition.

The general conclusions are that rehabilitation or restoration by planting tension ecosystems of grass-shrubs-trees can be successful on 2:1 slopes. This approach is more expensive compared to the usual seeding-only treatments for slopes and is probably not justified in rural settings. By way of comparison, in industrial-residential plantings (on flat ground) naturalistic plantings are price competitive with grass sod (Dorney 1983). In the ROW circumstances described in this paper, however, such a cost comparison with landscaped grass is misleading as the naturalized banks planted to native trees and shrubs received no regular weeding, periodic fertilizing, and periodic sprinkling. The utilization of the ROW for gardening and for open space trails does, however, shift the maintenance cost from the utility company to the user.

REFERENCES

Dorney, R.S. 1983. "Cost Comparisons Between Establishing Small Natural Woodlands and Grass Lawns." *Restoration and Management Notes* 1, no. 4:22–23.

The Texas Highways Department Wildflower Program
Craig Steffens

Texas has a long history of wildflower propagation. Wildflowers have been indigenous to Texas for millions of years, but the influx and propagation of wildflowers began when Texas developed a large beef cattle industry. Livestock has a tendency to overgraze, and wildflowers are the first things that come back when land is disturbed. If we look at ecological succession, whenever land is disturbed by overgrazing, industry, or agriculture, the first thing that reappears on the land if left fallow are annual wildflowers.

It was noticed in the 1930s that when land was disturbed, the first thing to come back was our state flower, the bluebonnet (*Lupinus texensis*). It was coming back profusely on our right-of-ways, and the garden clubs of Texas came to the highway department and beseeched us to preserve this. We were then probably the first state highway department in the nation to hire a landscape architect who worked directly with garden clubs. We also had a very sympathetic state highway engineer at the time, who was foresighted enough to recognize the beautiful resource that we had along our highways and to propagate and preserve the wildflowers that were coming back.

At the time, we did not know much about wildflowers, but we did know that if we allowed the wildflowers to reseed on our right-of-way, and if we curtailed our mowing until they had reseeded, we

Craig Steffens is a supervising Landscape Architect with the Texas Department of Highways and Public Transportation. His duties include highway landscape and development, wildflower preservation and propagation, and herbicide management and experimentation.

would have a bountiful crop the following year. We also knew that we could very easily and economically take these wildflowers from one area to another simply by mowing the plants down and taking what we call wildflower hay, containing seeds, from one location to another. We now have many different species that have expanded their range up to four hundred miles from their native habitat by our doing this over a period of sixty years.

Lupinus texensis, the state flower of Texas, is a basic lupin with a lot of names. It was called buffalo clover in the old days because buffalo, as they migrated south and north, overgrazed the land causing a change in the ecological system from climax vegetation back to primary communities. Lupin is named for lupus, which is the wolf, which has a lot of serious negative connotations to it. The early cattle ranchers wanted to get rid of it because they felt it competed too much with the grass that the cattle were eating. We know now that lupines and other wildflowers are very beneficial because they are legumes that take nitrogen from the air and stow it in nodules in the root system. When the annual dies, it releases the nitrogen to the soil as a fertilizer.

Wildflowers, native plants, and wildlife are very important in the scheme of things. Our highway program is very simple, and has been for many years. We never contend to know anything about wildflowers as an engineering oriented department, but we did know that we could recreate very simply what we saw out in the fields, because we had disturbed land. Over the years, we have created various habitats by benign neglect, delaying mowing, and moving the species on.

As a large agency, the highway department has basic philosophies and policies that have to be addressed. Number one is the preservation of the paved surface. We must have a transportation system; it is vital to the nation and the state. We must maintain the safety of the travelling public, so there are safety engineers on staff. We also have traffic engineers, pavement engineers, and structural engineers. With all these engineering interests to meet first, aesthetics comes way down the line. Safety and maintenance of the travelling surface come first.

We have to understand those basic principles in order to fit the aesthetic need for wildflowers into the highway system. In 1982 we found that the only way we could get the attention of anyone was to look at the economic benefits of wildflowers. All the scientists in the world can have all the greatest ideas in the world, but unless you hit somebody economically, especially a large department such as the highway department, with an annual budget over $2 billion, you will not get much attention. In other words, you can be a devil's advocate, but you also have to appreciate what their duties and responsibilities are and, since you are the low man on the totem pole, you have to incorporate into them.

First, we needed to change the engineering philosophy in which knowing something about aesthetics is perceived not to be a part of the job, so we looked at the philosophy of building a highway. The philosophy is as follows: Build a bridge; it will last a long time because it is made out of concrete and steel. But when you plant a roadside, although it will last a fairly long time, it is constantly changing. You cannot plant something and walk away from it unless you do homework based on timing, or annual events, or seasonal events, and can convince the engineers that it is very important economically as well as aesthetically.

We worked with the economic issue and came upon a wonderful word, management, that changed everything around. Maintenance means money, while management includes other concerns. We can work *with* mother nature and call it management, so we came up with a road sign for the "Vegetation Management System." We decided upon systems because at that time "system" was the big buzz word within the highway department. We had a maintenance information management system and we had a design management system. Using systems makes a big difference, because it fits vegetation management into the overall scheme.

In this system we looked at the problems and the economic issues. We were spending $34 million every year mowing 1,054,000 acres. We knew that we were reducing some mowing by allowing the wildflowers to grow, but we also knew that every employee we had in the highway department grew up with someone mowing the lawn every week. This is otherwise known as the front yard syndrome,

where it is ingrained in your mind that every blade has to be mown
in order to be maintained. Additionally, hardware stores and seed
companies are making a mint from purchases of fertilizer and
mowers. We had to change the philosophy so that it is okay for the
grass to grow a little taller and for everything to change with the
seasons. We first decided to reduce mowing, but the question still
remained over how to get the department personnel to go along with
us because of their ingrained thoughts that everything had to have a
manicured look.

First, we came up with a system that said all highways do not have
to look the same. Another catch phrase, "the unannounced right-of-
way," proved very functional for this. An unannounced right-of-way
is best defined through examples. If you cross the state line from
Oklahoma to Texas, it looks no different on either side. The man-
made line does not mean that the landscape changes, because the
environment does not change at any particular point. Similarly, when
you cross from Canada to the United States, you would not know the
difference at that point without the sign. It is an artificial man-made

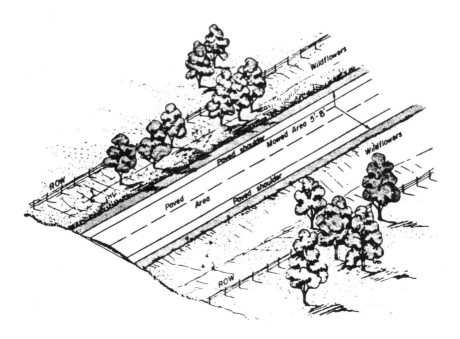

point. There is no reason why any highway right-of-way must look different from property adjacent to it.

We defined where we needed to have safety aspects of lower vegetation, where we could let things go fallow, where we could maintain at different heights, and we then used this unannounced right-of-way in a golf course situation. From a golf green that is highly maintained, to the fairway, the rough cut, and the deep rough, maintenance decreases in grades. The highway right-of-way has the same linear effect. The further out from the general purpose of the highway, the more maintenance defers into a management system. This type of thing started to catch on as something a mathematician or an engineer could analytically understand.

Then we pointed out that some people do not like the mowing. In fact, a lot of people do not like it, and we are also spending too much money, especially with the legislature always looking down our throat. Would you rather mow all the time, or build better highways? This got attention, so we took one particular county as an experiment. Texas has a legislative session every two years, and I noticed one spring that the interstate highway running through the capital, Austin, had overgrown grass and litter everywhere. It was a mess, while out on the farm roads they were mowing up a storm. With the legislature in session and all the politicians coming to town, the middle of downtown Austin looked awful, while we were mowing farm roads that may have only one hundred travellers a day. When I asked why, I was told that they generally start at mowing the southern part of the county, slowly moving north.

The first thing we did in the vegetation management system was to have our people prioritize their mowing. Take every road within a county and colour code it, so that the contractors know when to mow and where to mow. Mow first in the urban area — again, an unannounced right-of-way. Make the right-of-way blend with what is on the other side of the fence, such as in an urban area where people are taking care of their lawns in manicured condition. Do not mow the southern part of the county; leave it alone, and move the mowing through the winter months into position so that it will take care of the philosophy of the unannounced right-of-way. Make it look like what is across the fence.

Another thing that happens in mowing is that land starts eroding and we have to completely revegetate it, costing hundreds of thousands of dollars. They were not thinking about these things, and all we did was to put these ideas to work. We have 254 counties in the state covered by twenty-four highway districts. We asked each district to put one county into this program, and then, after a year, to compare the costs and the looks to the other counties. The results were a 28 percent reduction in mowing costs, which when projected statewide amounts to a $12.7 million reduction in mowing costs. That got their attention, and so did the fact that it did not look as bad as they thought it would.

You cannot go into anything with a large department and change it all at once. Our highway department is very autonomous, and we have district engineers in each of the twenty-four districts where it is their own bailiwick. They may not want to change, but if you get one or two of them to like the change, you then generate interest.

We first mow a ten to twelve foot strip, depending on the width of the right-of-way, for safety. You would be surprised at how good wildflowers look with a manicured strip in front, while wildflowers growing directly on the pavement look weedy. It is a compromise from the total environmental concept that would allow the wildflowers to just grow, because we have a functional requirement that must be addressed. Then, we begin transition mowing, in which we consider special requirements such as mowing around signs and into ditch lines. The rest of it is left alone. Shoulder strip mowing is mowing to preserve the safety corridor, so a car can get off the highway in an emergency without hitting an obstruction. Medians on interstate highways less than seventy feet wide are, for example, completely mown, because a fifty foot median with a four foot strip of native vegetation down the middle would look strange.

We put these guidelines into a booklet that we give to all of our maintenance personnel. Basically, we end up with a little bit of both, so perhaps you can have your cake and eat it too. In other words, mowing is essential for certain situations, but many other situations can be left fallow. By leaving areas that do not have to be mown all the time, we reduced our mowing in many cases from eight mowings a year down to two, one, and even to none in some areas.

Another very important point with wildflowers and native grasses, and especially with native bunch grasses, is that they have to be mown at a higher level. This is because all of their food manufacturing comes from one area. As they grow taller, low cutting eliminates the chlorophyll needed to produce the food for the root systems, so they will decline. Once this happens, grasses such as Johnson grass, which is a rhizome rooted grass, stores food in the root system and will out-compete the more desirable grasses.

Most of our programs have been very successful. Some of the looks we have include bluebonnets emerging in the early spring from an area left over the winter. The fears of the highway officials did not come to pass when they said that it would look ragged. We do not

Mowing should be performed over rural intersection or interchange areas as necessary to provide adequate site distances.

have the unkempt weedy look that they feared. The large areas taken out of maintenance and put into management cost nothing, and by utilizing the cost of mowing by acre, the more acreage taken out, the more money saved. It is something that is tangible, and something that we can put in the computer and notice a financial saving. Then we can go to the legislature for more money to build highways, able to demonstrate that we are saving money. This makes vegetation management a great tool for any department, because all we do is save money by putting it to better use.

Eventually, in some areas where we will never mow again, we get woody shrubs. Such areas that have been taken completely out of the maintenance spectrum are allowed to go completely back to forest. Hillsides, which are very dangerous to mow because the machine can roll over and kill the driver, are also left to fallow. We do not need them mown, and common sense says that a car cannot get up there anyway, so there is no point in trying to mow them. We can then get back into ecological succession, and eventually the area will be a reforested, ecological, climax community.

I want to impress upon you the important thing about mowing, essential for wildflowers. In areas where we have wildflowers, we have to mow once a year to stop ecological succession. That is the only point to mowing, and we do it after the first killing frost.

You would not believe the inefficiencies that can be found with a little investigation. Our native grasses try to put on a seed head in August, September, and October. With any of the bluestem or grama varieties, two weeks after mowing they are back to full height because they are trying to put on a seed head. We had one maintenance group mow a section of highway eight times between 15 August and 1 October. All they had to do was wait six or eight weeks until the first killing frost, mow it once, and it was clear from that point until April. Naturally, this was because they did not understand what the plant was doing, and because they were told to keep the plants under twelve inches. In this situation, they have to understand that timing is essential to the program.

We are now utilizing herbicide programs with a machine that takes areas out of mowing by controlling tall vegetation in the area. Then we have an overspray program in which herbicides are limited to only three, all environmentally safe. Personnel are certified by examination procedures through our Department of Agriculture, and we will not allow a herbicide to be used on the right-of-way until we have personally researched it for at least three years. These safeguards are very important, because the mention of herbicides scares every environmentalist to death.

The key to a good herbicide program is to keep the number of herbicide brands down. Our overspray program uses a nonselective herbicide in a selective way. We use either Roundup, Oust, or Velpar. The Oust and Roundup are used together, in a formulation of one pint Roundup and two ounces of Oust per acre, developed within the department to specifically kill Johnson grass, our major pest plant. By diluting the product we can use one herbicide and make it twenty different herbicides, just by the amount we put on per acre. It takes a lot of time and research to do this, but once done it gives the best of two worlds. It is a simple approach to herbicide operations with safe herbicides that can do many different jobs.

Next, I will consider the seeding of wildflowers, a very important task. Our most economic means is to take wildflower hay and move it from one area to another. Buying wildflower seed is very expensive. For instance, *Castellia indivisa,* one of our best species, has four thousand seeds per ounce. A double handful of that and a sneeze looses a lot of money. There are better ways, then, to seed. What we use now with purchased seed is a modified grain drill with eight bins. The reason it has a lot of bins is because wildflower seed is very diverse in size. When you use a combination of seeds, you have to use a combination of seed or seed mix in different bins in order to get a proper seed mix.

We incorporate the seeds directly into the turf because disturbing the ground while planting wildflowers releases the seed bank of weeds and everything else in the soil. Turf is also extremely good with wildflowers because it prevents erosion from washing all the wildflower seeds off, and it maintains moisture in the soil. We can also move soil to another location which captures a lot more seed than using just a hay mix. Some of the new equipment coming out includes a vacuum harvester that can go over a field blooming with any composite flower in which seeds mature at different stages and pull out the mature seed, leaving the immature seed.

We also retain all top soil used in our construction processes. It is stockpiled and in most cases we try not to bring in any topsoil from other areas. After construction is complete, we spread the topsoil back on. It is very important to use indigenous species and not introduce other species into the area that is of concern or under construction.

To reduce the cost of production we utilize row cropping, just to simplify production of seed. Lowering the cost of seed production is very important to any wildflower program. The state of Texas bought up most of the phlox seed in the world last year, and it all came from Europe. It is native Texas *Drummonds' phlox,* but the only place that produced it was in Europe. We are looking at California poppy, an excellent plant to be adapted to our western arid regions. We take a lot of care when we introduce plants, because they could become pest species.

Our seed mixes are gauged for a blooming succession to keep the wildflower season as long as possible. The only way to do that is to start a mixture of seeds that commonly bloom from March all the way through the growing season into October. All those seeds together will deliver a blooming succession. Amazingly enough, as the season progresses, the wildflowers that bloom in summer are taller than those that grew in spring. As the grasses start to grow, the different species of wildflowers have taken that into consideration genetically, so they are just a little bit higher in order to compete for sunlight. This continually covers the ugly brown colour remaining from each earlier bloom, which engineers do not like to see and want to mow down. Blooming succession is, then, a very important thing to consider when selecting a seed mix for any part of the country.

Every jurisdiction considering a beautification program should have a type of recognition or award system. Our Lady Bird Johnson award program will soon be in its nineteenth year, where she awards prizes to our maintenance foreman. It is at the grassroots level with the people who are out there working on the highways and maintaining our roadsides. We have a competition each year, and she awards

$1,500 to the district winner. She also, very importantly, brings in dignitaries from all over the United States to recognize our program.

Humans and wildflowers can live together. Any area that one time was mown and taken care of, and then abandoned, has wildflowers come back. Another area, full of livestock at one time, with probably not a blade of grass on the area, regains its wildflowers once humans are gone. We have introduced wildflowers to private dwellings, and they have worked. While a high-intensity area that is being walked around on can certainly have a maintained lawn, the other areas can be returned to wildflowers.

Private developers are utilizing wildflowers extensively. With an area planned for houses or an office park, utilize the area and plant the portions without buildings in wildflowers. They work exceptionally well. Or try golf courses. Areas between houses and a golf course should be planted with wildflowers. The members of the courses are extremely proud of these areas because they are unique. Or, right in the middle of a small town, there should be wildflowers growing on a vacant lot between two buildings. With the majority of our economic dependencies in Texas down right now, we are hoping that wildflowers can make up the difference.

REFERENCES

Texas State Department of Highways and Public Transportation. *Standards of Vegetation Management*. Austin: Texas State Department of Highways.

Forests as Living Filters for Urban Sewage
Dr. William Sopper

Many pollution problems in the United States have been caused by the discharge of sewage effluents from secondary treatment plants, and more of these plants will be built to meet increasingly stringent water quality requirements. Secondary treatment, of course, virtually eliminates the health hazard associated with raw waste, and it breaks down most of the organic matter into its components. However, it is the concentrated discharge of these secondary treated waste waters that enter our balanced aquatic ecosystems and causes ecological chaos, accentuating many of the water problems that did not exist before.

A significant amount of research has been done over the past twenty years which has shown that forests can be used as land treatment systems to renovate secondary treated waste water for direct recharge to the groundwater table. Although these waste waters contain a lot of plant nutrients that could be used, they also could contain trace metals and some toxic substances, and some concern has been voiced by the public over land application. Most of these concerns are related to agricultural systems, because the crops may go into animal feed and trace metals could thereby enter the human and animal food chain. Very few forest products go into the food chain, however, although one exception might be animals that are harvested and eaten by humans. Research has shown that you can

William Sopper is professor of Forest Hydrology in the School of Forest Resources, and an Environmental Scientist in the Environment Resources Research Institute, at Penn State University in University Park, Pennsylvania. He is the coordinator of university projects related to land application of municipal sewage effluent on forest land and crop land.

apply waste water in forested areas with very little health threat to animals or humans, and that these areas can really be used as greenbelts. They can be made open to the public for hiking, walking, and hunting, with a minimum number of safeguards. Some forest land treatment systems in Maine have even maintained trails that are open for cross-country skiing in the winter time.

A land application of municipal waste water provides many advantages to a community beset with waste water disposal problems. First of all, it provides an opportunity for water pollution abatement. It provides an opportunity for the recycling and beneficial use of the nutrients contained in the waste water. It allows for the replenishment of local groundwater supplies and for the preservation of open space or open greenbelts.

Our interest at Penn State University in land application treatments started in 1962. It began because of two local problems, both partly caused by the university. The university was growing and owned a waste water treatment plant which served the university, and the town of State College, Pa. The amount of effluent that was being dumped into Spring Creek, the only surface stream in the area, gradually turned a beautiful stream into an open sewer. That was one problem. The other problem in the early 1960s was that we were experiencing a seven year drought, where we had a deficiency of one and a half years of natural precipitation. The only water supply in the area was groundwater, and the groundwater was depleting from wells put in by the university and the town. At the same time as we were going through these two problems, we were discharging millions of gallons of sewage effluent from the local treatment plant for rapid transport to the Atlantic Ocean. This did not quite make sense.

What I would like to do is describe the Penn State system and discuss some of the research that has been conducted on these systems over the past twenty-five years. The concept we envisioned at Penn State was to determine if it was feasible to take the waste waters we were discharging into the stream and recycle them back onto the land. This concept became known as a living filter concept because we were not just trying to use the soil as a mechanical filter; we were trying to use it as a living filter. In other words, we applied the waste water in such a fashion that it would work with the natural system to irrigate forests and grow trees, or to irrigate crops and grow crops, and to then have that waste water renovated by the natural system through degradation by micro-organisms, chemical precipitation, ion exchange, biological transformation, and uptake of the nutrients by absorption through the roots of the growing vegetation. We planned to have the waste water directly recharge the groundwater, then between that recharge area and the point of use drill wells, enabling the use of the water again as groundwater. By doing this we believed it would be possible to recover and reuse 80 to 90 percent of the water over and over again.

The university treatment plant is a secondary treatment plant, a trickling filter design with a capacity of four million gallons a day. It treats both the university and the town. The university population is about 35,000, and the town population is about 35,000, so we are serving, when the students are all there, about 70,000 people. From the secondary treatment plant, after chlorination, the water flows by gravity to a pumping station. This pumping station has three electrical turbine pumps. Two are usually in operation when it is going full force, and they can pump 3,200 gallons per minute of waste water.

The pumps move the waste water to two sites. The first site, called the astronomy site, is two miles away from the plant. The water is pumped there through an eighteen inch buried pipeline. This is primarily an agricultural site, and the waste water is applied here usually during the summer. The crops we grow include reed canary grass, which loves a lot of moisture, and we harvest it as an animal feed. We also grow corn, primarily for silage rather than for the grain, because we want to keep applying the waste water for as long as possible to achieve the maximum amount of nitrogen uptake, which is the main constituent of effluent that one has to worry about in a land treatment system. Nitrate is very mobile, and it is the first constituent that will cause any groundwater pollution, so the whole idea of designing and operating any land treatment system is to apply it in such a fashion that takes up and stores most of that nitrogen, preventing it from moving down into the groundwater, allowing it to be either harvested or recycled within the system. Agricultural systems are, of course, very easy to manage, because applying waste water for irrigation all summer applies two hundred pounds of nitrogen. You then take off the two hundred pounds of nitrogen with the harvest, leaving little to be leached into the groundwater.

A forest system is a little more tricky, because there is no harvest and everything you apply in a forest system just moves from the leaves to the ground and back again. The second site is called the gameland site. This is a forested area and it is primarily used for winter irrigation. In this sixty-year-old natural mixed oak stand is our system, all solid set steel pipe where nothing is ever moved, even in the agricultural area, and where they harvest between the pipes that stay there all the time. For winter irrigation certain lines in the forest areas are installed on a 2 or 3 percent slope, so that after irrigating the line drains, preventing frozen and burst pipes.

The system covers over five hundred acres with sixty miles of pipe and over three thousand sprinklers. The waste water is irrigated on all of these areas where there have been crops or forest at two inches per week on an acre. Every acre of land gets just two inches a week,

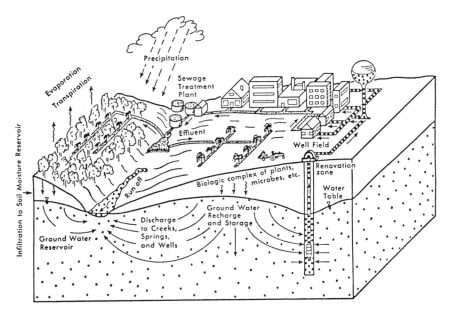

Figure 1. Diagram of the living filter concept.

then it has a resting period for six days, then it gets another application of two inches. That two inches is applied at one-sixth of an inch per hour, meaning that every day over the first twelve-hour period one acre is being irrigated, and then another is irrigated over the next twelve-hour period. In a week there are fourteen irrigation periods, and we irrigate all the time because there is no storage in the system. At any moment there are about thirty-seven acres being irrigated with waste water, regardless of the temperature.

Forest systems are tricky to monitor sometimes, and different forest ecosystems have different capabilities for accepting and renovating waste water. I want to consider three different ecosystems that we tested and how they differ in handling waste water. First is a red pine plantation, thirty-five years old. We had irrigated it for several years and found it did not do a very good job of taking up nitrogen. Everybody thinks trees are big and therefore they should take up a lot of nitrogen, but they really do not. After about six years we had a very severe snow storm in early November which took the whole plantation down, so we allowed it to come back into natural pioneer species of various hardwoods — pin cherry, aspen, and sumac — and continued to irrigate. The blowdown was in 1968, and today it is a dense young forest of hardwood species.

Let us look at how to handle the nitrogen. Figure 2 shows the concentration of nitrate-nitrogen after the waste water goes four feet through the soil. We are concerned with water quality, so our requirements are that it has to be drinking water at the four foot level. In other words, we have to take all the nitrogen out before it goes four feet in the soil so that the groundwater is recharged with good water. We started to irrigate the plantation in 1963, but Figure 2 does not show the first two years because we did not have instruments in at that depth. By 1968, after about five years of irrigation, nitrate levels were up to 24 mg/l at four feet, which meant that the pine plantation had stopped removing the nitrogen. Most of it was still moving through the system. Then we had the blowdown, and the new pioneer early succession coming in, and the nitrates immediately dropped the first year to 8 mg/l. In the second year the nitrates dropped down to 2 mg/l. Just taking the pines off converted it to a new type of vegetation perfect for renovation. It is now a beautiful land treatment system.

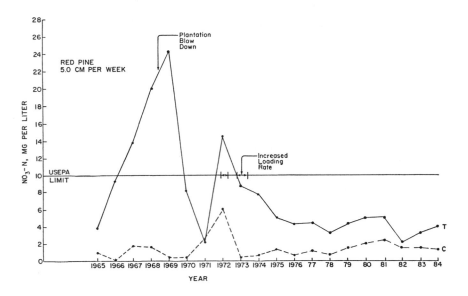

Figure 2. Average annual nitrate-N concentration of soil water at the 120-cm soil depth in the red pine forest ecosystem irrigated with municipal wastewater at 5 cm/wk during the growing season for the period of 1963 to 1984.

In 1972 we thought we ought to be looking at what happens when the system is overloaded to the point of collapse. How does one get it back to where it can be used again? Well, there are two options. You can either stop irrigating on the area and move on to five hundred other acres which are available, or you can reduce the rate of application and hope the system will recover. Most land treatment systems do not have the option of just picking up another five hundred or a thousand acres, so the only option is to drop back. In 1972 we increased all of the application rates by 50 percent, so instead of putting on two inches we put on three and a half inches. Of course what then happened, in 1972, was that tropical storm Agnes came through and thirteen inches of water fell in the three days we were doing this experiment. We repeated the experiment again in 1973, and the irrigated areas with the increased amount were getting nitrates at 8 mg/1, but we did not have a breakthrough.

In another area we worked with an old abandoned agricultural field where the forestry people had planted white spruce as an attempt to try to change it into a white spruce plantation. The trees were about three feet tall and scattered within little open areas, so we started to irrigate them, and, of course as was expected, tree growth increased dramatically. The one year terminal growth on the irrigated trees was almost thirty inches, which in white spruce is very good.

Constituent	Average Concentration mg/l	Average Annual Application[1] kg/ha	Total Amount Applied[2] kg/ha
Cu	0.068	1.1	22
Zn	0.197	3.2	64
Cr	0.022	0.4	8
Pb	0.140	2.3	46
Co	0.040	0.6	12
Cd	0.003	0.05	1
Ni	0.050	0.08	16
pH	7.5	—	—

[1]Total amount in forest ecosystems which received waste water applications at 5 cm/wk. (2 in./wk.).
[2]Applied over twenty-year period (1963 to 1982).

Table 1. Typical Chemical Composition of the Waste Water

Without the irrigation it would have been about twelve inches. Today, most of these trees are thirty-five to forty feet high. They have been irrigated for twenty years now and have diameters that are about ten to fourteen inches, while in the surrounding area where no waste water was applied the trees are only four to six inches in diameter.

This ecosystem of white spruce and herbaceous vegetation has done a beautiful job of renovating waste water without any harvest. In Figure 3 it is clear that throughout the whole twenty year period, from 1963 to 1982, we had very good renovation except for the two years when we increased the rate (1973 and 1974) and went above the drinking water standards. After we did that experiment we cut back from three and a half inches to two inches of application, which is the design rate, and the ecosystem took almost three years to get back to where the quality of water met drinking water standards.

It is very important, then, that these systems are not overloaded, because if you have to keep operating them it will take a long time to flush out the extra nitrogen and return to where it can recycle in a normal fashion. The only reason it works is because there is a desynchronization between nitrogen input into the forest and nitrogen release. In irrigating the forest from May up to October, nitrogen is stored in the trees and in herbaceous vegetation. Without irrigation in the winter and with the decomposing vegetation and needles, nitrogen is released into the groundwater at an acceptable rate. During the dry season the nitrate levels are very low, while in the winter they go up a little but are still within drinking water standards. They are still acceptable while releasing the nitrogen, so there is a balance with the input and output of nitrogen and no harvest is needed.

In a mixed oak stand we were interested to see whether we could irrigate a forest year-round, so we started to irrigate with two inches per week all twelve months of the year. It was too much nitrogen for the forest to get rid of and recycle, and nitrates within a couple of years went up to forty-two parts per million, which is very unacceptable. After several years we decided to stop irrigation for about a year and a half, and then start it up again to irrigate every summer or every winter to see if the system had recovered. Figure 3 is from such a forest system, which was irrigated every summer beginning in 1976 and then rested in winter, that was able to handle the nitrogen throughout a twenty year period. A forest area can, therefore, be used, but it must be given a resting period in order to get the nitrogen out of the system.

There has been a lot of concern about trace metals, and with our land treatment systems we have the same concerns. After twenty years of irrigation we decided we would take a look to see what happened in terms of trace metals. Table 1 shows the quality of the

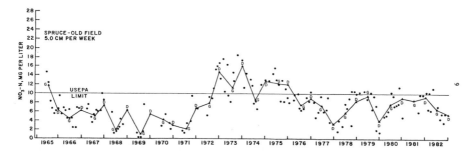

Figure 3. Average monthly and seasonal nitrate-N concentrations of soil water at the 120-cm soil depth in the white spurce-old field forest ecosystem irrigated with municipal waste water at 5 cm/wk during the growing season for the period 1965 to 1982. Growing season (G) and dormant season (D).

waste water for the seven major trace metals. They are very low because most of the metals end up in the sludge produced at the treatment plant. Also, trace metals are not very soluble in an alkaline solution, and most sewage effluent is neutral or alkaline. The annual amounts of trace metals we applied with the irrigations at two inches per week for thirty weeks per year was one pound of copper, three pounds of zinc, .05 pounds of cadmium, and so on. Over twenty years this amounts to one pound of cadmium, which is the element with the greatest health hazard. In Pennsylvania you are allowed to put three pounds of cadmium on over a lifetime. If we operated this system for sixty years, we would get only up to that three pounds. The EPA limit for this, however, would be ten pounds, so you could put ten pounds of cadmium on there without ever causing a health hazard for either animals or humans.

Looking at percolate water quality after twenty years of irrigation (Table 2), the amount of, for instance, copper in the waste water was

.07 mg/l after four feet. Irrigated it is at .01 mg/l, meaning most was taken out by the soil. In the unirrigated control plot the values are

Source	Cu	Zn	Cr	Pb mg/l	Co	Cd	Ni
Wastewater Quality	0.07	0.20	0.02	0.14	0.04	0.003	0.05
Wastewater Irrigated Plot	0.01	0.05	0.01	0.02	0.01	<0.001	0.02
Control Plot	0.01	0.05	0.01	0.02	0.01	<0.001	0.01
US EPA Drinking Water Maximum	1.0	5.0	0.05	0.05	—	0.01	—

Table 2. Average Annual Trace Metal Concentrations in Soil Percolate Water at 120 cm Depth for 1982 in the White Spruce — Old Field Plantation

identical, so even after twenty years of irrigation the water quality under four feet is exactly the same in both the waste water irrigated and the natural rainfall irrigated plots. These values all are within the drinking water standards.

Consider uptake in the trees and vegetation of, for example, the white spruce where the waste water irrigated copper concentrations were 3.3 mg/l while on the control unirrigated plot they were 3.7 mg/l. Zinc was at 21 parts per million in the waste water irrigated trees for twenty years, while in the control trees it was at 44 parts per million. This is biological dilution, because when you put the waste water on, and although you are adding heavy metals, you also increase the biomass. With increased biomass foliar concentrations are reduced, so the quality of the foliage or the crop is much better. In the control area with spruce trees, the amount of herbaceous vegetation after one year of irrigation is three, four, and five times that of the herbaceous material without irrigation. With many more leaves in the forest, and many more needles in the spruce trees, the trace metals are not really found.

What happened in the soil is that most of the trace metals were taken out in a very small layer of the soil, where they are held in insoluble complexes and cannot move unless there is a bit of acid precipitation. Most of the trace metals are taken out, and the controls in some cases are even higher. The normal range of cadmium in the soil is from .01 to 7 ppm in natural soils, so these concentrations are very low. Basically there was no significant adverse effect.

As I mentioned before, tree growth is increased tremendously. A red maple cross section of a control with ten years of growth compared to a red maple that was irrigated for ten years shows an increased diameter of two or three times and an increased volume of wood of four times. Wood quality is, however, affected. When trees are growing very fast, the wood produced is better for making pulp and not so good for structural timber because the specific gravity is less, making the wood less strong. It also causes some other changes in the ecosystem. We looked at micro-organism populations and found, for instance, that with keeping the soil moist in irrigated forests, something like four hundred earthworms per square metre were present, while normally there would be less than fifty earthworms in a square metre.

We have also looked at effects on wildlife, and found no adverse effects on the white tailed deer. Because these areas are open for hunting, we had to be able to tell hunters that the meat is not going to cause any health problems. We also looked at rabbit populations, and found that the rabbits are healthy in these areas with bigger populations because the quality of the food is better. Anyone who is familiar with trace metals will know that most trace metals accumulate in organs and not in the flesh. Cadmium accumulates, for instance, in the kidney and liver and sometimes in the bone, but hardly ever in the muscle. In the flesh of fish we found that there was no accumulation of trace metals that would prevent people from eating the fish. Of course, most of the trace metals end up in the organs which are discarded.

We have also looked at smaller mammals because we know that while a rabbit or a deer will naturally come and go and not get all its food here, a mouse will. We examined their organs and found no adverse effects on the health of these little animals in the waste water irrigated area. We also trapped birds, looked at the species of birds, took blood samples, and, again, found no problems. There were some changes in the types of birds, because in the forest where we irrigated with waste water in the winter the shrub layer is lost, so the birds that nest in the shrubs disappeared while the ground and canopy nesting birds increased. Birds are attracted to these areas because water is available at all times, so when there is no normal precipitation they come in for water. Even ducks come in and get wet.

There are only a few things we have found to be adverse, and one of them is as follows. Irrigation with waste water stimulates the growth of herbaceous vegetation which takes up a tremendous amount of nitrogen. This is good because it is the control in the system. On a normal forest floor there would be about two inches of leaf layer decomposing over several years, but with waste water irrigation there is hardly any forest floor cover. This is because in a normal forest there is a lot of carbon but little nitrogen. Low nitrogen levels limit decomposition, while adding nitrogen from irrigation increases the carbon-nitrogen ratio, leading to rapid decomposition. In the waste water plots after twelve months a leaf is 80 to 85 percent decomposed, something which normally takes about five years. The system rapidly reaches a new equilibrium where all the leaf litter is decomposed, so that after about ten years a leaf which falls in September is practically all decomposed by the next August.

This can be a problem in a system that is irrigated in the winter, because it is that insulating litter layer which keeps the soil from freezing. If you lost that insulating layer then you may not be able to irrigate the forest in the winter. What happens, however, is that the extra herbaceous material grows up and then falls down in the winter, providing a type of insulation which prevents soil freezing and allows us to operate. The bad thing is that you lose the forest floor by rapid decomposition, but it is replaced by something else, so in the end it was not a problem.

The main purpose of our system is to reuse the water. Table 3 shows the quality of the groundwater and the average annual nitrate concentration in the groundwater under the irrigation system. In 1963 1.9 mg/l was the average, and over the twenty years up to 1982 it fluctuated up and down between 2 and 4 mg/l, with no apparent trend. The fluctuation depended on the precipitation pattern of each year and on how much rain was there to leach nitrogen down. We find no adverse effect, and think that we could probably operate this system for another twenty years without any influence on groundwater quality. This also goes for the other elements because very few other elements move to the groundwater. They are more or less taken out. Chlorine might be the only other real mobile unit, but everything else is essentially taken out by the living filter system.

The amount of water is very important. We based our estimate

Year	NO=3-N (mg/l)	Year	NO=3-N (mg/l)
1963	1.9	1975	3.5
1964	2.3	1976	3.5
1965	1.4	1977	4.1
1966	1.8	1978	4.5
1967	2.9	1979	4.3
1968	3.1	1980	3.3
1969	4.0	1982	2.5

Table 3. Mean Annual Concentration of Nitrate-N in a Deep Groundwater Monitoring Well Adjacent to the Waste Water Irrigation Areas

upon the amount of waste water applied, natural precipitation, and evapotranspiration, and estimate that we recharge about 90 percent of the effluent back to the groundwater table. This comes out to be about 1.5 million gallons for every acre irrigated. With about four hundred acres being irrigated at two inches per week, there is a lot of water that goes right back into the groundwater. Between the irrigation area and the university we have put in some wells to take the water right back out. It is chlorinated and goes right back into the drinking water system of the university.

One last thing I would like to make a comment about is compatibility with neighbours. This system occupies about five hundred acres and it is surrounded on two sides by a housing development. Some of the irrigation system is two hundred feet away from a hedge row with houses on the other side. When we started in 1963 these homes were selling for about $70, 000. They now sell for about $190,000. There is also a resort area, a conference centre, and a golf course which we irrigate with the waste water. There is always a concern with land treatment systems that they will depress the value of surrounding homes because they are near a sewage treatment plant. Well, it is really not a sewage treatment plant. It is four miles away, it has no odour, and it looks like any farm irrigation system. No one has ever refused to buy a home because it is next door to a land treatment system. In fact, the people love it. At anytime you could find ten or twelve people either walking or running with their dogs or, during hunting season, hunting. They look at it as open space they can use and that it is a benefit, rather than a problem.

After twenty-five years of doing this research and operating this system I think it is pretty safe to say that forest areas can be used to treat waste water for the recharge of groundwater both in summer and in winter. Additionally, these areas can be used as greenbelts for limited use by the public, without any threat to their health or to the health of the animals which inhabit the area. It is a viable alternative to using waterways to dispose of secondary sewage effluents.

REFERENCES

Cole, D.W., C.L. Henry, and W.L. Nutter. Eds. 1986. *The Forest Alternative for Treatment and Utilization of Municipal and Industrial Wastes.* Seattle: University of Washington Press.

Sopper, W.E. and L.T. Kardos. Eds. 1973. *Recycling Treated Municipal Waste water and Sludge Through Forest Cropland.* University Park, Pa.: The Pennsylvania State University Press.

Sopper, W.E. and S.N. Kerr. Eds. 1979. *Utilization of Municipal Sewage Effluent and Sludge on Forest and Disturbed Land.* University Park, Pa.: The Pennsylvania State Press.

U.S. Environmental Protection Agency. 1981. *Process Design Manual for Land Treatment of Municipal Waste Water.* Cincinnati: EPA 625/1-81-031.

Integrated Pest Management
Dr. Linda Gilkeson

Pest Control Today

I am here today to speak on Integrated Pest Management, an alternative to dependence on pesticides for urban forests and gardens. The key to this talk is *alternatives* to dependence on pesticides, because there are some cases where the judicious use of pesticides is necessary. It is the dependence on pesticides, however, that has gotten us into some very serious problems.

As residents of a city or an urban area, we think of pollution in air, water, soils, and of the persistence of chemicals in the food chain. For entomologists, however, an incredibly serious problem is the changes that have been wrought in insect populations, such as the development of pesticide resistance. To date, there are over six hundred species of insects known to be resistant to the pesticides used to control them. Some local populations of those species are resistant to virtually any pesticide that is now used. Some of them even have resistance to pesticides that have not yet been commercialized. When these are used, they have no effect because the mechanisms developed to resist one pesticide offer the same protection from other pesticides. This happens in potato beetles, flies, and many other insects with which we are familiar, but a particularly frightening example is that of mosquitoes that carry malaria in many parts of the world. These mosquitoes are resistant to the pesticides used for their

Dr. Linda Gilkeson is a research entomologist at Applied Bio-Nomics of Sidney, B.C., which is a firm specializing in commercial production of and research on biological control agents.

control while the malaria organism itself is resistant to antimalarial drugs. The result is the super insect carrying the super parasite that we cannot kill.

Not only have we failed to control some pests with pesticides, but we have also made the pest problem worse. Pest resurgence, when the pest population bounces back to a higher level than it was before spraying, is a problem we do not really understand. Perhaps other, unknown species were controlling the pests. Maybe there were competitors in the environment for food, or for places to lay eggs, or for hiding places, that were also knocked out when the pesticides were sprayed, thus leaving open a big niche into which the target insect can spread. There are also secondary pest outbreaks, when pests not even known to be present break out after a pesticide directed at another species kills the natural predators. This produces two pests instead of one. We need to remember these phenomena, even in an urban context.

Integrated Pest Management

In response to these severe problems with pesticides, integrated pest management concepts have been developed. Put very simply, integrated pest management is the use of all available tools and methods to suppress, but not to control, insect populations and keep damage to acceptable levels using the safest, most effective and most economical means. That is a rather tall order, and it requires thought about all the kinds of controls that can be used. There is no one magic chemical or one magic bullet, or one magic predator, or one magic technique. We have to think about using many techniques together.

An example of pest management as it applies to an urban situation comes from work done by the Okowski's at the Bio-Integral Resource Centre, Berkeley, and who are leaders in the area of urban pest management. In California on any summer day, an average garbage can produces a thousand flies. These flies are attracted into the shade trees because of the honey dew produced by aphids feeding on the trees. As the aphid population increases the honey, dew also increases, and so does the fly population in the shade trees. This phenomenon has led to complaints from the public, because it becomes a nuisance.

One way they attacked the problem was to trap the flies with very effective fly baits. They also approached it by releasing a parasite to control the aphids which alleviated the honey dew problem. That, however, was not really the problem. The problem was the waste management to begin with, because that is where the flies came from. There are many facets to such problems, and the solution is not to just keep treating superficial effects.

Integrated pest management, as it applies to urban situations, is a fairly new concept. It was first developed for agricultural crops. Factors such as the cost of pesticides, value of the harvest, and the residues in the crop would be taken into account. In urban situations, it is rather different, and the thinking has been a bit different, but some of the basic principles still apply.

Now I want to emphasize the steps and components of an integrated pest management program as it applies to any situation. It is a different way of thinking about a pest, whether you consider it a plant out of place in a garden, rats, head lice on children, flies, or something attacking a whole forest. These steps can be very personal and they can also be done for whole systems, so anyone should feel able to institute integrated pest management into whatever system he or she is dealing with.

Plants in urban habitats are under stress in a lot of ways. They may be poorly adapted species. Plants under stress from poor nutrients and under-watering can be quite susceptible to certain diseases and insects, and plants that are over-watered and over-fed are also susceptible to pests. Plants put up with road salt, root compaction, airborne pollutants, propane, and many other threats to their survival.

Indoors, in malls, public offices, and other public spaces, plants are often planted because of a desire to be closer to nature. Yet these plants are often in environments that are much dryer, or warmer, or dustier, or have poorer light compared to their natural environment. Because of this, they are susceptible to pests, yet because of their close proximity to human beings, spraying is either very difficult to manage or forbidden. The company I work with ships a weekly order of biological control agents to public buildings in Alberta because no pesticides are allowed in any public office.

We also have community gardens, backyard gardens, and many of the urban agriculture efforts that are increasingly popular, conflicting with herbicide and pesticide treatments on adjacent property. You have the situation I experienced, where the people next door invited in the lawn care company to spray from the top of the tallest tree right down to the lawn. They soaked it all with pesticides, including the walls of the house.

I went to the people involved and asked them what the sprays were for. They told me that they were spraying for tent caterpillars, flying ants, spiders, and damselflies. Damselflies are only alive for two days. They come out of the water, mate, lay eggs, and die, so spraying for them is great for a pest control company because the pest will definitely disappear (until next year). It is the same with flying ants, which are seasonal migrants, while tent caterpillars are very difficult to kill with a water spray because they are protected in their webbing. The best way to control them is to cut off the branch or use a blow-torch to flame the nest. Spiders are beneficial predators, yet they were targeted as pests. Almost everything these people were using the pesticide service for was inappropriate. I am not sure whether the pest control company was being ingenuous or was lying to them. These people wanted that treatment, and I am sure they were not told why it would appear to be successful.

The Integrated Pest Management Program

Identification

These are the basic steps to develop an Integrated Pest Management (IPM) program. The first one, identification, is very important. It may seem simplistic, but it is not. If you spray for something you think is insect damage when it is really virus damage, nothing will happen. If you spray for spider mites when the damage is from an insect, nothing will happen.

The disgruntlement with alternate methods of control has often been caused by the fact that people have not properly identified the pest. Talk to more experienced gardeners, go to extension agents, go to university people in entomology or biology, but get some kind of identification before you proceed. Once you do that, learn everything you can about the biology of the pest. All insects have times in their lifecycle that are more susceptible to specific treatments.

Injury Level

The next step is determining the injury level. This is the level at which the unacceptable damage occurs. The action level, however, is the point at which you need to treat to stop the injury from happening. If you are treating with an insecticide, very often the injury level is the same as the action level because the effect is immediate.

If you are using a beneficial organism, the action level and the injury level are usually at two different times in the population cycle. Often the action level must be a lot earlier because the beneficial organisms must reproduce and have time to act on the pest population. The same applies with some habitat modifications. Taking away the garbage today will not stop the flies that are in the environment today, but will stop flies developing tomorrow.

The injury level is a very important part of urban IPM. It is primarily an aesthetic injury level in urban situations. In garden situations it is not necessarily an aesthetic level, but it usually is for most pests that we want to control. Most pests that do damage in garden crops do not do enough damage, especially in a city, to risk losing the crop. Some damage is severe but is not seen. Some damage is actually not that much of a problem to a plant, but it looks terrible. It depends also on the plant, whether it is a foliage plant kept in the house where one bite is really noticeable, or whether it is a plant a long way away where quite a few bites are not noticed.

The location of the plant is very important in establishing its aesthetic injury level. The plant on a roadside has a different aesthetic injury level than a plant in your house. Attitudes are also extremely important. It has been shown in several studies that with public education, pesticide use goes down. It is as simple as that. When people know what the insects are doing and how many can be tolerated, they do not need to use pesticides out of a fear that things will get worse.

The type of pest involved is very important in establishing the injury level. For example, mealybugs are slow to reproduce and they produce lots of a white fluff, although only in huge numbers do they do a lot of damage. People see the fluff on a plant a lot sooner than they will see spider mites, which are very tiny and can do a lot of damage rapidly under hot dry conditions. Aphids and other foliage pests on plants on the roadside of an arboretum go unnoticed by people driving by. It is quite a different situation in a botanical garden where someone is walking by very close to the plant.

Treatments

After identification and determination of injury and action levels, comes the treatment. There are a wide range of treatments that can be used in different ways. I want to emphasize that the last step, evaluation, is just as important as identification. It is also often forgotten. One must finish up, evaluate the situation, and make notes about what to do next year.

Resistant Pests

The most important treatment in an urban context is probably planting resistant plants. There has been quite a bit of work done on resistant ornamental plants. Norway and white spruce are resistant to eastern gall aphids. There are Douglas firs resistant to various midges and rhododendrons that are very resistant to root weevils. Consult nursery people to find out what plants are adapted to your area and their resistance characteristics.

There has been a real breakthrough in turf management, with new varieties of fescue and perennial rye grass that are extremely resistant to disease and insects because they grow in association with endophytic fungi (meaning that a fungus actually grows up inside the leaves of the plant in a symbiotic association). The fungus growing inside the grass accumulates toxins that enable the plant to resist weevils, aphids, armyworms, billbugs, many species of cutworms, sod webworm, and chinch bugs, as well as fusarium, blight, and brown patch diseases. The plants are also drought resistant, and some varieties actually produce very high quality turf. When you consider that the lawn care industry in the U.S. alone spends $40 million a year just on insecticides, and then you think about sitting on those lawns, these resistant varieties can be seen as a real breakthrough.

Habitat Modifiers

Habitat modification is the second treatment on the list. Under habitat modification comes naturalizing and waste management, such as removing the breeding sites of insects and keeping food away from cockroaches. The benefit of naturalizing areas is that you provide for an incredible number of beneficial insects, which is the beginning of the end of pest problems in the area. In fact, that is one mechanism behind companion planting for gardens. Most of the plants listed as good companion plants are plants that supply pollen and nectar to beneficial species. It is unbelievable how many insects are out there that we will never see or notice but that can be attracted into our gardens to control pests. It may look like the plant repels pests, whereas the plant was an attractant to the beneficial insect that controlled the pests.

Attitude Changes

Attitude changes are a very important tool, and in an urban situation the equivalent of extension to growers is in public education for residents of a city. Many people just do not realize that pesticides are not the best way to control pests. They tell you that they would rather not use pesticides, but that they are the only way. As soon as they find out there are alternatives, attitudes change very quickly.

Physical Controls

Physical controls such as fly traps, cockroach traps, and bait stations are very useful. Some of these things are effective in bringing down the breeding numbers of a population because the adults can be attracted into traps. Yellow sticky traps can be used for monitoring to tell what pests are in the greenhouse or garden, but when used in quantities, traps keep populations below the injury level.

Physical control that I do not see used very much are the dust products like diatomaceous earth and silica gel that kill insects by abrading their outer coating and causing them to die of dehydration. They are not chemicals, so are quite safe, and they never break down. If you put diatomaceous earth on grain it can be stored for forty years without insect damage. As long as the dust is there, weevils cannot survive. It is very effective in places which must be free of insects, such as in food, in cupboards, on pets. Diatomaceous earth is not appropriate for garden and outdoor uses because it kills any insect. This would harm many beneficial insects, and less than 1 percent of the insects in this world are directly harmful to humans.

Chemical Controls

Chemical control is the next thing on the list. As I mentioned before, most people do not realize that pesticides are not the best way to control pests. It is a bit like hitting a bug with a shotgun. Ninety-nine percent of the pesticide that is used does not hit the target pest because it cannot. What you are doing is spraying where the pest might be, which means you are getting it all over the leaves and into the air.

There are, however, places where pesticides can be used. (Strictly speaking, something like diatomaceous earth is a pesticide. It kills insects, and when used in appropriate places it will kill specific insects.) There are sprayers that deliver low volumes of spray in a large volume of carrier, so that very small amounts of pesticide are used more efficiently. The timing of pesticide application can be changed to hit the part of the pests life cycle when it is most suscep-tible. One well-timed spray will do where four were used before, and that considerably reduces pesticide use.

Some of the more recently developed pesticides are quite specific and have low residual toxicity. You can use them and then a week later put in beneficial organisms because the residues break down so quickly. Insecticide soaps will reduce certain pests, while dormant oil sprays are very important in the wintertime on trees. They prevent a lot of problems in the spring because they kill eggs and insects that are over-wintering in the bark of trees.

Botanical insecticides are becoming more easily available, such as pyrethrins and rotenone. Their beauty is that they break down very quickly, but some are still very highly toxic at the time they are used.

Just because some of these botanicals are safer in terms of environmental effects, they are not safer when being used. Good protective equipment is necessary when spraying these products.

Something that has been noticed in the San Francisco Bay area is that certain trees act as host trees for pest populations. They found that among groups of Norway maple, ash, elm, plum, linden, oaks, and hollies, only one tree in an area needed treatment. It is called the host tree effect. Why that tree needed treatment, why it was more susceptible, whether it was genetic or environmental, we do not know, but finding those trees and marking them, removing them, or spot-spraying them only has considerably reduced pesticide use.

Biological Control

Biological control is the last component. There are three main ways that we use biocontrol organisms, or that we can aid biocontrol. The first one, and the most important one outdoors, is conservation of native predators and parasites. The others are inoculation and inundation. Conserving beneficial populations is much easier than having to buy them and hope that they make it. To conserve the native population, plant food for them. Plant wildflowers, companion plants in your garden, or put a wildflower strip along one edge of your garden. Diversify your plantings.

As an example, I would like to run through the complex of native aphid feeding insects. These are native hardy northern species that will come and get aphids if you encourage them with attractive plantings. Most gardeners know aphids — they are easy to kill because they are soft, tiny, delicate things, but they have an amazing reproductive strategy, with the mother aphid giving live birth to nymphs. She can have five to ten a day, and they already have inside them the embryos of their daughters, so there is no time delay for eggs hatching and development phases. If one aphid survives a spray, you get a lot of aphids again very quickly. Also, when they become crowded the nymphs are born with the ability to sprout wings, fly away, and find somewhere else to eat.

There are many species of lady beetles hardy here. There is also a hardy native predatory midge that is such a good biological control agent that we are working on it in China and all over Canada for release outdoors and in greenhouses. You can probably find it anywhere in your garden among aphids.

We have syrphid flies, amazing little creatures that fly like hummingbirds and hover at flowers to get the pollen and nectar needed to lay eggs. Their larvae eat aphids voraciously. There are also many species of parasitic wasps that parasitize aphids.

To use biocontrol it helps to understand population dynamics. As the pest population increases, any beneficial populations will follow. It takes time for them to catch up to the pests so you will not get instant control. Then as the population of the pest drops, so will the beneficial population. The aim is to have a pest population curve that does not go so high that it causes terrible damage, but also not to have it crash so far that the beneficial species starve to death. Always having some pest insects around is desirable.

The other two methods of using biocontrol agents, inundation and inoculation, are relevant primarily in an urban situation, with interior plantscapes. The company I work with does a lot of work with commercial greenhouses and large conservatories. One of the best predators that has ever been developed for biocontrol is *Phytoseiulus persimilus,* a predatory mite. It controls the two-spotted spider mite, which is a very serious pest of many interior plants, vegetables, and flowers. It is such a good predator that we know it nearly always works. Another one that is particularly good is the parasite for white fly, called *Encarsia*. It is a tiny wasp that lays an egg in the white fly larva, which then turns black. We also have predators for aphids, mealybugs, scale, thrips, and several different kinds of mites.

I will finish with this final thought from Carl Huffacker: "When you kill off the natural enemies of the pests, you inherit their work."

REFERENCES

Common Sense Pest Control Quarterly. Bio-Integral Resource centre, P.O. Box 7414, Berkeley, Ca. 94707.

Frankie, G.W. and G. S. Koehler. 1978. *Perspectives in Urban Entomology*. New York: Academic Press.

The IPM Practitioner. Bio-Integral Resource Centre, P.O. Box 7414, Berkeley, Ca. 94707.

Steiner, M. and D. Elliott. 1978. 2nd edition. *Biological Pest Management for Interior Plantscapes*. Vegreville, Alta.: Alberta Environmental Centre.

Breaking the Technical Barriers:
Restoration of an Urban Green Space
Wayne Gall

I have been asked to react to the statement that "Urban wilderness is an area of urban space that is not managed in any significant way." Without questioning the size scales implied by the term wilderness, this definition may be appropriate for open spaces which have retained, during their history, primary control by natural forces. It would then seem to be a relatively simple matter to perpetuate such existing natural control. But how about urban open spaces which have had a checkered history of human disturbance, use, and abuse? I would like to relate how technical design and innovative planning are allowing a former municipal/industrial dump to revert to a wild state at Tifft Farm Nature Preserve, Buffalo, N.Y.

In 1972 the city of Buffalo purchased a 264 acre tract of land located three miles south of downtown Buffalo, an area which had been reverting to a wild state since widespread municipal and industrial dumping ceased in the early 1960s. The city's sole purpose, at least initially, was to provide a site for transferring about 1.6 million cubic yards of mixed municipal waste from the Squaw Island dump near the source of the Niagara River so a new secondary sewage treatment plant could be constructed there. One of the proposals was to spread the refuse out across much of the Tifft Farm site (Figure 1) to create a golf course, filling in all or part of the ponds which were remnants of

Wayne K. Gall has been the administrator of the Tifft Farm Nature Preserve for the Buffalo Museum of Science, in Buffalo, New York, since 1983. He is an avid field naturalist and educator, and is active in several environmental organizations in the Buffalo area.

shipping canals, destroying a productive seventy-five acre cattail marsh, which was a reminder of the once extensive wetlands along this area of the Lake Erie shoreline, and obliterating fields and thickets in the uplands.

In spite of the previous use and abuse of the Tifft Farm landscape as it evolved from dairy farm/stockyards to a transshipment terminal and then to a dump, the site retained significant natural value. In fact, for local residents and naturalists, it was an unofficial recreational preserve for bird watching, strolling, hunting (illegal as it was), and numerous other outdoor pursuits.

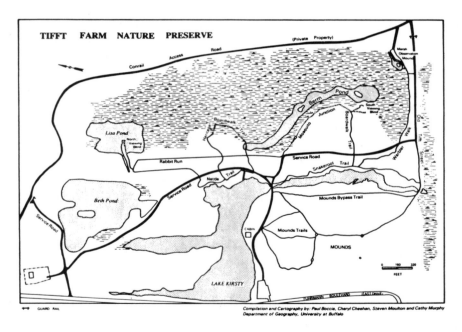

Figure 1. Tifft Farm Nature Preserve, 1987. The visitor centre (cabin) is on the south shore of Lake Kirsty, a remnant of shipping canals formerly connected to the Buffalo River. The Mounds area in the southwestern quadrant is the planned landfill constructed 1973–75. The western portion of Beth Pond originated as a borrow pit. A 75 acre marsh stretches across the eastern third of the 264 acre site. The Buffalo Harbor is west of Fuhrmann Blvd., just off the map.

An *ad hoc* coalition of citizen, environmental, and sportsmen's groups devised a conceptual plan to concentrate the refuse in the southwest quadrant of the site by mounding it up, rather than spreading it out, and at the same time covering the area which had been most severely affected by prior industrial and municipal dumping. The concept also included an active recreational area (ball fields, etc.) along the southern boundary and establishment on the bulk of the site a nature preserve and environmental education centre. The *ad hoc* coalition evolved into a Technical Advisory Committee containing key professional members who were successful in "selling" this plan to the City of Buffalo and the Buffalo Sewer Authority.

The conceptual barrier had been broken. A former dump and planned landfill would evolve into an urban nature preserve, satisfying both municipal and citizen needs. But what about the technical barriers? How best could such a massive amount of waste be transferred in an environmentally acceptable manner? Concerns were raised that leachate generated by the mixed waste would contaminate the ponds, marsh, and uplands which were the very object of protection and rehabilitation. Where would the clean material come from to cover the mounds of garbage and to ultimately cap it? How could soil erosion be prevented from exposing the landfill?

The mode of transport selected for transferring the 1.6 million cubic yards of refuse was barges rather than by rail. This method took advantage of Tifft Farm's proximity to the Buffalo waterfront and the convenient water connection to Squaw Island afforded by the Black Rock Canal and Buffalo Harbour. The additional disturbance of installing new rail facilities into the Tifft Farm site was also eliminated. From the landing dock deployed in the Buffalo Harbour, the waste was trucked across Fuhrmann Blvd. where earth movers sculpted it into four mounds.

The leachate problem was addressed by trenching around the perimeter of the mounds until an impervious layer of clay was reached (about twenty-two feet) and pouring a bentonite clay slurry which hardens into an impervious wall. Inside the leachate barrier, a collection system of perforated pipes was laid horizontally, to intercept leachate and transmit it under gravity from the perimeter to a single pump station on the site which, in turn, pumps the leachate into the municipal sewage treatment system. Monitoring wells were installed along the leachate collection system to allow access for sampling.

To provide cover for the refuse, soil was excavated from a borrow pit established at the north end of the site and trucked via a haul road, constructed with slag, to the mounds area. As a result of the soil removal, an existing pond was enlarged to add to the site's aquatic habitats. The pond was configured and the shore sloped to promote the establishment of rooted aquatic plants along its margin. Some old concrete foundations were encountered during the borrow operation and the configuration of the shoreline was modified to include a peninsula and island to avoid the cost of removing these structures. Although initial disturbances to plants and wildlife from the borrow operation were significant, this area continues to become more valuable to wildlife as aquatic and terrestrial habitats evolve. The haul road is now utilized as a service road and provides access for maintenance, security patrols, and handicapped persons in permitted vehicles.

After two feet of final cover was placed on the mounds to create an impervious cap, and about three feet placed along surface drainage paths, the cover was tamped, seeded, and mulched to minimize erosion. A mixture of grasses and legumes (clover and bird's-foot trefoil) was initially planted. After this herbaceous vegetation became established, trails were mowed, trees and shrubs were planted in clumps to provide food and cover for wildlife, and a winter sledding/tubing run was established. No other improvements are planned in this area (Figure 2).

As the construction of the mounds neared completion in 1975, a master plan for Tifft Farm Nature Preserve was issued. It provided technical guidelines for management and phasing of additional site developments such as a water level control system for the marsh, construction of a visitor centre, proposed trails, etc. Key elements of the master plan include defining the purpose and prioritizing uses of the site as a wildlife sanctuary, environmental education centre, and passive recreation area; zoning the site for different intensities of use; and listing policies for planning and management.

Figure 2. Looking north from the top of the mounds toward downtown Buffalo in 1983, eight years after completion of solid waste transfer. In foreground, note establishment of dense herbaceous vegetation, clumps of planted trees, and a mowed nature trail on the left. In the centre is the visitor centre on the south shore of Lake Kirsty. The former Cargill grain elevator in the upper right corner is along the Buffalo River.

The biggest technical barrier since the establishment of Tifft Farm Nature Preserve in the early to mid 1970s had to be broken in 1983. Barrels of solidified industrial waste became exposed during shoreline work near the log cabin visitor's centre. The Erie County Health department recommended closing the preserve until identification and removal of the waste was completed. From April to October 1983, about 116 barrels were sampled and removed. Naphthalene, the constituent of moth balls, was the only hazardous material found in the barrels in relatively high concentration. Surface soil and fish samples were also analyzed as the property was intensively scrutinized. After review of the sampling results by the U.S.

Figure 3. Children's class studying the preserve's 75-acre marsh from the Heritage Boardwalk. Note smokestacks of inactive steel mill in background.

Centres For Disease Control in Atlanta, the Erie County Health Department lifted its advisory and the preserve re-opened.

Tifft Farm Nature Preserve is still rebounding from the effects of prolonged and often negative publicity. Now that many technical barriers have been broken, this difficult situation has given the Buffalo Museum of Science, which administers the site, the challenge and burden to break some educational barriers: we can now transmit the message, loud and clear, that urban green space can be reclaimed from disturbed sites as long as nature's capacity for renewal is not overwhelmed (Figure 3). How even more significant Tifft Farm's urban wilderness would be if, through long range planning and proper management of solid waste, it was not allowed to be so seriously disturbed in the first place.

REFERENCES

Gall, Wayne, Karen Geiger, and Catherine Ansuini. 1986. *Tifft Farm Nature Preserve: Self-Guided Nature Trail and Wellness Walk.* Buffalo: Tifft Farm Nature Preserve.

Technical Report for the Tifft Farm Nature Preserve Master Plan. 1975. New York: Ecoplans Incorporated.

The Tifft Farm Guide for Kindergarten Through Sixth Grade. 1980. Buffalo: Tifft Farm Nature Preserve.

Wolf, Teresa L. and the Tifft Farm History Committee. 1983.*Tifft Farm: A History of Man and Nature.* Buffalo: Tifft Farm Nature Preserve.

Establishing Ecology Parks in London
Jacklyn Johnston

People need nature in the city. Children and adults benefit from contact with the natural world in their everyday life, from seeing common birds in their back garden and street trees coming into leaf, to the antics of squirrels in the local park. But many are divorced from the cycles of nature and have had few opportunities to enjoy wildlife. Ecology parks are being established in London to help bring more wildlife into city neighbourhoods.

Ecology parks are small parcels of land, usually a few hectares or less, located in the inner city or further from the city centre but in heavily built-up areas. Most ecology parks are "created from scratch" on vacant land. In some cases, areas of naturally colonized vegetation will be retained, and in others the park will be developed "from a clean state." The design will generally incorporate mounding of the landscape to create visual interest and several habitats, including a pond, meadow, and woodland area. Pathways lead visitors to explore the habitats without trampling or disturbing more sensitive species.

Ecology Parks in London

Britain's first ecology park, the William Curtis Ecological Park, was built during 1977 near Tower Bridge on the River Thames. The park was created as part of H.M. the Queen's Silver Jubilee celebrations

Jacklyn Johnston works for the London Ecology Unit and is a Trustee of the London Ecology Centre. She is particularly interested in neighbourhood use of city nature parks and gardens.

and located along the route of "Jubilee Walk" through central London.

William Curtis Park was located on one hectare of temporarily vacant land which was earmarked for office development. The Ecological Parks Trust (now the Trust for Urban Ecology) was responsible for the project and employed the British Trust for Conservation Volunteers to build it for a small fee. From the outset, the park was staffed and records kept of both visitors and changes in the vegetation.

To create this park, volunteers broke up concrete and tarmac, dug a large hole for a pond, spread subsoil throughout, and then planted about 150 types of plants. Many species self-seeded into the park, swelling the list of invertebrates, birds, and mammals recorded. By 1984, twenty-one species of butterfly had been seen.

Sadly, the park closed in 1985 to make way for office development. Throughout its eight-year life, William Curtis attracted fifty thousand visitors, one-third of which were local school children. It also acted as an inspiration to many interested in urban ecology and a demonstration of possibilities for a small inner-city vacant plot.

Gillespie Park is another early example of an ecology park. Established during 1981 by the London Borough of Islington, the park was created through the parks department system in the same way as more formal open spaces. However, the park is different: native plants have been used instead of more traditional bedding plants and shrubs, and the overall design is much less formal.

Gillespie Park is 1.6 hectares and supports areas of grassland, shrubs, woodland, and a pond. Formerly a goods yard used for the storage and transport of coal, the park has been established on a layer of coal dust up to one metre thick. It is frequently used for school visits and local residents are encouraged to use it like other local parks — to walk the dog, sit on the grass, have a picnic, or even play football.

Two further ecology parks have been established: Lavender Pond Nature Park and Stave Hill Nature Park, both in London's docklands. Since the decline of London as a major shipping centre, the docklands have become derelict, but in recent years vast tracts of land have been redeveloped for residential, office, and light industrial use.

Redevelopment has included establishment of two ecology parks with another proposed during the next few years.

Lavender Pond Nature Park (1.0 ha) includes a large pond and wetland area as a central feature, with boardwalks providing access to visitors. Flower-rich grassland and a band of woodland delineates the boundary of the park on one side, with an expanse of mown grassland on the other. A full-time teacher and warden manage the park and conduct visits for school children.

Stave Hill Nature Park is the most recent of London's ecology parks — established in 1986 — and the largest at 2.3 ha. The park is still relatively new and, as such, many habitats are just starting to take shape. It has been designed to incorporate a variety of different habitats with a series of management regimes. The aim is to record success rates to help further research in the establishment of naturalistic vegetation.

Camley Street Natural Park

Camley Street is London's most famous ecology park. It is often cited in Britain and abroad as a remarkably successful example of the benefits of inner-city renewal and the potential of urban land for environmental education. It is located in King's Cross, on the northern edge of central London, which has large areas of derelict land and a grey mixture of busy roads, gas holders, a waste transfer station, and miles of railway lines — an unlikely place for a wildlife haven!

The history of the park began in 1981 when a local wildlife group "discovered" the site. A derelict coal yard vacant for about twenty years, it had become a tangle of colourful wildflowers with a fringe of willows near the roadside. The strategic planning authority (the former Greater London Council or GLC) identified the site for development of a coach park with a small area of parkland, but later agreed that it should become a nature park. During 1982, plans were drawn up by GLC landscape architects and ecologists (now the London Ecology Unit) in consultation with the local wildlife group.

Establishment of the park was delayed when "travellers" occupied the land from April to September 1983. It was November before work began with clearance of several metres of mattresses, tires, and various articles of domestic refuse dumped during previous months.

Little of the original colourful vegetation could be saved as construction of the park continued over the winter.

The central feature of the park is a large pond, fed by the adjacent Region's Canal, with a fringe of reeds and other aquatic plants. The pond grades into a marsh and then meadow at the northern end, and other areas of meadow lie alongside the main path and behind the nature centre. Shrub and woodland areas surround the pond and a small "children's garden" has been established near the centre.

The nature centre includes a classroom, interpretation area, small kitchen, office, and toilets, and is fully accessible to the disabled. An extension to the nature centre has been built and is used as an additional meeting room/youth club and base for the park's nature club. Paths and timber walkways have been constructed around and across the pond to provide access. After crossing the pond, the path leads up to a steep mound giving attractive views, and returns to the nature centre through an area of woodland.

The park is run by the London Wildlife Trust, a voluntary organization that employs a manager and project officer on site. The Local Education Authority fund a teacher who works full-time at the park. About ten thousand school children and five to ten thousand adults visit each year. Camley Street is open seven days a week during daylight hours but is locked at night.

The main objectives of management are nature conservation, recreation, and education. Wardening and day-to-day management of the vegetation are carried out by park staff who also oversee work by volunteers from the Camley Street Support Group. A comprehensive management plan has been written and sets out a management regime for each habitat. Although the park is seen mainly as a local facility, it attracts a much wider audience and functions as a demonstration project for interested people from all over Britain. Visitors come from Europe, North America, Australia, and Japan, too.

Local residents tend to visit on weekends or come to special events. Most people who live nearby know of its existence either by word of mouth, through local publicity, or via their children's experience there as part of the school curriculum. Staff and support group members encourage everyone in the community to use the park and have particularly tried to reach disadvantaged groups with special needs.

Recently, the future of Camley Street has come into question as the landowners push ahead with plans to sell the land. Recent plans to redevelop the King's Cross area will also affect the park greatly. Although the chosen developers have demonstrated their intention to retain the park, British Rail hopes to build a new rail line underneath, which would require the park's destruction and reinstatement. A highly vociferous campaign has been mounted to save Camley Street.

Establishing an Ecology Park

Camley Street Natural Park and other ecology parks in London serve as useful examples for formulating general guidelines for their establishment in other cities. Experience shows that before embarking on such a project, however, a feasibility study should be carried out with particular considerations given to the following factors:

* community interest
* ownership and leasing arrangements
* location in relation to schools and centres of population
* difficulties and dangers
* size
* finance
* intrinsic nature conservation value of the area

If the feasibility study shows that there are no major obstacles and that there is sufficient support, the next phase should include setting up a steering committee, community involvement, site design and facilities, and an assessment of costs and staffing requirements.

Steering Committee

Once a suitable site has been chosen and approved, a steering committee should be formed to oversee the progress of the project. The committee could include representation from local government councillors and employees, teachers, local residents and voluntary groups, and organizations knowledgeable about ecology and environment. By forming a committee it will be easier to incorporate suggestions from a wide range of interested individuals and organizations. However, it is vital that one member of the committee be prepared to act as the key person to whom all questions and suggestions can be referred.

Community Involvement

One of the main objectives in establishing an ecology park is to provide local people with a facility that they will use and enjoy. Accordingly, proposals should be publicized and the steering committee should be prepared to make changes according to suggestions from local people.

Once the outline proposal for an ecology park has been approved,a public meeting can be arranged. The committee should enlist the support of local amenity groups, youth clubs, environmental organizations, residents associations, and individuals living or working near the project. Notices of the meeting can be posted throughout the community and advertised in the local press.

One of the reasons for involving local people in these projects is the belief that this will decrease vandalism. Evangelists of community involvement believe that with power comes responsibility and a belief in the future. The idea is that some people who are not involved in their own environment will take out their frustrations on that environment, and there are many examples of this syndrome. Ecology parks in London confirm the benefits of public participation for they have suffered little vandalism on the whole, particularly where relations are good between the community and park managers.

Key Ingredients for a successful Ecology Park

Experience in London shows that there are several key factors which contribute to the establishment of a successful ecology park:

1. Staffing — wardens/teachers to keep the park open seven days a week
2. Balance between wildlife and people — encouraging success without disturbing the wildlife that people come to see
3. Nature centre — to act as a base for all activities

4. Management and maintenance — nature areas need long-term caring management

5. Community involvement — ecology parks should provide people with a facility that they will use and enjoy

6. Key person — to keep the project running smoothly and act as a pivotal point for everyone involved

7. Interpretation and publicity — to bring the park alive for visitors and ensure that everyone is given the opportunity to visit

8. Security of tenure — necessary for establishment of vegetation

FURTHER READING

Bradley, C. 1986. *Community Involvement in Greening*. Birmingham: The Groundwork Foundation.

Chandler (Johnston), J.D. 1988. "Urban Renewal in Sympathy with Nature." *London Environmental Bulletin* 4, no. 4: 5–8.

Emery, M. 1986. *Promoting Nature in Cities and Towns*. London: Christopher Helm. (Available from Trust for Urban Ecology, below.)

Goode, J.A. 1986. *Wild in London*. London: Michael Joseph.

Johnston, J. D. In press. *Nature Areas for City People*. London: London Ecology Unit.

HELPFUL ORGANIZATIONS

London Ecology Unit, Berkshire House, 168–173 High Holborn, London WClV 7AG, Tel. (01) 379–4352

London Wildlife Trust, 80 York Way, London N1 9AG, Tel. (01) 278–6612

Trust for Urban Ecology, P.O. Box 514, London SE16 1AS, Tel. (01) 237–9165

Toronto's Ecology Park
David Gordon

Part A: Planning and Planting a Park

What is Ecology Park?

Ecology Park, located at 10 Madison Avenue in the downtown Toronto neighbourhood known as the Annex, is a Pollution Probe Foundation demonstration project to show the potential of natural landscaping in an urban environment. Located on what was once an abandoned construction site, the naturalized landscaping follows the tradition established for ecology parks in 1977 in London, England. It challenges the conventional approach to public open space with a natural, ecologically sound landscape — one which does not require large amounts of water, energy, synthetic pesticides, and fertilizers.

How the Toronto Ecology Park came to be is the subject of this section. Since the creation of an ecology park offers a unique opportunity for individuals and organizations to practise environmental restoration in a cooperative community environment, the aim of this section is to encourage others to have a go at it.

Site Description

The location of Toronto's Ecology Park owes almost as much to fortuitous circumstances as it does to the efforts of the staff and volunteers of the Pollution Probe Foundation. It is on property owned by the Metropolitan Toronto government, the second tier municipal level government in the Greater Toronto area responsible for regional urban concerns such as transit, major roadways, and water and sewage systems. The property was left vacant after construction of the Spadina subway line was completed in January 1978. Because it was directly above two subway tunnels that in places were as shallow as four feet below grade, engineering restrictions severely limited construction opportunities. Ownership of the undeveloped site was retained by Metro Toronto for future use by the Toronto Transit Commission (TTC) as a turning loop for a proposed Light Rail Transit (LRT) line on Spadina Avenue.

The retention of the site as a vacant lot was unrelated to the development of Ecology House, a demonstration project of the energy efficient retrofitting of a downtown single family home. Ecology

Figure 1. View of Ecology House and Ecology Park from south-east prior to any work beginning on the park. Madison Avenue is bottom right, Spadina Avenue is behind vacant lot in upper left. The trombe wall is on the south exposure of Ecology House, and the Spadina subway station bus platform is behind brick wall in centre left. Photo by Stephen Hall.

House was opened in 1980 by the Pollution Probe Foundation at 12 Madison Avenue, the lot immediately north of the current site of Ecology Park. The only indication in the design of Ecology House for any planned use of the adjacent vacant lot was the construction of a trombe wall on the south exposure of the house which, as a passive solar heating mechanism, captures direct sunlight across the vacant lot. There was no conscious effort on the part of the Pollution Probe Foundation, which occupies Ecology House, to link the development of Ecology House to future plans for the neighbouring vacant lot, although it was clearly in the best interests of the Ecology House project to see that no development occurred on the site.

Site Acquisition

Almost as soon as Ecology House was occupied by Pollution Probe staff and volunteers in 1980, they expressed interest in the site at 10 Madison Avenue. An urban organic garden had been established in the small back yard of Ecology House and had begun to encroach on the neighbouring lot. As the vacant lot was increasingly recognized as both an eyesore and an opportunity to develop a community green space project complementary to the aims of Ecology House, Probe staff and volunteers began to investigate the possibility of leasing the site for a community open-space project.

Since Pollution Probe was receiving an increasing number of requests for information on pesticide-free urban agriculture and naturalized landscaping, the lot at 10 Madison began to be seen as a potential site for a project to demonstrate alternatives to conventional landscaping and gardening. Such use of the site was implicitly supported by a 1981 City of Toronto report that identified the Annex neighbourhood as being short of both existing park space and of locations where parks might be developed. Restoration of derelict urban sites in the United States and Britain as community gardens and ecology parks suggested that such a demonstration project was feasible.

In 1981, the staff of Ecology House began to pursue the bureaucracy of Metro Toronto and the City of Toronto for permission to develop a demonstration green space project on the 10 Madison site. Although some support from the city was evident, neither the Toronto Transit Commission nor Metro Toronto expressed interest in approving a lease for the temporary use of the site by Ecology House. As a result, in 1984 Probe made an explicit decision to abandon the bureaucratic route in favour of a political approach. This was also, in part, a response to yet another bid to lease the land for parking, and indications that Metro supported the proposal. Probe's political effort included a campaign to build community support for the project and to obtain the backing of area representatives from all four levels of government.

The choice to pursue the political route also coincided with an upcoming Toronto municipal election in 1985. The election was the first for a restructured municipal council which collapsed the existing two alderman seats for the Ecology House ward into one. As a result, the two incumbent aldermen (one of whom also sat on Metro council) were candidates for a single council vacancy, and both campaigned as strong supporters of the Ecology Park project, promising to pursue the issue at the council level. In addition, Pollution Probe developed and retained the support of the local residents' association and neighbourhood businesses. Thus, it was difficult for the political representatives to be anything other than enthusiastically supportive of the project at both the City and Metro levels.

The political effort paid off and both municipal councils instructed the appropriate agencies to investigate the Ecology House proposal, which was formally presented to the Metro Land Use Committee in April 1985. In connection with this presentation, Probe volunteers distributed five thousand flyers to neighbourhood residences urging active political support for the proposal. Thus, Pollution Probe's presentation included endorsement of the project by the Annex Residents' Association as well as several local businesses and the Ecumenical Council of Canada. In May 1985 Metro Council gave approval for Probe to lease the 10 Madison site. Use of the site by Ecology House had three preconditions: that the cost of the lease would be one dollar each year; that the lease could be cancelled upon one month's notice; and that Pollution Probe would be required to obtain liability insurance for any eventualities at the site.

With the lease in place, a volunteer steering committee was struck at Ecology House to guide the planning and development of the site. This committee was supported by a number of Probe staff members, but it was primarily composed of volunteers with a strong interest in seeing the project through to completion. The work of this committee, and of several volunteer advisors, guided the entire planning, development, and implementation of effort for the Ecology Park project.

Getting Started — A Chronology

1981

- Ecology House solicits support for Ecology Park idea from neighbours in response to the proposed use of 10 Madison as a parking lot.
- Alderman asks Metro Land Use Committee to reject use of site as a parking facility.
- Annex is identified in a City of Toronto report as a priority area for parkland.

1982

- City of Toronto Housing Committee explores purchase of the site for public housing.
- Ecology House requests TTC to lease the site for one summer only.
- Metro Toronto opposes City of Toronto redesignation of zoning for the site from "Low Density Mixed Commercial-Residential Area" to "Park."

1983

- Ecology House requests Metro Toronto Land Use Committee to allow use of the site as a park.

1984

- Alderman Kanter asks Metro Land Use Committee to support use of the site as a park and requests the City to investigate purchasing the site from Metro.
- Ecology House writes to Alderman Hope for support of park idea for site.

1985

- Ecology House canvasses five thousand local homes for residents to appear at Metro Land Use Committee hearing to support park plan.
- Alderman Hope asks Metro to support Pollution Probe plan and identifies three conditions for lease approval.
- Annex Residents Association strongly endorses the Ecology House plan.
- Ecumenical Council of Canada endorses the plan.
- Pollution Probe makes a formal proposal to the Metro Land Use Committee to lease the site.
- May 15: Metro Parks and Recreation Property recommends that Metro enter into an agreement with Pollution Probe for temporary use of the site.
- June 2: ceremonial ground breaking, attended by two aldermen, Member of Parliament, Member of the Provincial Parliament, and media.
- Steering committee formally convened.
- Technical advisors approached regarding involvement in Ecology Park.

The Conceptual Ideal

The development of the working goals, objectives, and designs for Ecology Park was by no means a clear and definitive process. Many possible plans and functions for the park were discussed over the five years of effort by Pollution Probe to obtain use of the site, but no final design had been developed by May 1985 when the licence was granted and the ground breaking took place. However, urged on by the need to obtain funding for the project, Probe volunteers, staff, and advisers developed the following outline of needs, goals, and objectives in the spring of 1985. It represents an ideal for the project and was intended to appeal to the broadest possible range of potential funders. While it differs from the formal working proposal eventually developed by the steering committee, it served as a source of ideas for the final site plan. Because of this, and because it also represents many of the ideals and values which can be achieved in any ecology park, it is worth examining in detail.

A Needs Assessment for the "Ideal" Plan

The range of needs identified to support the development of the 10 Madison site as a demonstration of alternative urban landscaping highlights the extent to which ecology parks can address a variety of urban problems. Many of these needs were expressed by the people who sought specific information on alternative landscaping and gardening techniques from Pollution Probe. Others were reflected in emerging trends of urban landscape design in ecology parks elsewhere. The identification of these needs provided social and environmental justification for development of Ecology Park in downtown Toronto.

Energy Conservation

The manicured, fertilized, and weed-free turfgrass lawns of traditional urban landscaping consume large amounts of nonrenewable resources, demand power-hungry machines, and the non-native species used require large applications of energy-intensive pesticides and fertilizers. Ecology Park will show attractive alternatives to the energy-intensive conventions, including demonstrations of how plantings reduce the heating and cooling needs of adjacent buildings and extend growing seasons through the creation of microclimates.

Environmental Protection

Chemical pesticides and fertilizers are potential health hazards if not handled properly, and their residues can contribute to the toxic loading of regional environments. Ecology Park will show how use of toxic garden products can be reduced or eliminated through the choice of hardy and native plant species well-adapted to our climate, precipitation, and soils. Organic gardening principles which rely on companion planting, healthy soils, habitats for beneficial insects, compost, green manure, and other soil amenities to ensure healthy, contaminant-free produce will be given visible form in the park.

Water Quality

Conventional landscapes, especially turfgrass lawns, require a lot of expensive drinking water for their upkeep. Again, there is a missed opportunity because the root systems of naturalized areas absorb and retain water for their season-long use, thereby adding to the capacity of municipal sewage systems to deal with storm water surges. Ecology Park will have woodland and prairie native plants able to survive in local rainfall conditions and a grey water recovery system to lessen the gardening burden on the drinking water supply.

Wilderness Appreciation

Current landscaping practices tend to create a sterile "green desert and lollipop tree" environment which attracts few species because it undoes the natural diversity of wilderness by using a minimum amount of a few different plant species, many of which are not native. Such an environment attracts few native flora and fauna, many of which are dependent upon a close association with native vegetation. Ecology Park will have native woodlands and prairies with accelerated succession to attract wildlife in general and, specifically, a variety of bird and butterfly species.

Food Supply

The incorporation of edible species into landscapes for decorative purposes is currently rare. Ecology Park will show how vegetables, herbs, fruit trees, and berry bushes can be integrated with decorative plants to create functional gardens that are aesthetically pleasing.

Information Services

Ecology Park will be a source of information about alternative gardening and landscaping approaches for urban residents, landscapers, and institutions.

Social Alternatives

Ecology Park will be an example of how private and volunteer resources can be organized to create and support a public park. It will also be designed to suggest ways in which parks can be more attuned to visually and physically impaired people.

Coordination

Existing efforts to promote environmentally sound management of landscapes tend to be piecemeal. Government agencies which have an interest in land use include Environment Ministries, Energy Ministries, Natural Resources and Wildlife Ministries, Housing, Agriculture, Recreation, Urban Affairs, and Social Services. Municipalities focus on urban flood control, reduction of toxic loading in sewers, and landscape diversity. Business interest in ecological landscaping is minimal but growing. Ecology Park will coordinate these interests in one project, demonstrating that diverse concerns can be addressed in an integrated manner.

Goal and Objectives

The goal of the Ecology Park project was to transform a vacant downtown lot into a community park that could demonstrate ecological approaches to urban landscaping. A number of objectives were developed to guide the design process. These were:

- To broaden public awareness of and exposure to environmentally sound alternatives to conventional urban landscaping. The alternatives:
  - are resource efficient in terms of water and energy requirements
  - do not invite use of toxic pesticides or chemical fertilizers
  - help to abate air pollution, control storm water surges, and reduce soil erosion
  - are cost effective

- supplement food supplies
- contribute to the heating and cooling of adjacent buildings
- have aesthetic and social value
- are based on natural or wilderness planting principles

- To heighten the urban dweller's sense of connection to the natural environment.

- To increase the involvement of nonprofit organizations, community volunteers, and donors of commercial goods and services in the creation and operation of parks as an alternative to sole dependence on government agencies for park services.

- To expand the opportunities for people without personal green space, especially the physically disabled, the aged, and apartment dwellers, to visit and help maintain an urban park.

- To augment the amount of park space, beneficial vegetation, and landscape diversity in areas of dense residential, institutional, and commercial use.

- To improve the recreational use and aesthetic appearance of vacant urban land.

- To advance the state of the art in urban ecology by monitoring plant species' performance in a polluted environment, energy and water savings related to low-maintenance horticulture, and other measurable aspects of the demonstration park.

The Reality of Design

With the needs identified, goal and objectives established, and the site acquired, work had to begin on developing a design for the park which followed these guidelines and could be accomplished with available resources. As a starting position, three options for what the new park could offer (outlined in the spring of 1985 by Pollution Probe staff) were adopted by the steering committee. These were:

1. A venue for plays, films, seminars and music presented from a stage in front of the Ecology House trombe wall

2. A garden for everyone rather than a neighbourhood community garden

3. A demonstration of environmentally appropriate urban landscaping systems including indigenous ground covers as an alternative to lawns, the use of restoration/rehabilitation ecology in reclaiming a derelict site, and edible landscaping, or Permaculture.[1]

These three options were adopted by the steering committee as a working model for the design of Ecology Park. All design elements considered initially conformed to the working model and were either retained in or dropped from subsequent designs on the basis of changing circumstances and available resources. The process by which specific design elements were proposed, selected, or rejected was complicated and involved evaluative feedback to the steering committee by a variety of advisors, designers, and interested individuals. It was clearly not a formalized review framework, but rather an ongoing process in which designs were circulated for comment throughout the fall of 1985 and into the following winter and spring. Indeed, this design process did not end in the spring of 1986; the design was still being adapted to resources and opportunities even as it was being implemented.

Design Parameters

A number of physical and social factors had to be considered in the development of the site design. While some of these concerned neighbourhood and community needs which might be met by the park, others related to the physical constraints of the site. These included not only factors arising from the urban nature of the surrounding environment (Figure 2), such a air pollution, but also the microclimatic characteristics of the site and their implications for the location and selection of ecological communities. The major social and physical parameters considered in the development of the design were as follows:

Social

The site has a central downtown location immediately east of a busy subway station, on the edge of a twelve-thousand-household residential community known to lack parkland, and surrounded by educational, religious, and social services organizations. Within one block there are three senior-adult and two public housing units, as well as many small and large commercial outlets. The granting of the lease on the site was also a significant precedent, the first time that Metro had given permission to an organization willing to become involved in surplus lands.

Physical

The site was immediately downwind from airborne pollution generated by the adjacent bus station, through which up to fifty-six buses pass each hour during peak weekday hours. Two subway tunnels curve through the property only four feet below grade, while the little topsoil present had a very high sand gravel content with no nutrient value. Much of this soil was immediately above a layer of subsurface asphalt, while throughout the site the soil was littered with concrete slabs, bricks, and gravel pockets remaining from the subway construction. The lease allowed construction of no permanent structures. Areas at the south end of the site received four to six hours of daytime shading from an adjacent building and an existing row of mature hardwood trees.

Design Elements

The 1985 formal proposal for the Ecology Park project identified a number of specific elements for inclusion in the design of the Park:

- Plaques to explain features and to acknowledge contributors
- Seating area(s) for lunching, reading, and passive recreation for local workers and residents
- Pathways to encourage pedestrian through traffic and exhibit exploration
- An edible landscape, or "permaculture," including herb plants, fruit trees, berry bushes, and certain vegetables, all as food for humans and birds, to demonstrate the incorporation of agriculture into aesthetically pleasing gardens
- Wilderness areas, including a woodland and prairie with all indigenous and some endangered species

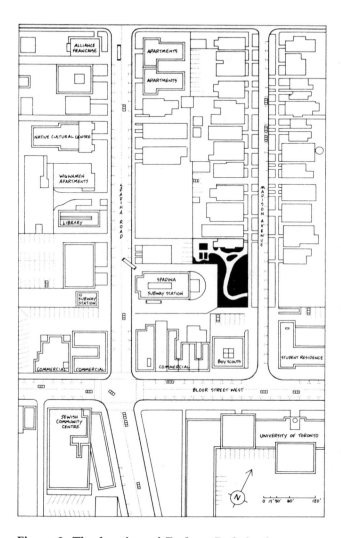

Figure 2. The location of Ecology Park in downtown Toronto. To the north is the Annex neighborhood, comprised of single family homes, many of which have been made into apartments. North along Spadina Avenue are numerous highrise apartments, while south of Bloor Street is dominated by institutions, including the University of Toronto. Note the Spadina subway station immediately west of the park, and the commercial strip along Bloor Street.

- An aroma walk for the visually impaired and raised garden beds for the physically disabled
- Planned microclimates, created by plants and berms, to show how the sun can be trapped to extend the growing season
- Plantings to demonstrate how properly placed trees and vines can lower heating and cooling costs in adjacent buildings
- Species which supply colour and attract birds in the snowy winter months
- vegetable growing areas for local adults and children, especially those from nearby public housing and institutions
- A recycling depot for waste metal cans and glass containers

A number of these elements did not survive the review process and do not appear in the final design.

Design Development

The development of a final design for the site took place under the direction of the steering committee throughout the fall of 1985 and the winter of 1986. In selecting elements for inclusion in the design, efforts were directed toward identifying who would use the site (home owners, neighbourhood apartment dwellers, professional architects, landscape designers) and how the interests of these people could be stimulated into action by providing concrete examples of ecological practice.

Ecological communities were established in a realistic setting. For example, the vegetable and herb garden, together with the edible landscape, were placed behind Ecology House in an area more protected from random access, just as they would be by a homeowner. In order to biologically control problem insects in the vegetable garden, a pond added to the design in spring of 1987 was also located in the "backyard" portion of the park to provide a home for beneficial insects and amphibians. The largest portion of the site was reserved for the prairie and woodland communities. This was considered necessary to the effective simulation of the desired communities as well as to demonstrate large scale alternative landscaping for institutional and residential settings.

Part of the initial proposal promoted the park as a wheelchair-accessible green space with brick pathways and raised garden beds as well as sensory walks for the visually impaired. It also called for the installation of a water pipe, lighting, a grey water recovery system, and an amphitheater. These amenities were dropped from the design early in the planning process for a number of reasons. The major barrier to their development was the fact that the land was still being held for public transit use, and Metro Council would be unlikely to allow the construction of any fixed structures. Since testing the willingness of Metro Council to approve the construction of any such amenities was not a part of the steering committee's mandate, all structural elements were eliminated from design consideration.

The Prairie element (Appendix A) was placed adjacent to Madison Avenue along the centre of the park's street frontage. A berm was

Figure 3. Looking south from Ecology House during the spring 1986 planting. Woodchip path bisects the woodland; the prairie is immediately left of the potted shrubs. Light coloured building on the left is commercial; brick building with chimney in centre background is the University of Toronto. Note the mature row of trees along the south border. Photo by Henny Markus.

created from clean fill donated by the city, and planted as a transition zone from the woodland element surrounding the central pathway to the prairie species adjacent to Madison Avenue. The prairie itself was planned to achieve a "wave" effect apparent in natural prairies, with undulations from tall grass and associated species to shorter grasses and their associated species. Two experimental methods were used to plant the prairie species, both using seed donated from another experimental prairie. The first, tried using tall species, was to predetermine the location of individual species on a grid, and to then plant each species according to its appropriate location on the grid.[2] The second was used primarily with the short and medium species, in which seeds were mixed together and randomly scattered across the designated area. The aim was to determine experimentally the relative advantages and disadvantages of the two planting styles. This information was to become part of the education effort for professionals and others who wished to develop prairie ecosystems for their landscaping.

The Woodland element (Appendix B), which covered the bulk of the leased site, was divided into two areas. A shaded woodland was planted along the south end of the site, while a young woodland, of the type that existed in the Toronto area prior to European settlement, was planted along the west side, across the central pathway and up to the berm border with the prairie. Since a richer soil than that of the donated topsoil was required in order for many herbaceous woodland species to survive, the soil was fortified with six to eight inches of triple mix followed by four to six inches of leaf mold. Many of the species in the woodland, especially herbaceous plants, were obtained in plant rescues from development sites surrounding Toronto. A small network of botanists and conservationists aware of the project supplied these plants as they became available from development sites.

The Trombe Wall garden element (Appendix C) had a dual function. One was its design as an example of how foundation planting could be used to improve the climate of buildings. Vines which grow up a trellis attached to the trombe wall perform this function. In the summer, shading from the leaf mass reduces solar overheating while passive solar heating in winter is maximized when leaves are not present. The other role of the trombe wall garden is as a demonstration of Permaculture — a system of "self-perpetuating food producing landscapes, foodscapes really, based on ecological rules of cyclical renewal."[3] The garden surrounding the trombe wall was planted as a permaculture garden, with fruit trees, berry bushes, edible groundcovers and other nutritious plants along with plants to provide a full season of sequenced flower blooms. In a small plot immediately south of the trombe wall, a self-fertilizing, no-mow, herbal lawn presents an alternative to turfgrass landscaping.

The Backyard Garden (Appendix D) was intended as a demonstration of the efficient use of limited urban space to organically grow nutritious produce for urban dwellers. It included four experimental techniques in its first season — raised bed and square foot organic vegetable gardening, a herb section, and a variety of dwarf fruit trees and native berry bushes. Associated with the garden was a greenhouse attached to the back of Ecology House and a composting system. During 1986 and 1987 the produce was cared for by Pollution Probe staff and was donated to area nonprofit housing units.

The Pond (Appendix E) was a late addition to Ecology Park, added to the design and dug in 1987 after most other planting and construction had been completed. The primary purpose of the pond was to help with the biological control of pests by providing a habitat for beneficial insects and amphibians close to the garden. In design terms, the addition of the pond made the backyard area of Ecology Park a "complete" organic food production area. It was also to be an experiment that would test the ability of aquatic plants and amphibians to survive and reproduce over several years in an urban environment.

The evolution of the Ecology Park design through several intermediate steps (Figures 4 and 5) to the final site plan (Figure 6) was a dynamic process of give and take. Each proposed element had strong committee support, but not all could be included in the final design. The wealth of proposed elements stemmed from both the variety of interests represented on the steering committee and from the range of ideas solicited from Ecology House staff and the technical advisors. In the end, individual design elements were included or eliminated on the basis not only of their specific relation to the initial objectives

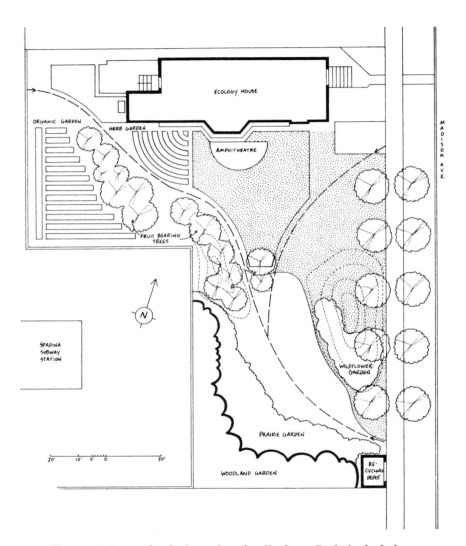

Figure 4. An early design plan for Ecology Park included an amphitheatre, brick pathways connecting the park to Spadina Avenue, and numerous small gardens. Many of these structures were dropped from the design early in the process.

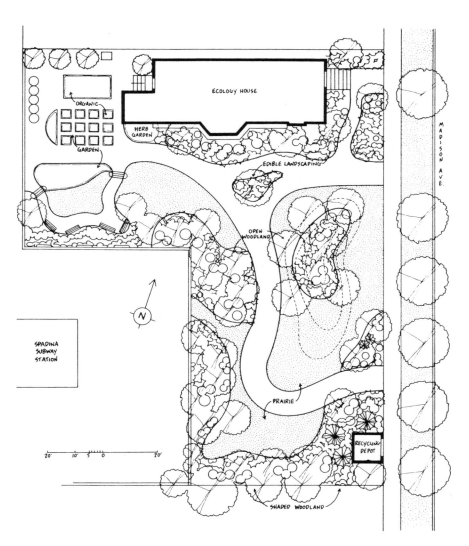

Figure 5. The final design for Ecology Park that emerged in the Spring of 1986 had no pond and still included brick pathways. This was the plan used to guide the plantings during 1986 and 1987.

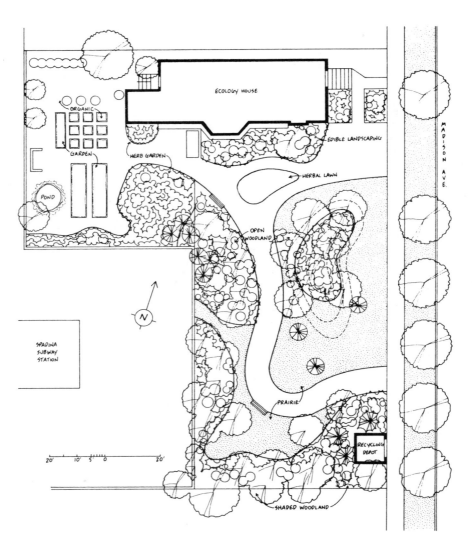

Figure 6. Ecology Park as it was in 1988. The changes from Figure 4 indicate modifications made during the plantings in 1986 and 1987. Note the woodchip pathways and the pond.

of the design, but also on constraints imposed by technical, legal, and financial considerations.

Planting Sequence

Prior to any actual planting in the park, there was a substantial amount of preparation of the site in the summer of 1985. Initially, the existing weeds were mown, the trees and shrubs pruned, and the surface litter removed, to give the site a cared-for look. There was also some exploratory digging and a soil test to identify growing capabilities. The digging revealed that much of the site was covered by a large subsurface asphalt layer, along with assorted concrete debris remaining from the subway construction. Additionally, the soil test revealed the nutrient value of the soil to be negligible. Because these conditions, especially the asphalt, severely limited the choice of design alternatives for the site, the decision was made to remove the asphalt and to add substantial amounts of topsoil. With a rented jack hammer and donated tractor and haulage services, several tandem truckloads of debris were removed from the site during the summer. Other debris, such as concrete blocks, was either buried or put aside to be available for use in the final design of the site. Finally, eleven tandem truckloads (175 cubic yards) of topsoil were brought in to cover the inadequate site soil.

An initial "occupation planting" was done in the late summer of 1985, after the site had been prepared by the removal of debris and the addition of topsoil (Figure 7). This planting had little relation to the final design, which had, in any case, not been developed at this time. Numerous donated trees and shrubs were planted, while a commercial wildflower seed mix (a mix of both native and non-native species) was experimentally scattered over a fifty square-foot area. The remainder of the site was seeded with buckwheat and rye grass as green manure, the former to be mowed and then turned under in the fall of 1985, the latter to be turned under in the spring of 1986. The purpose of this initial "occupation planting" was to provide a concrete demonstration to supporting residents and politicians of Probe's commitment to the site. For much of the summer after the lease acquisition, the site remained an ugly and derelict eyesore while the debris was removed and the soil brought in, and it was considered

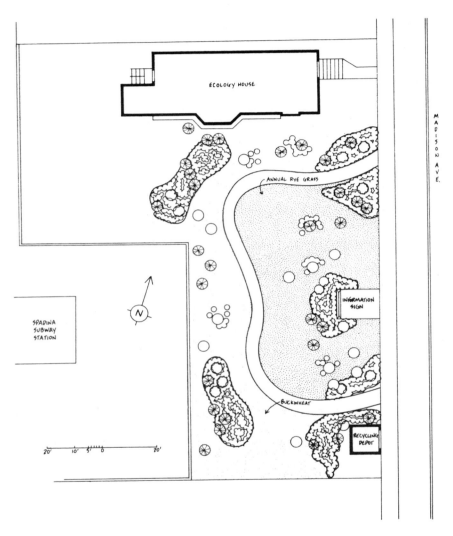

Figure 7. The design used for the 1985 "occupation planting" was based on beautification and information. Grasses and wildflowers were planted over fresh topsoil and a large sign indicating future plans for the park was placed next to Madison Avenue.

politically important to demonstrate some beautification as a temporary measure while final site plans were being developed.

The majority of the final planting of the park was done in the spring and summer of 1986, after the final design was approved. Prior to this planting, an additional six tandem truckloads of triple mix (one-third peat, one-third topsoil, and one-third manure) were spread in the backyard garden and trombe wall area. To create a three-foot berm, three truckloads of clean fill followed by three truckloads of sandy loam were used, leaving the entire site with an average one foot of amended topsoil. In April of 1986, the first two full-time project employees were hired on a government summer employment grant to oversee and supervise the entire process of site development. One person directed planting schedules, volunteer work, and supplies reception for the prairie and woodland elements, while the other developed the edible landscaping, permaculture, and urban agriculture elements of the park.

Part B: People and Priorities

The Supporting Cast

Environmental activism in all its forms is often driven by dedicated groups of volunteers. These volunteers, in turn, nurture support in a variety of forms from other groups, organizations, and individuals who might not otherwise be either aware of or involved in an issue. The development of support for Ecology Park was no different. It began with people who believed in the ideals of and need for ecology parks, and who then volunteered their time to see the idea through to fruition. Involvement was then extended to those who contributed physical labour or some specific expertise, and to the businesses and

Figure 8. Over 120 volunteers put in more than 1,000 hours of labour in 1985, 1986, and 1987. Here, volunteers construct garden boxes and plant fruiting shrubs immediately behind Ecology House in 1986. Residential apartments are in background. Photo by Henny Markus.

organizations which donated goods and services. In one way or another, most community constituencies got involved voluntarily.

Such a coalescence, around this project of groups with different goals, upset the assumption that "alternative" and "ecological" approaches are of no interest and little value to mainstream businesses and community institutions. Interestingly enough, the mix of traditional business values and environmental concerns that attracted many groups to the Ecology Park project foreshadowed our current realization of the need to combine these priorities.

Volunteers

There were three distinct groups of volunteers in the development of the Ecology Park project. The importance of these volunteers, and their different levels of involvement and expertise, cannot be over-emphasized. With the exception of one contract staff person in the fall of 1985 and the winter of 1986 and two Project Managers during the spring and summer of 1986, the entire development, design, and implementation of the project was undertaken by volunteers.

The first "level" of volunteers were the more than 120 occasional workers who laboured on the excavations and plantings at the site. Students were the largest component of this group, but neighbourhood residents, interested individuals, some staff from Pollution Probe, and all members of the steering committee also contributed. Recruiting these volunteers was an ongoing effort involving radio public service announcements, a recruiting booth at numerous neighbourhood and environmental events (particularly successful at university campuses), using contacts found by the Ecology House volunteer coordinator (who was herself a volunteer), and offers of help from people who happened by the site while work was underway. Most of the volunteers pitched in on "work weekends" in the late summer and fall of 1985, and in the spring and summer of 1986 when a series of tasks for volunteers to complete was planned in advance by the project managers. Supplies and tools were arranged beforehand, and the volunteers, up to thirty on any day, were directed to specific tasks and given complete choice over the length of any day's work.

The second group of volunteers were individuals on the steering committee. Members of this committee were responsible for collectively refining the goal and objectives of the project, developing the final site design, and preparing the plans and schedules needed to accomplish development tasks. Individually, members of the committee designed specific elements based on their respective expertise. For instance, an expert in historical and alternative cultivars of fruit and vegetable plants guided the selection of appropriate species for the trombe wall garden; a landscape architect provided academic work on sustainable rural design as the basis for site design principles; a herbalist/horticulturist undertook responsibility for the design of the herb garden; and individual ecologists designed the woodland/prairie and the trombe wall/pond elements. In addition to this substantial volunteer workload, as a group they all laboured for many hours in the summer of 1985 to prepare the site for planting.

Steering Committee (1985 – 1986)

Jan Anderson
    Curator of Horticulture in Training, Metropolitan Toronto Zoo

Roy Gucciardi
    Principal, Landscape Alternatives

Jo-Anne Lennard
    Assistant Manager, Karma Food Cooperative

Maria Nicolussi
    Horticulturalist/Herbalist, Blue Willow Farms

Roman Kaczynski
    Head Gardener, Black Creek Pioneer Village

Rebecca Sora
    Gardener, Department of Parks and Recreation, City of Toronto

William Bradley, Henny Markus, and Jim Savage
    Staff, Ecology House, Pollution Probe Foundation

The third group of volunteers were members of the Technical Advisory Committee. This group provided essential professional ecological and landscape design feedback for ideas generated by the steering committee. Composed of academics and landscaping professionals, members were either part of a regularly consulted core of advisors or were engaged on single occasions for specific purposes. As core advisors, Robert Dorney, Jim Hodgins, and Larry Lamb were instrumental in providing advice for the design and the plant material which could not be obtained through donations.

Financing

A question remains as to how much the whole project cost — the overall value in dollars of the cash, goods, and services raised or donated for the park. To define this sum would be pure guesswork, since meticulous records of the corresponding dollar values of each donated good and service were never kept because they were never needed. It is sufficient to say that had the costs been met in cash only, the final total would have been prohibitive. A look at Appendix F, which was the proposed budget used for fundraising in 1985, indicates a cost of more than $200,000 without any land purchase. If the value of the land is included, the costs escalate to unrealistic levels. As a measure of this, consider that the approximate value of land and building which Ecology House currently occupies is over $600,000.

The important fact is that the dollar costs were met by an overwhelming outpouring of community, business, and institutional support. With local governments and residents behind the project, and with the substantial fundraising expertise available at Pollution Probe, donations from the business community were readily available. The land was provided virtually free of charge. Over one thousand hours of voluntary labour went into the site. Employees were paid through available government grants. Foundations and related clubs and organizations came up with generous cash donations, and the required botanical and planning experts were interested enough in the project to offer their professional services in the name of urban greening. To attach a dollar value to all of these services is unnecessary, and probably impossible. The point remains that needed goods and services were presented free of charge because the project had widespread support, was well conceived and organized, and the need for such a demonstration was widely recognized.

In planning or considering such an ecology park project, it is important to remember that the main barrier is not financial. Although the apparent costs may at first seem excessive, these costs will be covered by the public and private sectors if the necessary community and political support is nurtured first. Toronto's Ecology Park became a reality because all the constituencies which had contact with the project believed it was worth supporting and were willing to do so.

Accomplishments

It is worthwhile to conclude with a consideration of what the Ecology Park project accomplished. Does the presence of the park address the needs identified and fulfill the goal and objectives selected? This is an important question with more than simply academic implications. The answers will bear on how and whether ecology parks can realistically contribute to urban greening as well as the extent to which such demonstrations can help to remedy the systemic social and ecological inadequacies of urban design.

First and foremost, the park was built, and it was built as a demonstration of alternative and ecological landscaping. The needs identified for such a demonstration — energy conservation, environmental protection, water quality, wilderness appreciation, food supply, social alternatives, and information services — have all, in part, been addressed simply by the fact that the park exists. Given that these needs arise from systemic inadequacies within urban design, this is as much as can be expected from a single demonstration project. It demonstrated that there are workable alternatives which address the needs. Similarly, the goal of transforming a vacant lot into a demonstration of ecological landscaping was also met. The physical presence of the park and its use of native communities for landscaping accomplished this goal.

The project objectives remain as specific tasks to be reviewed for positive impacts beyond those evident from the physical presence of the park. Such a review indicates a concentration on activities to move ideas and techniques into the public eye so as to counteract and offer positive alternatives to the inadequacies of current urban landscape practice. These objectives were to broaden public awareness, to heighten our connection to nature, to increase community involvement in urban parks, to expand opportunities, and to augment urban park space. They had in common a reliance on outreach communication and the need to deliver the demonstrated ideas and techniques to those who already understood the needs. As well, it was hoped that the park could bring the message of urban ecology (along with the ideas and techniques) to those whom the presence of the park would make receptive. Mechanisms would be required for academics and landscaping professionals, institutional representatives and homeowners, that would bring them to see the demonstration and then provide them with the tools necessary to pursue the ideas represented in the park. How much of this the outreach efforts achieved is an important footnote to the completion of the demonstration project.

Outreach

As the project moved on through 1985 and 1986, the one clear message from the Ontario garden supply industry was that they had little knowledge of how to design and plant a naturalized landscape or garden. Given that Ecology Park was always to be a temporary demonstration,[4] education and outreach were critical to encouraging the implementation of demonstration landscapes elsewhere. However, while an extensive and long-term outreach program was envisioned, one was never systematically implemented. At least partially as a result of this, it is unclear whether the project achieved any extensions of the ideas demonstrated. There were, however, some programs and events through which possible diffusion of information may have occurred.

Media interest in the park was substantial, and coverage of the development and dedication of the park was widespread. Ecology Park was featured on the popular CBC show "The Nature of Things," and on the PBS network in the U.S., giving it television coverage across all of North America. CBC radio attended the dedication ceremony, while members of the steering committee appeared on numerous radio talk shows in the southern Ontario area. Rogers, the local Toronto cable network, produced an hour-long video on the park which appeared on downtown Toronto television, and the park was featured in an Ontario Ministry of Natural Resources CWIP video which was distributed all over Ontario. In the print media, articles appeared in over a dozen newspapers, magazines and journals including: *Now* (10–16 Oct. 1986, 15–21 May 1986, 18–24 June 1987), a popular Toronto arts and entertainment magazine, the *Annex Town Crier* (13 June 1987), *Canadian Heritage* (Aug.-Sept. 1987), *Equinox* (Sept./Oct. 1987), *Landmarks* (Winter 1987/88), *Restoration and Management Notes* (Summer 1987), *Canadian Art* (Winter 1988), *Probe Post* (2, no. 9) and *Toronto Life*. Each publication and television program has widespread academic and household distribution to an audience likely to already be receptive to the objectives of the park and to pursuing some of the ideas themselves.

Ecology House undertook a number of outreach efforts, both as the park was being planned and developed and also immediately after its completion. In the fall of 1985, two brochures of the "Ecology Park Notes" series were produced covering the topics of lawn alternatives and natural landscaping, and an introductory brochure and map for visitors to the park was made available in 1986. These were widely distributed, are still available at Ecology House, and focus on inspiring readers to educate themselves and implement some demonstrated alternatives. Signs on site were constructed to explain the different elements of the park, identified donors, and direct the curious into Ecology House where several relevant books are sold. Tours were also offered on request for school and other groups as part of regular Ecology House tours , and several well-attended organic gardening courses were offered at Ecology House by members of Canadian Organic Growers.

Professional and institutional interest in the park was unclear, since there was no specific outreach program from Pollution Probe to these groups that would give them the inclination and knowledge to implement some of the demonstrations. It is probable that the extensive use of regional suppliers over two years for the project helped to stimulate awareness, and also genuine interest, within the landscaping profession of alternative and ecological landscape design. Interestingly enough, as the park developed in parallel to a similar naturalization project at Kew Beach primary school in Toronto, a degree of positive momentum developed which helped to spur on to implementation a similar park at the University of Waterloo which had been stalled for many years. In the summer of 1988 the Robert Starbird Dorney Ecology Garden was dedicated on a site next to the Environmental Studies Building at the University of Waterloo as a permanent feature of the University campus.

Important recognition of Ecology park came in 1988 when Pollution Probe was given the CWIP "Project of the Year" award. This recognition was extremely important to one goal of the green cities movement, that of bringing nature into the city, the centre of power and decision making, in order to help foster a wilderness consciousness in those who have power. It broke the popular assumption, and one on which the CWIP program had to a large extent operated, that wilderness is not a part of the city. Recognition of this urban wilderness enhancement project by a government ministry with virtually no urban presence, but which is the major institution responsible for wilderness and wildlife policy in Ontario, was an important step towards developing institutional awareness of an available niche for an urban wilderness policy.

Plans to monitor successional changes which would occur in the park communities over time, in order to be able to document the capacity of native species to survive intact in an ecologically insulated urban environment, were discussed but never developed. Similarly, visitation has not been monitored, although it is clear that the simple presence of a park on what was once a vacant lot has attracted visitors. Who these visitors are is a matter of conjecture. Any monitoring is currently done on an *ad-hoc* basis by volunteers. No effort was made to collaborate with an outside source of botanical expertise to formally monitor changes in the park communities over time. Similarly, any effect the park may have had on consumer demand (already perceived to be increasing when the project began) for, and on the availability of, native species in local garden supply centres is unknown. It is safe only to say that the park, and any education which occurred, contributed to a small but probably growing trend.

And Finally

At first glance, it might appear as if the outreach programs initiated by Pollution Probe inadequately met the objectives first established. While it is easy to indicate what was not properly achieved, considered within the context of a volunteer based demonstration project it is even more important to indicate that much was achieved. This is not an unreasonable view given that project was only viewed as temporary, that it lasted longer than envisioned by its designers, that the lease imposed restrictive conditions (for example, what substantial efforts in education could be undertaken with no space available in Ecology House and with no building allowed on the site?), that it was primarily dependent on the resources of the volunteer sector, and that it was to be a demonstration only of alternative landscaping techniques. It is also a valuable viewpoint considering that the measurement of the less tangible results of the outreach efforts, such as increased consumer demand for ecological landscaping services, could not have been measured as solely attributable to the Ecology Park project. The outline of accomplishments above should, within such a context, serve as an inspiration, while any inadequacies should be viewed as possible points of departure for future projects.

As a demonstration of possibilities, and as a vehicle for attracting interest in these possibilities, Ecology Park is a credit to the initiating individuals, to the volunteers, and to the ability of Pollution Probe to positively respond to an idea with substantial merit. Few environmental organizations other than Pollution Probe would be able to accomplish such a project. Similar urban naturalization projects in the United States and Britain, also developed with significant community and volunteer input, are often conceived and initiated under the sponsorship of a municipal government agency which has the security of access to government resources. Pollution Probe had no such support, and while problems may be perceived, they resulted more from some overextended objectives and the intangible results of outreach efforts, rather than because of inadequate effort. There can be little doubt that the skill and reputation of the organization were central to the success of the project, and that Toronto's Ecology Park is an inspiring first small step toward the greening of the city.

NOTES

1. The word "Permaculture" is a registered trademark throughout much of the world. Commercial use is reserved for successful graduates of Permaculture design courses. Completion of a design course and further work with regional Permaculture groups can result in designer certification.

2. The "grid" used was made up of irregular shapes of variable sizes, into which one species was planted.

3. White, Robert. 1982. "A Blueprint for a Self-Sustaining Foodscape." *Probe Post* (June).

4. The meaning of temporary is unclear. While the funding proposal reviewed earlier suggests expectations that the site would be available for five to ten years, no such time frame was ever envisioned by those most closely involved with the park. At best, five years was viewed as a maximum time limit which would include the years taken to prepare and plant the park.

Appendix A

Ecology Park Prairie Species

Tall Grass Prairie

Andropogon gerardi	Turkeyfoot/Big Bluestem
Andropogon scoparius	Little Bluestem
Anemone canadensis	Canada Anemone
Asclepias syriaca	Common Milkweed
Asclepias tuberosa	Butterfly Weed
Aster azurenus	Azure Aster
Aster ericoides	Heath Aster
Aster laevis	Smooth Aster
Aster novae-angliae	New England Aster
Aster novae-angliae "Harrington Pink"	Harrington Pink New England Aster
Baptista australis	Blue False Indigo
Baptista leucophaea	False Wild Indigo
Blephelia ciliata	Downy Wood Mint (rare)
Coreopsis lanceloata	Lance-Leaved Coreopsis/ Tickseed
Coreopsis lanceolata "Sunchild"	Sunchild Coreopsis
Coreopsis tripteris	Tall Coreopsis
Desmodium canadense	Showy Tick-Trefoil
Dodecatheon meadia	Shooting Star
Echinacea pallida	Pale Purple Coneflower
Echinacea purpurea	Purple Coneflower
Erigeron spp	Fleabanes
Filipendula rubra	Queen of the Prairie
Fragaria virginiana	Common Wild Strawberry
Gallardia aristata	Blanket Flower
Geum triflorum	Prairie Smoke
Helianthus spp	Sunflowers
Hypericum kalmianum	Shrubby St. John's Wort

Juniperus virginiana "Canaertie"	Canaertie Red Cedar
Juniperus horizontalis	Andorra Juniper
Liatris aspera	Rough Blazing Star
Liatris spicata	Dense Blazing Star
Monarda fistulosa	Wild Bergamot
Monarda "Prairie Night"	"Prairie Night" Bergamot
Oenothera biennis	Common Evening Primrose
Panicun virgatum	Panic Grass
Penstemon spp	Beard Tongues
Petalostemum spp	Prairie Clover
Potentilla argentea	Silvery Cinquefoil
Potentilla fruticosa	Shrubby Cinquefoil
Phlox divaricata	Blue Phlox
Prunella vulgaris	Self Heal (alien)
Pycnathemum tenuifolium	Narrow-Leaved Mountain Mint
Pycanathemum virginana	Virginia Mountain Mint
Ratibida columnarius	Red Mexican Hat
Ratibida pinnata	Gray-Headed Coneflower
Rhus aromatica	Fragrant Sumac
Rosa spp	Rose
Rudbeckia hirta	Black-Eyed Susan
Rudbeckia subtomentosa	Sweet Coneflower
Silphium perfoliatum	Cup-Plant
Silphium laciniatum	Compass Plant
Siphium terebinthinaceum	Prairie Dock
Solidago canadensis	Common Goldenrod
Solidago gramnifolia	Lance-Leaved Goldenrod
Solidago juncea	Early Goldenrod
Solidago nemoralis	Oldfield Goldenrod
Solidago rigida	Hard-Leaved Goldenrod
Solidago speciosa	Showy Goldenrod
Sorghastrum nutans	Indian Grass
Tradescantia virginiana	Spiderwort
Tradescantia ohiensis	Ohio Spiderwort
Verbena hastata	Blue Vernain
Vernonia fasciculata	Ironweed

Appendix B

Ecology Park Woodland Species

Woody Plants

Acer rubrum	Red Maple
Acer saccharinum	Silver Maple
Acer saccharium	Sugar Maple
Amelanchier alnifolia	Saskatoon Serviceberry
Amelanchier candensis	Downy Serviceberry
Celtis occidentalis	Hackberry
Cercis canadensis	Red Bud
Cornus alternifolia	Pagoda Dogwood
Cornus racemosa	Gray Dogwood
Cornus stolonifera	Red Osier Dogwood
Fraxinus americana	White Ash
Fraxinus pennsylvanica	Green Ash
Lonicera spp	Honeysuckle
Ostrya virginiana	Ironwood
Populus balsamifera	Balsam Poplar
Populus tremuloides	Trembling Aspen
Prunus pensylvanica	Pin Cherry
Prunus virginiana	Choke Cherry
Quercus alba	White Oak
Quercus rubra	Northern Red Oak
Rhus aromatica	Fragrant Sumac
Rhus typhina	Staghorn Sumac
Sambucus canadensis	Elderberry
Thuja occidentalis	Eastern White Cedar
Viburnum dentatum	Arrowood
Virburnum lentago	Nannyberry
Virbunum trilobum	Highbush Cranberry

Vines

Adlumia fungosa	Allegheny Vine
Campsis radicans	Trumpet Vine
Celastrus scandens	Bittersweet
Clematis virginiana	Virgin's Bower
Parthenocissus quinquefolia	Virginia Creeper
Vitis riparia	Wild Grape

Woodland Wildflowers

Actaea alba (pachypoda)	White Baneberry
Actaea rubra	Red Baneberry
Adiantum peltatum	Maiden Hair Fern
Aqrimonia spp	Aqrimonies
Anemone canadensis	Canada Anemone
Aquileqia canadensis	Eastern Columbine
Aqilequia	McKana Mixed Giants Columbine
Arisaema triphyllum	Jack-in-the-Pulpit
Asarum canadense	Canadian Wild Ginger
Asclepias syriaca	Common Milkweed
Aster cordifolius	Heart-Leaved Aster
Aster ericoides	Heath Aster
Aster iaevis	Smooth Aster
Aster novae-angliae	New England Aster
Aster novae-angliae "Harrington Pink"	Harrington Pink New England Aster
Baptista australis	Blue False Indigo
Carex spp	Sedge
Chelidonium majus	Celandine
Chrysanthemum leucanthemum	Ox-Eye Daisy
Clarkia amoena	Farwell-to-Spring
Coreopsis lanceolata	Lance-Leaved Coreopsis
Coreopsis lanceolata "Sunchild"	"Sunchild" Coreopsis
Coreopsis tinctoria	Garden Coreopsis
Daucus carota	Queen Anne's Lace
Echinacea pallida	Pale Purple Coneflower
Echinacea purpurea	Purple Coneflower

Epilobium spp	Willow-Herb
Erigeron annus	Daisy Fleabane
Eupatorium maculatum	Spotted Joe Pye Weed
Eupatorium perfoliatum	Purple Boneset
Euphorbia marginata	Snow-on-the-Mountain
Fragaria vesca & virginiana	Wild Strawberry
Galinsoga ciliata	Galinsoga
Gallardia aristata	Blanket Flower
Geranium robertianum	Herb-Robert Geranium
Geranium maculatum	Wild Geranium
Geum macrophyllum	Large-Leaved Avens
Helianthus divaricatus	Woodland Sunflower
Hesperis matronalis	Dame's Rocket (alien)
Jeffersonia diphylla	Twin Leaf
Lilium philadelphicum	Wood Lily
Linum lewissii	Blue Flax
Linum medium	Flax (rare)
Lobelia cardinalis	Cardinal Flower
Lobelia inflata	Indian Tobacco
Lobelia siphilitica	Great Lobelia
Lupinus perennis	Perennial Lupine
Maianthemum canadense	Virginia Blue Bells
Mertensia virginica	Wild Lilly-of-the-Valley
Monarda fistulosa	Wild Bergamot
Monarda "Prairie Night"	"Prairie Night" Bergamot
Oenothera biennis	Common Evening Primrose
Oenothera lamarckiana	Evening Primrose
Opuntia humifusa	Prickly Pear Cactus
Papaver nudicaule	Iceland Poppy (alien)
Physostegia virginiana	Obedient Plant
Podophyllum peltatum	May-Apple
Polygonatum biflorum	Solomon's Seal
Potentilla argentea	Silvery Cinquefoil
Prunella vulgaris	Heal-All (alien)
Polystichum acrostichoides	Christmas Fern
Pteridium aquilinum	Brachen Fern
Ranunculus acris	Common Buttercup (alien)

Rubus odoratus	Purple Flowering Raspberry
Rudbeckia hirta	Black-Eyed Susan
Rudbeckia subtomentosa	Sweet Coneflower
Saponaria officinalis	Bouncing Bet
Solidago canadensis	Canada Goldenrod
Solidago flexicaulis	ZigZag Goldenrod
Solidago graminifolia	Lance-Leaved Goldenrod
Solidago juncea	Early Goldenrod
Solidago nemorallis	Gray Goldenrod
Solidago rigida	Hard-Leaved Goldenrod
Solidago speciosa	Showy Goldenrod
Smilacina racemosa	False Solomon's-Seal
Smilacina stellata	Starry False Solomon's-Seal
Tiarella cordifolia	Foamflower
Trillium erectum	Red Trillium
Trillium grandiflorum	White Trillium
Verbena hastata	Blue Vervian
Viola pubescens	Downy Yellow Violet
Waldsteimia fragarioides	Barren Strawberry

Appendix C

Ecology Park Trombe Wall Species

Trees

Amelanchier canadensis	Downy Serviceberry
Malus "Heritage"	Heritage Apple
(M-2 rootstock)	
Prunus verasus "North Star"	Northstar Cherry
Pyrus spp	Bosc Pear

Shrubs

Buddleia davidii	Butterfly Bush
Elaeaqnus umbellata	Autumn Olive
Juniperus horizontalis	Andorra Juniper
"Plumosa Compacta"	
Ribes spp	Red Currant
Ribes sativum	White Currant
Ribes uva-crispa "Pixwell"	Gooseberry
Rosa rugosa "Hansa"	Rugosa Rose
Rubus ideaus "Heritage"	Everbearing Raspberries
Sambucus canadensis	Elderberry
Vacinnium spp	Highbush Blueberry

Vines

Parthenocissus quinquefolia	Virginia Creeper
Parthenocissus tricuspidata	Boston Ivy
Polygonum auberti	Silver Lace
Vitis spp	Grapes

Herbs

Aloysia triphylla	Lemon Verbena
Ettaris cardamonum	Cardamon
(var. *miniscula*)	

Fragaria spp	Strawberry
Mentha spp	Mint
Ocimum basilicum	Purple Basil (annual)
Symphytum officinale	Comfrey

Perennial Vegetables

Allium schoenoprasm	Chives
Allium sativum	Garlic
Asparagus officinalis	Asparagus
Rheum officinale	Rhubarb

Appendix D

Ecology Park Herb Garden Species

Achillea millefolium	Yarrow
Achillea tomentosa	Wooly Yarrow
Ajuga reptans	Ajuga
Alchemilla vulgaris	Lady's Mantle
Allium schoenoprasum	Chives
Althaea rosea	Hollyhock
Anethum graveolens	Dill
Angelica archangelica	Angelica
Antemis nobilis	Roman Camomile
Anthriscus cerefolium	Chervil
Armoracia lapathifolia	Horse Raddish
Artemisia abrotanum	Southernwood
Artemisia absinthium	Wormwood
Artemisia dracunculus	French Tarragon
Asperula odorata	Sweet Woodruff
Berberis aquifolium	Barberry
Borago officinalis	Borage
Calendula officinalis	Calendula
Calluna spp	Heather
Carum carvi	Caraway
Chelidonium majus	Celandine
Chrysanthemum balsamita	Costmary
Chrysanthemum cinerariifolium	Pyrethrum
Chrysanthemum parthenium	Fever Few
Convallaria majalis	Lilly-of-the Valley
Coriandrum sativum	Coriander
Cuminum cyminum	Cumin
Delphinium consolida	Larkspur
Digatilis purpurea	Foxglove
Echinacea angustifolia	Echinacea
Euonymus atropurpureus	Wahoo

Galium verum	Bedstraw
Hamamelis virginiana	Witch Hazel
Helichrysum angustifolicum	Curry
Humulus lupulus	Hops
Hyssopus officinalis	Hyssop
Inula helenium	Elecampane
Isatis tinctoria	Woad
Lauris nobilis	Bay
Lavendula vera	Lavender
Levisticum officinale	Lovage
Ligustrum vulgare	Privet
Lippia citriodora	Lemon Verbena
Lupinus perennis	Wild Lupin
Mahonia aquifolium	Mahonia
Marjorana hortensis	Marjoram
Marrubium vulgare	Horehound
Matricaria chamomillia	German Camomile
Melissa officinalis	Lemon Balm
Mentha piperita	Peppermint
Mentha pulegium	Penny Royal
Myrica cerifera	Bayberry
Myrrhis odorata	Sweet Celery
Ocimum basilicum	Basil
Origanum vulgare	Golden Oregano
Origanum vulgare	Oregano
Pelargonium spp	Scented Geranium
Pimpinella anisum	Anise
Pulmonaria officinalis	Lungwort
Rhus typhina	Sumac
Rosmarinus officinalis	Rosemary
Rubia tinctorum	Madder
Rubus spp	Blackberry
Rubus idaeus	Wild Raspberry
Rumex acetosa	French Sorrel
Salvia officinalis	Sage
Salvia sclarea	Clary Sage
Sambucus canadensis	Elder

Sanguinaria canadensis	Blood Root
Sanguisorba minor	Salad Burnet
Santolina chamaecyparissus	Santolina
Satureia hortensis	Summer Savory
Symphytum officinale	Comfrey
Tanacetum vulgare	Tansy
Thuja occidentalis	Eastern White Cedar
Thymus citriodorus	Lemon Thyme
Thymus vulgaris	Thyme
Tussilago farfara	Colt's Foot
Viburnum opulius	Viburnum
Vinca minor	Vinca
Viola odorata	Violet

Appendix E

Ecology Park Pond Species

In and in Immediate Contact With Water

Acorus calamus	Sweet Flag
Butomus umbellatus	Flowering Rush
Caltha palustris	Marsh Marigold
Elodea canadensis (anacharis)	Elodea
Iris pseudacorus	Yellow Flag
Iris versicolor	Blue Flag
Lemma minor	Duckweed
Nasturtium officinale	Water Cress
Nymphaea alba	White European Water Lilly
Nymphoides cordata	Floating Heart
Sagittaria latifolia	Broad-Leaved Arrowhead

Adjacent Plant Material

Matteuccia atrathiopteris	Ostrich Fern
Onoclea sensibilis	Sensitive Fern
Tussilago farfara	Coltsfoot
Vaccinium corymbosum	Highbush Blueberry

Appendix F

Proposed Ecology Park Budget (Fall 1985)

Category	Fall 1985 – Summer 1986	Fall 1986 – Summer 1987	Fall 1987 – Summer 1988
Labour			
staff salaries and benefits	30,000	31,800	33,700
contract staff	5,000	10,600	11,200
Site Development			
design and plant materials	16,000	12,000	2,000
equipment rentals and purchases	2,500	1,200	500
haulage	2,900	400	0
furniture and building materials for signs, raised beds, brick path and tool shed	600	11.000	0
volunteer hospitality	200	300	400
rent	12	12	12
insurance	300	300	300
replacement and repair	0	500	500
lights (if necessary) and hydro	0	0	14,000*
Education			
production costs of:			
- brochure	150	0	200
- fact sheets	200	200	200
- tour script	1	000	500
- technical manual	0	0	4,000
- newsletter	0	1,500	1,800
- audio-visual	1,500	2,500	0
- displays	700	300	0
- seminar calendar	750	800	850
- poster	3,000	0	0
- office supplies	200	300	400
- telephone	1,500	1,600	1,700
Evaluation			
printing and distribution of report	0	0	6,000
	66,512	75,812	63,762
Total (excluding *)			206,086

* an option which may not be possible because permanent structures are forbidden by the lease

Part Three:
Effecting Change — Breaking the Barriers

This section offers examples of how local organizations have overcome institutional and social barriers to their attempts to realize visions of the green city. Examples from London, New York, and Toronto detail attempts to enhance communities through urban greening. We see that where institutions with the power to implement change begin to operate proactively to address community needs, they can help citizen groups to anticipate and circumvent barriers to change. Where groups have entered into working partnerships with such institutions, there occurs a horizontal diffusion of power that supplants top-down planning and encourages urban greening.

Two contributions to this section challenge our conventional notions of urban land use. Robert Dorney informs us that our perceptions of urban land use do not necessarily match reality and, thus, that our urban land use policies are often less than useful. Similarly, Harry Pelissero suggests that our perceptions of the farmer and the countryside are almost exclusively urban in origin and frozen in a romantic time past to such an extent that they are a barrier to realistic exploration of the agricultural potential of cities.

Finally, a view is offered of contemporary North American efforts to plan a green city. Something very unique appears to be happening in San Francisco. Dozens of groups representing many specific causes have come together to develop a detailed green city program for the San Francisco bioregion. Peter Berg suggests that in San Francisco they are beginning to do what has for the most part only been discussed elsewhere. They have defined their green city, identified specific greening projects, and developed a program to overcome the barriers to implementation. Here we return to our theme of exportable knowledge. The San Francisco process, modified for varying local conditions, could work for any city — including yours.

Gaining Public Support
for Wildlife in the City
Jacklyn Johnston

Awareness of the variety of wildlife in cities is not a new phenomenon. People have been advocating the benefits of nature and identifying and recording species living in urban areas for many years. In London, natural historians were recording species in the early seventeenth century and a flora of London was published by the botanist William Curtis in the late eighteenth century. The London Natural History Society was formed in 1858 and continues to keep comprehensive records of the capital's plants and animals today.

What *is* new is the widespread interest in urban wildlife. What was once of interest to relatively few botanists, zoologists, and amateur naturalists, is now fascinating to a much broader audience; more people are interested in identifying plants and animals, and others are keen to campaign to preserve open space, establish new nature areas, and help manage habitats. Public support for wildlife in the city is steadily growing. But why bother to encourage public acceptance and support? What are the benefits to people? And what are some of the obstacles to gaining much more widespread support for nature in the city?

Urban Wildlife — Who Needs It?

Acceptance of wildlife in the city has grown in recent years, but there are still many people who question the need for this. Through demonstrating the benefits that people gain from contact with nature, further support can be won. Winning public support can have practical benefits such as assistance with managing nature areas (physical work or administration), help with wildlife surveys, contributions towards funds, and assistance with lobbying politicians or others in positions of power.

People who become involved in caring for a wildlife area can be essential to its success. For example, where resources are scarce, volunteers can help to keep a nature reserve operating and assist with all aspects of management. Often, volunteers become protective and act as informal watchdogs too, helping to deter vandalism. In urban areas, most people are aware of what is in their local patch and can spot changes in their surroundings. If conversant with their rights, and aware of who to contact, local people can play a vital role when wildlife is threatened. This active political support is arguably the most important role that a member of the public can have; politicians react to their constituents and most take notice of what matters to their voters.

Winning public support for wildlife has practical benefits, but it is also beneficial to the individuals involved. Researchers have investigated the reasons why contact with nature in the city is beneficial to people. It has been shown that people benefit in four different ways: emotionally, intellectually, socially, and physically (Mostyn 1979). It has also been found that people develop a sense of identity with place and community from their (passive or active) involvement in urban nature areas.

Many believe that direct and frequent experience with nature as a child is crucial to concern and sympathy for the environment in later years, and that almost the entire urban population has a strong desire or even psychological need for contact with nature. What is clear is that people need contact with wildlife on an everyday basis and on a scale which fits in with their everyday living pattern; most people need a nature area within a five or ten minute walk of home. If this is so, it follows that all remaining areas of natural habitat should be jealously protected and new areas created in places where the former green has been replaced by man-made development.

Practical Ways to Gain Support

Urban wildlife enthusiasts can get their message across to the public in numerous ways. Some methods of enlisting support will elicit a passive response from people, whereas others will get them out and taking part. Ways to win support (from passive to the most active) include:

- Publishing printed materials: Attractive books, leaflets, posters, and maps are one of the best ways to communicate with a large audience.

- Mounting an exhibition: Erect it in places that people visit regularly — banks, libraries, post offices, public transport stations — not just traditional exhibition halls.

- Using the media: Make personal contact with editors and keep them informed. Organize press launches.

- Setting up an Ecology Centre for activities: Use it as an information exchange centre, meeting place, and public venue for events.

- Organizing talks, lectures, and wildlife workshops: Bring the subject alive and foster enthusiasm.

- Arranging excursions: Take people outdoors and encourage them to have a first-hand experience of the natural world.

- Organizing fun events: Activities might include batwatching or an owl prowl, barn dancing or a barbecue, or perhaps an annual wildlife day with lots of activities.

- Keeping the momentum going on a wildlife site: Activities might include fundraising for new facilities, painting signs and murals, building sculptures, or bird hides.

Response in London

Londoners have responded enthusiastically to the idea of nature in the city. In less than ten years, urban wildlife issues have been transformed from a marginal issue to the concern of many. Several organizations have contributed to fostering this public support, but notably the London Ecology Unit and London Wildlife Trust.

The London Ecology Unit has worked mainly within local government to influence policy decisions and stimulate good practice in land management and other aspects of government work. The unit has gained considerable public support, particularly through high-profile projects such as a survey of all wildlife sites in the capital, and the establishment of the London Ecology Centre and the widely known Camley Street Natural Park. The London Wildlife Trust is a membership and campaigning organization. One of the Trust's main objectives is to spread awareness of London's wildlife through the media and to organize events in which the public can take part. Together, these organizations helped to convince people that urban wildlife was no longer a fringe concern.

There is tangible evidence of recent changes in attitudes:

- Results of public inquiries: Many nature areas in London have been threatened by development. In most cases, where a public inquiry has been held, a decision has been taken to preserve an area because of its value to people and wildlife. For example, in a recent inquiry, the inspector stated that there was a new public awareness of the value of nature conservation and, accordingly, the nature reserve should be preserved.

- Ecology in local plans: Policies for preserving wild areas, managing land to further its nature conservation value, promoting awareness of ecology amongst the public, and developing new ecology parks and nature centres, are becoming commonplace in London Borough local plans or statements of intention. Once embodied in such a document, these policies provide a basis for planning and all land-use decisions.

- Campaigns: Public campaigns to preserve natural areas are more widespread than ever before. Although partly due to an escalation in the number of threats to develop even the smallest patch of wild land, it also reflects a growing willingness of people to stand up for an area that they value.

- Visitor levels: Demand for use of nature areas is on the increase. Some ecology parks are now booked for school visits up to nine months in advance.
- London Ecology Committee: This is the first committee of its kind in Britain (established in 1986) which deals specifically with ecology and nature conservation matters. By joining the London Ecology Committee (which oversees the work of the London Ecology Unit), politicians demonstrate their commitment to enhancing opportunities for wildlife in London.
- Membership of organizations: Since its inception in 1982, membership of the London Wildlife Trust has grown steadily. Similarly, other environmental organizations based in London report rising memberships and interest in their work.

Changing people's attitudes is time consuming and can be a slow process. The success of programs which set out to encourage more widespread awareness of urban wildlife depends on several factors: how much money is being spent on information; the sympathies of those in power; the enthusiasm of local people; the effectiveness of educational initiatives; and understanding what people actually want and responding to those needs.

Barriers to Wildlife in the City

Given the demonstrated need for and benefits of urban wildlife, it is surprising that there are still many barriers to break through before nature conservation becomes totally integrated into city living. Some of the most difficult obstacles to overcome include problems with funding; competition for land; how nature is perceived by different groups in society; confusion about terminology or in explaining what urban ecology is; and other priorities which take precedence over access to wildlife:

- Funding: Wildlife programs cost money. Establishing and managing nature reserves, interpretation, employing ecologists, producing publications, and carrying out surveys, all require a financial commitment. Often the assumption is that nature is free and available to everyone and, therefore, requires no funding. However, in the city, natural areas aren't accessible to everyone; they may need to be provided. Both capital and revenue expenditure will be required.

- Competition for land: Development pressures are intense in urban areas, particularly in the inner city. Shortage of development sites results in an escalation in land values and those who can pay most have a better chance of implementing their plans. Clearly, a nature area is difficult to establish, or keep, where land has considerable value for alternative uses. It is unrealistic to expect a nature area "to pay its way" like other more commercial land uses; a more realistic parallel is with other common property, like parks and play areas. One of the most effective ways to ensure that sufficient land is set aside for nature is to zone for nature conservation in local authority plans and adopt policies which prevent development there.

- How urban wildlife is perceived: Urban wildlife has a loyal following of people who are convinced that this is vital for enhancing the quality of city living. However, numbers of enthusiasts are still low relative to numbers of urban dwellers. This has led some to see the movement as élitist and the preserve of the educated middle class. However, visitor profiles at nature parks and reserves show that the whole community enjoys this activity. It is vital to ensure that nature areas are open, accessible, and welcoming to everyone so that all sectors of the population are encouraged to visit.

  Access to nature is everyone's concern and everyone's right — rich or poor, black or white. To gain greater acceptance and support for wildlife, the benefits to people need to be clearly understood and articulated.

- Wild — untidy and dangerous?: To the uninitiated, wildlife areas may look untidy, mismanaged, and dangerous. Thick bushes and straggly weeds, dead wood and rotting leaves, may be anathema to the tidy-minded city dweller. To those accustomed to the evergreen trees and "evergreen" grass of public parks, the brown and dishevelled remains of summer wildflowers may not seem quite right. Educating the public about the objectives of promoting urban wildlife, and the reasons for managing land in a specific way, is vital for gaining their support.

Some urbanites are also fearful that wild and seemingly overgrown places present the perfect hideaway for vagrants, drug-users, and criminals of various kinds. There are also fears for the safety of children near ponds, beside canals or rivers, or where there are dangerous structures. To obviate these fears, nature areas should look well maintained and cared for and site design should promote safety.

There is also considerable confusion about terminology. "City Greening" can mean formal landscaping around office blocks and planting of street trees to establishing new ecology parks and designating nature reserves. "Urban wilderness" conjures up images of unkempt derelict land which is out-of-bounds (and unattractive) to the general public. "Nature areas" may symbolize traditional city parkland and open space instead of relic natural habitat or places created with the purpose of attracting wildlife. "Ecology" sounds scientific and the concern of people carrying quadrats and clipboards. Getting the right message across is the key to gaining widespread support.

- Many people in cities have basic needs for food, shelter, and employment, which are not met. These social needs must be satisfied before people can examine the environmental dimensions of their life in the city. An application to develop much-needed public housing on an area valuable to wildlife illustrates how difficult it may be to decide political priorities: which is the more important land use?

Urban wildlife areas are not a panacea for rejuvenating a decaying concrete jungle, but they do have an important role to play in this process. They also have an important place in smaller towns or new settlements in or around established cities. These areas are not miniature pieces of countryside but an assemblage of plants and animals unique to the particular conditions found in cities; as such they can be studied and enjoyed for what they are.

People enjoy seeing nature in the city. In London many have responded very positively to the initiatives of urban wildlife groups. There are still challenging obstacles to overcome before nature conservation gains wider acceptance, but the indications are very favourable indeed.

REFERENCES

Harrison, C., M. Limb, and J. Burgess. 1987. "Nature in the City — Popular Values for a Living World." *Journal of Environmental Management* 25:347–362.

Johnston, J.D. In Press. *Nature Areas for City People.* London: London Ecology Unit.

Mostyn, B. 1979. "Personal Benefits and Satisfactions Derived from Participation in Urban Wildlife Projects: A Qualitative Evaluation." London: Nature Conservancy Council.

Smyth, B. 1987. *City Wildspace.* London: Hilary Shipman Ltd.

Friends of the Spit: The Greening of a Community-Based Environmental Group
Jacqueline Courval

Friends of the Spit was formed in 1977, by a small core of individuals, to preserve the Leslie Street Spit as a natural park and wildlife reserve. Over the years, the group has evolved into a sophisticated political force and has built a broad constituency of supporters. The group, which started as a one- issue organization, is now considered one of the prime grassroots environmental resources in the Toronto area.

An Accidental Wilderness

The Leslie Street Spit is a five-kilometre peninsula, or spit of land, that juts into Lake Ontario, minutes from the busy downtown core of Toronto in the middle of a bleak industrial area. To the thousands of Torontonians that have come to love the place, it is simply known as The Spit.

Paradoxically, the Spit did not even exist thirty years ago. It was started in 1959 by the Toronto Harbour Commission (THC) to create a harbour for the expansion of commercial shipping facilities. Tons of material was dumped into the lake: construction debris, excavation material from building the subway, silt dredged from the lake bottom, and all manners of refuse generated by a booming metropolitan area.

Jacqueline Courval is co-chair of Friends of the Spit and a community activist in Toronto.

As dump truck after dump truck rumbled farther and farther into the lake along the spine road of the Spit, nature was quietly but busily at work. Vegetation started to appear on the newly created moonscape. Then birds, at first mainly gulls and terns, began nesting on the inhospitable-looking scrubland.

By 1972, when the Spit was completed to its present length, there were already definite signs of rapid plant succession and wildlife diversity. While the landscape was not yet entirely vegetated, in some areas more evolved species were starting to replace pioneer flora.

In 1979, nearly two hundred species of birds had been recorded at the Spit, including Sanderlings, Yellowlegs, Sandpipers, Plovers, Long and Short-eared Owls, and over-wintering Snowy Owls, as well as many types of waterfowl. Some 150 species of plants had been found, forty-one of which had not been recorded previously in the Toronto area, including a number considered rare nationally or provincially. Willow and cottonwood trees had established themselves and harboured migrating warblers and field birds such as Savannah Sparrows and Horned Larks.

Less than a decade later, the number of species of birds recorded had jumped to over three hundred and more than 275 species of plants had taken root, including fall-flowering aster, goldenrod, white sweet clover, purple loosestrife, and bushy cinquefoil. Several kinds of amphibians and reptiles had been spotted as well as ten different kinds of mammals, such as rabbits, voles, muskrats, and foxes. A huge variety of insects — damselflies, bees, ladybugs, grasshoppers, leafhoppers, and thousands of migrating Monarch butterflies — added to the ecological diversity of the area.

Most of the Spit is grassland, uncommon in the built-up Toronto area. The Spit starts with a narrow neck more than one kilometre long that widens into a series of meadows and four lagoons with sandy beaches and shallow waters on its leeward side. On the windward side, which drops sharply into cold, deep water, containment cells have been constructed to receive the highly polluted dredge from the mouth of the Don River. Studies are underway to determine whether marshes and habitat creation would be possible once the cells are filled and capped.

And the People Came

Only a few years after the start of construction, it had become evident that new port facilities would not be needed, due to a sharp decline in commercial shipping. In 1968, the THC unveiled an ambitious plan to build a second spit to the west and establish a huge residential development and an airport on the newly created land. The project, called A Bold Concept, was soon abandoned because it would have proved too costly. However, the THC decided to continue building the Spit, with the grateful approval of the construction industry that found it a cheap (ten dollars per truckload) and convenient dumpsite.

Apart from a few hardy souls who, no doubt, sneaked under the fence, at the risk of being charged with trespassing by the THC, the Spit remained the preserve of dump trucks and wildlife until 1972. That year, after many representations, the Beaches Bicycle Club (the Beach is a community close to the Spit, in the east end of Toronto) managed to convince the THC to allow its members to tour the site, under THC supervision. A few other groups were also cautiously permitted to inspect the Spit later that year.

In 1973, the THC allowed access to the public in a limited way, by sponsoring bus tours on Sunday afternoons, from June to September. Nearly 2,300 people saw the Spit from the window of a bus that year.

The following year, cyclists and hikers were allowed onto the Spit for the first time. The season lasted for twenty Sundays. Observation sites were marked and a descriptive brochure was distributed. Only individuals over eighteen years were admitted (children had to be accompanied) upon signing a release form. Despite these limitations, and the fact that vegetation was still sparse, the number of visitors increased, which prompted the first of a number of questionnaires about the possible uses of the park. The majority of those who replied favoured low- intensity recreation. "Suggestions were 100% in favour of flowers, trees, birds and wildlife," reported the THC in its newsletter. Visitors wanted no cars and no garish commercial uses.

The Spit had already become a mecca for bird watchers who, with naturalists and cyclists, would constitute the initial core of Friends of the Spit. At the same time, the Ontario Sailing Association, a lobby group funded with public money, was working to establish extensive boating facilities on the Spit.

Friends of the Spit Founded

In 1977, Spit enthusiasts managed to get the Spit opened to the public during longer hours and on Saturdays as well, and the season extended into November. That year 9,471 visitors were recorded, half of them cyclists. Another questionnaire showed again a majority in favour of low-intensity recreation.

While a number of nature-oriented groups such as the Toronto Field Naturalists were publicizing the Spit as a wildlife park among their members and the public, the need for an advocacy group that would take on the issue had become evident. The founding meeting of Friends of the Spit (FOS), in late 1977, attracted two hundred people. A steering committee was appointed (five of the eight original steering committee members are still with FOS). Membership in FOS was $2.00. A pamphlet was produced to recruit new members.

"The group has two goals," said Steven Price, who was spokesman for FOS. "The long term one is to let the Spit grow naturally, without intensive development. We're not against sailing at all. What we are against is exclusive use of the Spit — parking lots, cars or sheds on shore — for one relatively small but highly influential user group. Our short term goal, year to year, is to keep the Spit open on weekends. We've never been sure that it wouldn't close. I think that without the Friends we wouldn't have the number of days or hours or any of the concessions we've managed to get from the THC.

"There were a number of groups involved in this lobbying ... but the Friends did most of the pushing. Our steering committee would show up at City Council meetings, executive meetings, THC meetings. We attended meetings a lot of other groups skipped."

By the end of January 1978, the steering committee had prepared a brief to the Metropolitan Toronto and Region Conservation Authority (MTRCA), which had been given the responsibility of "developing" the Spit by the Ontario government. The brief called for the abandonment of the proposed MTRCA $22 million Aquatic Park, which included a hotel, an amphitheatre, government docks, private yacht clubs, parking for two thousand cars, a water-skiing school, camping, and many other amusement facilities. "Our commitment is to 'passive' recreational use of the Spit (e.g. hiking, cycling, jogging, etc.), while the Spit develops naturally into a near wilderness in the heart of the city. The Spit is our last chance for an undeveloped, peaceful area where city-dwellers can be in harmony with nature," FOS stated in its brief.

This position was actively supported by groups such as the Conservation Council of Ontario, the Metro Labour Council, and the Association of Women Electors. Reception of the brief by the MTRCA was generally unsympathetic, however. According to an FOS newsletter of February 1978: "Some members [of the MTRCA] seemed to see us as an élite group of 'birders and fitness freaks.' The MTRCA is overpopulated by those already committed to 'playground development for the people'." A decade later that same attitude would continue to prevail among the larger number of members of the MTRCA board, who seem to feel very threatened by those advocating conservation and informal use of parkland.

The 1978 season brought new challenges. After numerous representations, FOS was successful in getting the MTRCA, the THC, and the City of Toronto to come up with the funds required to keep the Spit open to the public and the special bus running "to make the Spit more readily accessible to the very young, elderly, handicapped, weary, and plain indolent." A new pamphlet "to help people learn more about the Spit and to enhance their enjoyment and appreciation of the site" was printed and distributed. Exhibits to make the public aware of the Spit were put up at City Hall and other locations. Several naturalist and recreation groups were approached to give coverage of the issue in their newsletter and to sponsor tours of the Spit.

People or Cars

The issue of cars driving on the Spit was another hurdle that required enormous time and energy from the young organization. In the summer of 1978, some fifty mooring spaces had been created on the Spit by the THC, and sailors requested car access to their boats. After meetings with THC officials, a compromise was hammered out whereby sailors could drive their cars on the Spit before and after public hours. "Such a compromise seemed unavoidable this year," stated the FOS newsletter of May 1978 — the "compromise" still goes on more than a decade later.

The number of visitors topped eighteen thousand in 1978, double the figure for the previous year. They included "not only individuals seeking a quiet afternoon but various naturalist groups ... and a busload of geologists attending a convention being shown the scientific aspects of shoreline erosion by a provincial government geologist." Yet another survey, by the THC, showed once more a majority of visitors in favour of low- intensity recreation.

Responding to boaters pleas for more mooring space on the Spit, FOS commented: "When you compare the 18,000 who went to the Spit for other uses and the tiny handful of boaters, it's a disproportionate concern. The issue is not birds or boats. It's people or cars."

Keeping the Faith in the Early 1980s

The number of visitors at the Spit steadily climbed, mostly through the publicity efforts of FOS, which prompted a number of newspaper and magazine articles and feature films. The group was operating on a shoestring — membership dues remained at $2.00 until 1984, when they were raised to $3.00. The newsletter consisted of a single photocopied sheet published about twice a year. However, membership continued to increase.

During that period most of the efforts of FOS were expended on wearying skirmishes, such as fighting the THC closing the Spit to the public one year (alleging potential damage claims if someone got hurt), boaters driving their cars on the Spit during public hours, or attempts to discontinue the free bus service. The burnout rate of steering committee members was high as the fate of the Spit remained in limbo.

Public opinion remained strongly in favour of no development on the Spit. A poll conducted in 1983 by the daily newspaper *The Toronto Star* showed more than 90 percent of respondents asked to "Let it Be." An overwhelming number of deputations from groups and individuals at meetings called by Toronto City Council — which was preparing its Central Waterfront Plan — also requested preservation of the Spit as a "public urban wilderness," a new term put forward by FOS.

Another issue that was to be very high on the environmental agenda in the ensuing years also emerged: the dumping of contaminants into the lake. There were disturbing studies showing that the fill material was highly polluted with heavy metals, PCBs, and other toxic substances.

1984: The Watershed Year

Simultaneously, the three key players — the MTRCA, the THC, and the City of Toronto — started forging full steam ahead with plans about the Spit. The MTRCA set up a task force to produce a master plan for the development of the Spit. Over fifty deputants were heard, more than two-thirds of whom called for a no-development and no-automobiles approach; the other third were boaters, who asked for marinas and parking lots.

The THC announced plans to construct a twelve-hundred-boat marina on a new lakefill beside the Spit. Friends of the Spit and all user groups including small-boat sailors were in agreement that the huge development, which would include power boats, would ruin the enjoyment of that part of the waterfront. However, the sailing groups did not attempt to mount any significant protest because they were afraid of antagonizing the THC, from which they were leasing shore land.

The City of Toronto started proceedings for land use zoning of the Spit. FOS, supported by its allies, proposed that Council adopt a new zoning designation "PW," for Public Wilderness, that would ban automobile access and allow no development on the whole of the Spit. This was a bit too revolutionary for its time, but a victory was scored in that City Council adopted a motion forbidding the use or parking of private vehicles on the Spit. (Unfortunately, that decision was to be overturned by a right-wing dominated Council elected a few months later.)

Meetings and More Meetings

From 1985 on, life became frantic for the Friends as threat upon threat hit the Spit. The MTRCA started a five-phase planning exercise, which included a large number of public meetings. Time and time again, FOS members and allied groups were asked to attend meetings, write letters, and make phone calls in an attempt to convince the MTRCA board to vote for a no-development option.

Two options had been retained by the MTRCA: preserve the whole Spit in its natural state; and designate the first half of the Spit for marinas and other intensive recreation and the other half as "natural resource" area (with a heavy emphasis on "management" and "created landscapes").

It was evident from the onset, however, that the MTRCA planning exercise would inexorably lead to a "carved" Spit, in spite of the extensive lobbying campaign initiated by the Friends, which included a major brief "A Better Concept," unveiled at a well-attended news conference and sent to all the MTRCA board members and City of Toronto politicians. "The Better Concept" described the Friends' vision of an all-natural Spit: minimal management and intervention, a modest interpretive centre, no private vehicles, free public access for low-intensity recreation, and informal nature education. The solution for sailboat clubs, the brief said, was to allow them to remain on shore land west of the Spit, within a waterfront park complex, or to relocate them on the THC marina arm under construction.

While "The Better Concept" was very well received by all supporters and got major coverage by the media, it was to have little effect on the MTRCA decision makers. Their final plan had car traffic allowed half-way down the Spit to a large interpretive centre with parking lot, and boating facilities along two of the embayments. To accommodate boating clubs, the MTRCA was to lakefill an environmentally significant area (a tern nesting site), which the MTRCA had designated as such previously. The $6 million plan also included a large amount of planting and landscaping in the natural area that would be left at the end of the Spit, "to enhance the natural experience of visitors."

The FOS newsletter of January 1987 states: "This grotesque plan is being put forward despite the repeated requests from the public to 'leave the Spit alone.' Time and time again, survey after survey, public meeting after public meeting, the majority of the public has said it wants the Spit to remain a Public Urban Wilderness. These wishes have been totally ignored by the MTRCA for the sake of political expediency ... The list of 'strengths and weaknesses' to justify this plan is a classic example of doublespeak. For instance, one strength is a 'large natural area,' but one weakness is a 'somewhat smaller natural area.' Another strength is 'park walking distances reduced' (of course, the park is smaller)."

On 29 January 1988 the MTRCA board approved the divided Spit option, after a six-hour meeting where some thirty-five deputations were given. FOS reported in its next newsletter: "The meeting confirmed again that the MTRCA's 'consultation' process is nothing but a sham, and that neither the quality nor the fairness of the arguments put forward by the 'Let it Be' groups and individuals (who constitute the vast majority) were going to change a mindset ensconced since the very beginning of the planning exercise. It was evident that the MTRCA board members had consistently refused to acknowledge the many weaknesses in the plan and in the public consultation process."

Struggles on Many Other Fronts

Meanwhile, FOS continued to be involved in a number of other issues. For instance, it fought (unsuccessfully) the THC allowing hydroplane races beside the Spit, lobbied the provincial Ministry of the Environment for an end to the dumping of contaminated fill into the lake, continued to oppose the huge twelve-hundred-boat THC marina and, with other environmental groups, participated in the public debate on water quality.

FOS also extended its vision to the waterfront lands west of the Spit (owned by the THC), which were starting to come under development pressures. The group lobbied extensively the City of Toronto to designate the area as public parkland, which would act as a buffer for the Spit and permit low- to medium-intensity recreation (beaches, cycling paths, sailboarding, dinghy sailing, etc.). The City has now applied land use zoning to that effect, including a new designation for a large part of the area and the waterlots along the Spit, which allows only "conservation lands" and forbids lakefilling. However, the City seems powerless or unwilling to enforce its zoning to prevent the THC from opening its marina, which is built on land zoned for conservation.

Significant Achievements

Friends of the Spit, which now numbers more than twelve hundred members, has gathered ever-widening support from a broad range of environmental and citizen groups, which include, among others, the Federation of Ontario Naturalists, the University of Toronto Botany Conservation Group, the Sierra Club, the Toronto and Area Council of Women, resident and rate-payers groups, and cycling organizations. FOS members now represent a wide cross-section of the public, spanning all age groups and income levels, from casual park strollers to renowned naturalists.

FOS is entirely supported by membership, now $5.00, which covers a bimonthly newsletter that occasionally goes to four pages. All work is still performed by volunteers, out of their homes since the group cannot afford renting an office. Through well-planned media campaigns, FOS has kept the issue of the Spit in front of the public, who comes to the Spit in ever-increasing numbers (visitors topped fifty thousand in 1988).

First, to recognize and publicize the Spit as an educational resource, FOS prepared several brochures to help people understand and enjoy "nature in the city." It received grants from Environment Canada to hold viewing days, which aim at familiarizing first-time visitors with the Spit's wildlife and encouraging them to come back. The viewing day, held in June 1988 with the theme "Come, Explore the Spit" attracted several hundreds of first-time visitors.

While remaining informal and nonbureaucratic, FOS has become one of the best-known and respected environmental groups in Toronto. It has been approached by many governmental and community organizations for advice and input.

For instance, it was approached by the City of Toronto to participate with other environmental groups in the drafting of a Waterfront Remedial Action Plan, that made recommendations to all levels of government for cleaning up Lake Ontario. The plan was subsequently adopted by City Council. As well, members of FOS have been asked to be guest speakers at many meetings of environmental and community groups and invited to speak to school, college, and university classes.

FOS and the Future of the Spit

The Friends are gearing up for their next major battle: the environmental assessment of the MTRCA plan to develop the Spit. While the MTRCA has yet to file the environmental assessment documents with the Ontario Ministry of the Environment, FOS has established a broadly based coalition of environmental and community groups that intends to challenge the MTRCA development plans every step of the way.

Many other challenges are emerging as these lines are written. They include Toronto's bid for the 1996 Olympics, which calls for locating a number of facilities near the Spit, the THC's plans for turning the area around the Spit into an amusement park and commercial development, and heavy pressures from developers to take over the waterfront lands by the Spit for residential highrises.

Meanwhile, at the the Spit, wildlife continues to evolve, and the Friends are resolved to use all the means at their disposal to preserve this last chance for an underdeveloped, peaceful area where city-dwellers can be in harmony with nature.

Urban Agriculture and Urban Land Use
Dr. Robert Dorney

Consider this to be a journey of discovery for urban agriculture that requires a certain number of assumptions, which I will provide and make explicit. I mention this because it is important to remember that with other assumptions the argument could evolve from another direction. This is not necessarily to drive everything into a southern Ontario paradigm, but only to suggest that this is an analytical paradigm that may be helpful to other countries. We have applied it, to some extent, in Costa Rica, as well as in Japan.

The first assumption is that I am considering the next fifteen years. The next five are predictable because they are already in the planning process; they are already being built, and they are already being approved in design, so we cannot argue about the next five years, only about a ten year period after that. The next assumption is that we are working at a scale covering the entire area called southern Ontario. I will use an ecosystem model, which is really a fancy way of working with a systems dynamics approach.

This model has five components. Technologically, I will assume that agricultural productivity will continue to rise, probably dramatically. Our institutions will survive and be flexible, or willing to listen and to adapt. Our economics will have no surprises, with no major collapse in world markets. Our population will finish growing by the year 2000, and then flatten out to a very slow decline. There will probably be equal employment, and feminism will probably be one of the driving forces in the dynamic, by changing our paradigm from production to nurturing, which is a very different paradigm. The last assumption is that the new poverty groups, which include young women with children and the elderly, who are mostly women, are, for demographic reasons, really a new social dynamic that must be addressed.

Ecologically, the system will not collapse, although it could and there are certainly good reasons why one might suggest that it will. I am assuming that the information system we have will increase productivity, putting downward pressure on forestry, mining, and other resources, which potentially increases our standard of living. The stress on land is, therefore, amenable to a decrease because of all these dynamics, and the wasteful calorie flow systems we have invented over the last thirty to forty years in Ontario do not have to be perpetuated.

With all that in mind, there are then a certain number of tensions in the model. The land development dynamic is one of the definite tensions in the system. If you can take land and roll it over from $4,000 to $40,000 per acre, there are obviously a lot of people who are quite happy to do so. The import/export free-trade dynamic is another tension. Since we have an export driven agricultural sector, the question is over whether that will be exchanged for an import substitution dynamic. It is a tension yet to be resolved. The family farm versus the industrial farm is another tension in the model. Lead in children's food is, in my judgement, unacceptable and quite alarming. Finally, the farm economic crisis is very real. With this set of basic assumptions in mind, the following set of arguments will develop what might be a set of solutions for our urban agricultural system.

Part of the reality in this whole discussion is where we bound the problem, since each system has a boundary across and within which different things happen. Bounding a system is very important, and with what may be a point of departure, we looked at a city bounded by a number of compartments. The first is obviously the built city, or the downtown. We then have an urban fringe of mixed land uses which we define as being within the legal city limit. The lands within the city limits may have industrial agriculture being practised on them, for example, as on the University of Waterloo campus. That land is worth in the marketplace, however, anywhere from $14,000 to $25,000 per acre, and the farm production is so low as to be trivial. As a result, the economics of the urban fringe drive agriculture into a very peculiar and rather perturbed dynamic. The urban shadow is quite a different reality. It is outside the urban space which is controlled by the Regional Official Plans. There is a different political process there, so it requires a different bounded space.

Once we understand these three boundaries, we can begin to examine how urban land use physically looks on a map. With the 1981 Statistics Canada data for southern Ontario we took our boundaries to the outer fringe. We also took the commuting zone, the range from which people will drive to get to a meeting or work, to the outer boundary. If you look at where people are driving to go to a city for employment or for cultural activities, it looks like Figure 1. It is quite apparent that the conglomerate around Toronto is one large urban space which is driven by urban economics for social perceptions, and a whole series of urban realities which are functional, such as newspapers. The model also shows that the periphery is tending to collapse. There are cities with decreasing populations. There are also

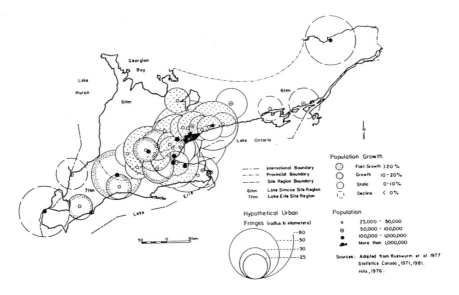

Figure 1. Urban Ecosystem Zones based on 1981 population data, with four growth classes indicated for the period 1971 to 1981. In this decade the first declining urban centres appear on the periphery of the area, and, as well, intensification of growth appears around Toronto, now having more than one million people.

Source: *Environments* 16 (1984): 9-20.

certain zones, Bruce County and Huron County specifically, which
are outside the urban zone and require special consideration.

There are some other interesting aspects. When you start to look at
land within the city, you can map it, and with this mapping one
discovers that agriculture is the dominant land use within the city.
Agriculture is not dead and gone within cities at all. It is just a matter
of where you bound the system, so agriculture now becomes a very
dominant land use, in terms of percentage area, but a very temporary
land use in a perceptual sense.

What is also interesting is that the land blocks are not small. Often
people think of urban agriculture as being on tiny parcels of land, but
here the parcels are on the scale of three thousand acres for single
development companies. In some cases large institutions like the
University of Guelph or the University of Waterloo own these large
blocks of land.

Table 1 shows that, for 1981 in Waterloo, agriculture was the largest
land use within the city boundary, within the legal city. The urban
savanna, the treed suburbs, is the next largest ecological system, and
then natural areas such as woodlots and wetlands form the third
dominant system. Then we get into abandoned agricultural land, and
we had 9 percent dereliction of agricultural land in Waterloo in 1981.
Multiplying 9 percent by 15,011 acres gives well over one thousand
acres of abandoned capacity one, two, and three agricultural land. It
is not a small space, and ranks fourth in the city. Last are the buildings, parking lots, and the built spaces which we consider to be the
city.

Another thing we discovered, then, is that agriculture is a
dominant land use in many cities. The statistics from Madrid verify
this for Madrid as well as for the regional metro area of Madrid. The
same is true of Chiba, on the east side of Tokyo Bay, as well as for
some cities in Costa Rica. What we are beginning to discover is that
agriculture is already a dominant land use within the legal boundaries of many cities, as opposed to our perceptions of cities as being
just built spaces. It is an important discovery because of the political
control exercised by cities over their land.

If we extend this, and again pull from Statistics Canada data, we
can begin to look at what happens within counties that are identified

Biotic Land Type	Waterloo, Ontario (%)
Agriculture	35
Urban Savannah (Treed Suburbs)	18
Remnant Ecosystem/Natural Island (Woodlots)	13
Derelict/Weedy Grassland (Abandoned Agriculture)	9
Cliff/Organic Detritus (Buildings, Parking Lots)	8
Mowed Grassland	7
Landscaped/Parkland	3
Abiotic/Weedy Complex (Dumps, Inorganic Fill)	2
Rail-Highway Grassland	2
Urban Forest/Plantation	1
Lake-Stream/Aquatic Complex	1
Dump/Organic Detritus (Sanitary Landfill)	1
Derelict/Savannah (Abandoned Orchards)	1
	$\overline{101}$
	[figures have been rounded up]

Table 1. Biotic land types for the built and urban fringe zones of Waterloo, Ontario, 1981 mapping (15,011 acres).

Source: *Environments* 16 (1984): 9-20.

as urban. Consider Halton, Peel and York, which together are the bounded area around Toronto, the three counties outside of the urban model. Looking at the value of products sold, Table 2, you can get some idea of what was happening over the last twenty years. The amount of investment which went into these farms is on the scale of 1,000 percent, but these numbers are real dollars, not adjusted dollars, so inflation is included. An economist could review this in one of two ways. One is that Halton, Peel, and York farmers are brighter because they did not invest large amounts of money only to go bankrupt later. Alternatively, it shows that the farmers are not producing as much food because they are not investing as much money. I think, however, that it is most interesting because there is no disinvestment occurring. There has been a very substantial rise in agricultural products in this urban fringe, suggesting that agriculture is certainly not dead. It may be stagnant, or it may be robust, depending on your mindset.

Selected Counties Inside Urban Ecosystem Limits	Value Production* Per Hectare in 1976 Dollars			Expenditures** on Census Farms in Actual Dollars		
	1961	1971	1981	1961	1971	1981
Halton	67	319	2853	4.9	9.4	37.5
Peel	75	266	1968	5.6	11.1	43.9
York	70	182	3143	10.9	16.5	61.0
Percent Changed Over Period	+3656%			+565%		

* Source: LeBlanc, G., 1983. By 1976 dollars is meant an index calculated by dividing the total value of agricultural products by the equivalent 1976 value. For example, the indices for 1951 are .275, for 1962 .377, for 1971 .707, for 1976 1.00, and for 1981 2.427.
** In millions

Table 2. Comparative selected county economic statistics for census farms inside urban ecosystem limits.

This begins to show that there are perhaps ways of explaining some of these phenomena. Table 3 is from a case we presented to the St. Catherines annexation hearings before the Ontario Municipal Board, which began to look at part time farmers in the Niagara Peninsula. In 1971 the percentage of agricultural sales which were derived from part time farmers was very high. These are people who are trivialized in the agricultural industry as only gentleman farmers

% Total Part-Time Farmers	Product	%Total Agricultural Sales
64	Greenhousing	58
54	Poultry & Eggs	72
56	Livestock	51
41	Dairying	37
63	Other	70

Source: Rich, S.G., Editor, 1979. Research reports of the Niagara Region fruitlands. Ecoplans Ltd., Waterloo, Ontario, 186 pp. (Presented to O.M.B. regarding St. Catharines Annexation Hearing).

Table 3. Part-time farmers' contribution to total 1971 agricultural sales in Regional Municipality of Niagara.

or hobby farmers. It is very interesting. They produce a significant amount of economic cash, not to mention the employment and the investment.

What does it all lead to? When playing around with the different possibilities, again based on the many assumptions which are open to complete challenge, we came up with the following zoning scenario as an opening for discussion. In the first zone it may be possible to look at an industrial farm style on soils and geomorphological landscapes which have the potential for low erosion rates, low eutrophication rates for aquatic ecosystems, and a relatively low component of sensitive areas. This industrial style of farming would then use the best of technology, perhaps partly export driven. It would at least utilize large spaces with large machines and be very capital intensive with highly specialized skills.

There is also the possibility of a family farm zone, which would be identified and explicitly funded, with a potential then to diversify production and move to specialty markets in the city. These are in some cases high value, import substitutions, such as strawberries. There is a lot of money to be made here, but in our judgement rather that allowing a complete *laissez-faire* approach, a little bit of a policy direction approach would probably accelerate the evolution of this zone. The other dynamic, of course, is that the family farm has a strong political/sociological context which would build into the nurturing concept, which then builds in with the assumptions about emerging social dynamics. Cooperative charitable institutions within the city boundaries could be established on land which is relatively impermanent in its long term potential, and which would need to draw on the skills and talents of various community groups in order to work. Lastly, there are the garden projects which have backyard specialty connotations, for people who want to utilize that approach.

What we are suggesting, then, is that there might be different ways of opening up the argument from a spatial, economic, social, and technological point of view. From this it is possible to explore the potentials of moving in this new direction that could support urban agriculture.

Urban Agriculture in the Green City
Harry Pelissero

I always like to ask a few questions at the beginning of a presentation. How many of your friends were raised on a farm? How many have been on a farm vacation within the last twelve months? How many have stayed on a farm for longer that one day? How many have visited a farm in the last twelve months? I ask these questions because the people who are reading this are the decision makers. They are the decision makers either from a planning perspective, as a pressure group, or as a lobby organization. We all have to wonder, carefully, what greening the city means. Also, what does urban agriculture mean? Obviously, we have not figured this out yet.

There are several important issues around competing land uses that I would like to address. What does it mean to grow food within the city, and what does it mean to be a "part-time farmer" versus a "full-time farmer," if there are any of those left? Consider this in light of a report released last year by the Ontario Agricultural Council showing a general breakdown of family farm incomes and farmers' incomes. The report showed that even those who considered themselves to be "commercial farmers" received almost 50 percent of their income as nonfarm income, or outside investment. Almost 50 percent of farm income in Ontario is from nonfarm sources. One premise

Harry Pelissero became a Member of the Provincial Parliament of Ontario for the riding of Lincoln in September 1987, was appointed Parliamentary Assistant to the Minister of Tourism and Recreation for one year, and is now vice-chairman of the Ontario Legislature's Standing Committee on Finance and Economic Affairs. He is past president of the Ontario Federation of Agriculture and most recently chaired the Federal/Provincial Crop Insurance Review Committee.

would be, then, that there are not many full-time farmers left, leaving one to wonder about the implications of this in terms of land use.

Also, the University of Guelph held a conference about the Third World and world hunger. Remember that fifteen or twenty years ago we were issued a challenge as farmers. We even had a report in Ontario, *The Challenge of Abundance*, calling on farmers to produce more food while the government would find a way to get it around the world at a profit. The bottom line from that conference was that it is no longer a production problem. It is a distribution problem. We do not have a shortage of food. We have inadequate networks to distribute the food.

What does all that have to do with urban agriculture? There are some urban fringes, and we must decide what is the appropriate use for land in these fringes. Anybody who puts forward the idea of trying to grow all a city's food within that city's boundary is not living in reality. There was once a pamphlet, called *The City Farm*, which said there is potential in the backyards of cities to grow all the vegetables that are required in Canada. That would come as a bit of a surprise to the vegetable growers within Ontario and right across Canada, and it would certainly put them out of business.

Assuming everyone becomes a backyard gardener, what, then, does one do with that excess production? Either you give it to your neighbour, or you sell it through the cooperative farmers market, where it somehow finds its way into the system. Then it either directly or indirectly competes with all the individuals who make their income from farming. I take this to mean that the term "yuppie" has just begun to filter its way into the farming community, because that concept of urban agriculture is nothing more than a nice yuppie concept of getting an individual's hands dirty and of getting back to nature.

There are all kinds of questions which are raised, and assumptions that are made, as to what we should be doing with this urban fringe land. At one time in Sudbury, they were growing mushrooms in the abandoned mine, so from a farmer's point of view there is no shortage of land. I also do not think there is a shortage of food. I just think there is a shortage of adequate distribution systems and of how we get that food to individuals. This raises more of a social costs question than it does a production question.

We all carry around a very romantic myth of what farmers should be — Ma and Pa Kettle, a few small chickens, and some goats. That is, in fact, not the case. Farming is a highly specialized and highly capitalized industry. In the Niagara region, where we went through an experience trying to develop a regional plan, there are still some conflicts when the local municipalities try to bring their bylaws and plans into conformity with the region as a whole. The individual farmers and landowners get caught in this, where at one time they are told that land can be used for one purpose, then all of a sudden, for whatever reason, perhaps because it looks nice on a chart and it is going to map out beautifully, the use is changed. In my mind, that almost becomes expropriation without compensation.

In New Jersey they have a special fund. If there are competing factors for a piece of farmland, for example, if a developer wants the land at $40,000 per acre while the farm production value is $4,000 per acre, the fund will pick up the difference or pay the farmer $36,000 for the development rights. To the farmer who is producing $4,000 worth of goods but who can roll one acre over for $40,000, there is no other incentive not to do that. In Ontario, a right to farm policy including a no- severance policy is hard for a farmer to understand. If he is operating one hundred acres, how can that one acre which may be severed off to keep the other ninety-nine acres afloat have an impact on world production in terms of food, distribution, and any shortages?

The Ontario Institute of Agrologists has just completed a study of Ontario agriculture and the shape it was in from 1985 to 1986. They felt that Canadian agriculture needed an immediate injection of about $4 billion to keep it where it is today. They also made some very interesting recommendations. For example, individuals living in the city seem to want to keep the park-like setting where they can and jump into the car and drive out to Huron or Bruce county to see the nicely kept fields, the nice harvest, the blue harvest stores, and the tractors. That is an enjoyment that people seem to like. If they want to keep that atmosphere, however, then they should pay farmers to keep it. Do not expect me as an individual who is in the *business,* and

I use the word business because it is as much a way of life as a business, to take this way of life to a bank manager and say I am saving farmland for future generations, so will you cut my premiums in half. That is just not going to happen. If you pay me to keep that farmland doing something, we might be willing to talk.

That is what we need to look at in Canada, because the bottom line for me as a farmer is the profit. When we start talking about nonprofit cooperative marketing systems, the hair on the back of my neck gets up. I am in farming as much for a profit as for a way of life.

As a farmer and lobbyist, this is a double-edged sword. If it ever came down to a vote, with less than 2 percent of the population involved in agricultural production, it is the other 98 percent of the population who are voting, and if they want to carry around the myth of the romantic farmer, the nice simple farmer, the country bumpkin who does not like to go to the opera, I have a difficult time debunking that because I use it to my advantage when I am talking to the city politicians. That is the image they have. They think that milk comes from the store and that bacon comes from the factory.

Overcoming these images is a real challenge. It is a responsibility that farm organizations and governments have to take. They have in many ways accepted that challenge, and have jointly sponsored a program of the Ontario Ministry of Agriculture and Food and the Ontario Federation of Agriculture called AgriFood week. The program sponsors farm tours where the farmers open up their farms for people to come in and understand how farming is done. It seems that only through continuing education, consultation, and consideration, will we be able to solve some of these conflicts, and then perhaps define what is meant by urban agriculture.

The Green City Versus Soccer Fields
Tupper Thomas

In talking about Green Fields versus Soccer Fields, people often ask which is going to win. The answer is that both should win. The question is really, what do *people* need from their open space and where should it then be? Soccer fields, we must remember, are symbols of active recreation.

Frederick Law Olmsted, the designer of Central Park, Prospect Park, and Mount Royal Park, is one of the few landscape architects who wrote about the meaning and the social importance of urban green space to people. Olmsted believed that mankind needs to have green space in order to have the sense of enlarged freedom needed to survive the urban environment; that without that sense of enlarged freedom, without that ability to return to nature, the human soul will crumble. He wrote this in the 1860s, during the Industrial Revolution, when he could see the negative effects of industrial development happening in the major American cities of New York, Boston, and Chicago. Certain that these cities were going to be in big trouble if the pattern continued, he was able to convince the city fathers that those open spaces should be set aside for the people.

Olmsted was the first American landscape architect, and he taught himself. He went to England and walked from Liverpool to the south of England, going to all of the fancy estates that were designed with the Victorian concept of the romantic, pastoral landscape. These es-

Tupper Thomas is the Administrator of Prospect Park in Brooklyn, New York. Her duties include overseeing the multimillion dollar restoration of the park, increasing usership, coordinating all department resources to improve and maintain the park, and raising private funds to assist restoration and community outreach.

tates belonged to individuals who could go out on their estates and have a lovely time walking through the woods, or in the open meadows, or by the lake, and his feeling was that this is what the common person needed. He built his parks to look and feel the same way as those that a wealthy Englishman would have had, feeling such parks would give people the uplift that would make them productive and "civilized." He convinced some very tough people who wanted to see development get going in places like New York, Brooklyn, and a number of other locations across the country, that they must set aside land to be made beautiful. It must have trees, meadows, water running through it, and it should have recreational activities where people could come and get the fresh air that they needed.

There is now a whole group of people who stick absolutely to Olmsted's plans, believing that parks planned by Olmsted are historic and must, therefore, be treated as landmarks, with any restoration or redesign true to the initial designs. As an alternative, perhaps what we must all do is look at his philosophy. Then, restoration or redesign considerations would first consider his desire for people to use the beautiful big green space, and then determine what people today need in large urban green spaces.

Prospect Park is an excellent example. I have been managing Prospect Park for seven years and am responsible to the Park Commissioner for just about everything that goes on there. I am responsible for the maintenance and management of the park itself, for park forestry, horticulture, fund-raising, community outreach, and major capital improvements. The job requires that I am able to cut across all the lines of government that are normally vertically oriented. This is a system of management that has been used in Central Park, and it has proved very useful because one person is making all resources work together for one park.

The construction of Prospect Park started in 1866 and was finished in about 1872. It is 526 acres in the heart of the City of Brooklyn N.Y., and the major regional park for 2.2 million people. It is a year-round facility where you may experience, among other things, relatively undisturbed nature. The park was developed by Olmsted, who was able to argue both economics and civic pride in order to get it developed. With Central Park in Manhattan, Olmsted believed that the people of Brooklyn deserved a great park. The second selling point was that property values around a park will increase and that development will occur because of the proximity to a very beautiful place. Seven years ago there were 1.7 million annual visits; we think now that visitation is up to about four million visitors a year. The majority of visitors, about 80 percent, come to the park for some sort of passive recreation. They are there to walk, to play, or to picnic. People just want to be out in the park to sit under a tree, to read a book, to talk to friends, and to do whatever they wish in a very beautiful place.

Throughout the last hundred years of the park, very few people have understood the maintenance required of such a varied and natural landscape. Although sections of the park were well maintained, management had not maintained the woods, the lakes, and the turf, so that the park is now in very poor condition. It still has most of the hills, the meadows, and the lake areas, but all of those areas are under enormous stress; people understand flower gardens, but a natural environment that is built by man needs to be repaired by man on a continuing basis. Even in the days when we had a large number of gardeners, all they did was annual bed plantings. They did not get back into the woods to replace the understory and to prune the trees. They did not worry about dredging the lake areas, so that as eroded silt travelled into the man-made lake, it became more and more swamp-like. In some cases this was good, because we now have wonderful bird-watching habitats in the swampy areas. In other cases it was a disaster, because some trees are falling over for lack of soil around their roots. It also means that we have to embark upon a major capital restoration of the landscape, which is a very difficult task.

About 140 or 150 acres of woods have to be rehabilitated. This is not an easy concept, because the park was built with stones and boulders covered with soil, and then trees, shrubs, and vines were planted. This system must be maintained in order to survive. We still have big old trees, some of them older than the park, with no understory and the soil rushing away from the edges. We have worked for a long time with the Audubon Society and the Brooklyn Bird Club to come up with areas that could be left on their own in a more natural state and areas which need to be restored. This brings us to the issues which must always be addressed: politics and education.

The public has to want to be in a park, in an open space. They have to know that they need it. They may know this instinctively, but they do not necessarily know to fight for it, so park managers should work closely with city agencies to be sure that parks are safe and well maintained so that when people arrive, they feel comfortable. In the first two years that I was the administrator of Prospect Park, we worried about security and maintenance. We developed a horticultural crew and roving maintenance crews. We figured out which areas were most heavily used and had those cleaned every single day, and we developed a seven-day work week rather than a five-day work week. That was the first step in the politics of having people want their park. We worked with the city police to get the crime rate cut in half.

The next step was to start doing plantings and to make it look like something was happening. We have spent over $200,000 of the private funds we raised on plant materials that our horticultural crew has put in, and on pruning shrubs. For example, a leggy high shrub must be cut all the way down before it will grow up thick again. In doing this, however, there is a controversy as the public observes the cutting of these shrubs. Immediately, that is when education begins, and the horticultural crew must be the kind of people who can talk to the public and explain to them how the same shrubs will look next year.

We have also done $17 million worth of restoration so far, and all of it has been in facilities and buildings except for about $3 million which has gone into landscape. We did not want to start with the landscape right away because we wanted to first develop a master plan in order to better understand exactly what was in the park. We did, however, want to pick up on the momentum that had the people of Brooklyn demanding something for their park in 1979. If we had not done something pretty fast, we would have lost the whole thing, so we restored the facilities in the park. We have five playgrounds, of which two have been restored. Three buildings have now been restored, and as people walk into the park they immediately notice them. Although they now feel good about coming to the park, they also think we are finished. The next effort is to get the public to realize that it is just the beginning, and that what we really want out of the park is not facilities, but the improvement and preservation of the natural environment.

How does one do that? We have a master plan that we started on about five or six years ago. Working with local groups, we formed the Prospect Park Advisory Committee, which is made of the political organizations around the park including the five surrounding community planning organizations, each one of which sends at least one representative. The organizations include the Friends of Prospect Park, which is very big on historic preservation; the Audubon Society; the Brooklyn Bird Club; the Limaen Society; the Caledonia Hospital Advisory Committee; the Bikers and Runners of the Park; the representatives of the Little League Baseball Teams; and the Playground Committees chairs. Anybody who shows an interest gets invited to these meetings.

We started with what we thought would be the most controversial issue. Our ball fields are right in the middle of a big meadow and are very unsightly. Suggestions ranged from moving the ball fields elsewhere to adding more ball fields. We expected chaos, because the ball players were screaming about élitist snobs while the historians were screaming that an Olmsted landscape is a national landmark in which you cannot put ball fields. We were able to get the groups to work together with a landscape architect to come up with a compromise plan, finally ending up with two additional ball fields and one additional soccer field backed up along the edges of the big meadow. They have grass in-fields, not clay. A number of unattractive paths were removed, and all the fussing is gone. In addition, everybody felt better because each had gotten what they wanted, to a degree, and they had all worked together to achieve it.

We came out of the process with a good project, and started an educational process that will be essential when we move to the development of the much more environmentally sensitive parts of the park. We have developed a Volunteer in Prospect Park Program, or VIPP. The Volunteers in Prospect Park is another great way to get people involved in the park and to educate them at the same time about what we are trying to accomplish. Our volunteers come from every background, every walk of life, and every age level. People have come out just to show they love the park and because they want to work in nature. They want to be out there with the soil to do the planning and to even clean garbage! People just want to get out and get involved, and the VIPP organization has now become a very strong part of our office and of our efforts to restore the park.

The Urban Park Rangers program began in 1979 and was actually a concept that Olmsted started with park keepers. The Park Ranger is basically an environmentalist who is trained in environmental issues and goes out to talk to kids about why they are not supposed to throw stones at ducks or tear branches off trees. They deal with many "quality of life issues," like picnic tables in the lake, garbage cans thrown down the hills, or teachers who come to the park with a large group of kids and tear branches off a magnolia tree to show the kids what a pretty branch it is. The Urban Park Rangers also offer tours to school children and adults. In winter they take the park to the classroom. They do not have guns and they do not make arrests; they just talk.

We have another kind of ranger who can give a summons for environmental infractions. Our people can give a littering summons, or a summons to people whose dogs are off leashes. They have, because of the summonses, become an important part of the educational process. We have an environmental centre run by a man named John Muir, a distant relative of the famous John Muir, who operates a nonprofit organization that is in the park but is managed separately from the New York City Department. Last year they had twenty thousand school visits to the park, which means that all those children are beginning to learn about the significance of their environment, and the significance of their park, and are developing an appreciation for the park.

Another aspect of park management is how to encourage people to get involved. This has to do with public relations and special events, all of which most people in the environmental world do not want to deal with but which very important to a park. Olmsted was a great believer that music and other entertainment was appropriate in a park. That does not mean having an entire meadow filled with 300,000 people; rather, it means having activities that are of interest to the cultural backgrounds and heritage of the people around the park. We have started, therefore, to develop a series of small events that bring people to the park to enjoy the event and the park, and to then come back again and again. It is important to remember that 80 percent of those people have come there just because they want to do something quiet, so the entertainment is only a small portion. But because we want people to come back and to care about the park, we do press releases, posters, newspapers advertisements, and really get out there and learn the ropes of public relations. If you can sell Coca-Cola, you can sell Prospect Park.

There is no reason that one should not approach the issues that we all consider important from a public relations perspective with attractive brochures and flyers. I think New York City's Parks Department has gone a very long way in doing that. People feel as though there are informed people running the organization who know what they are doing and thereby feel more confident about giving support. In the long run, this means support from the elected officials who put money into the budget for what needs to be done.

The final thing that we have been trying to accomplish is the establishment of what we were going to call the Prospect Park Alliance, an organization of business and community leaders at a very high level who will be a board of trustees for the park. They will begin to raise substantial funds for the park from the private sector. They will also be here through administrations, through mayors, and through any future times when the existing political commitment to the preservation of natural open spaces is not guaranteed. This organization will be able to assure that this can happen. Some people are mayoral appointees, while the Prospect Park Administrator and Park Commissioner are on the board. Hopefully, this will be the sort of final step in assuring us that the park will continue on into the twenty-first century.

The Greening of the Big Apple
Terry Keller

According to Webster's dictionary, green as an adjective is "of colour between blue and yellow; grass coloured; emerald coloured; containing its natural sap." The noun "green" can mean a communal piece of grass-covered land, as in a New England green, or the putting green in golf.

As an adjective, green can also be "unripe; inexperienced; easily deceived; sickly; wan." When I am most discouraged those words describe the Big Apple, New York City. "Unripe, hard and bitter," although in the summer one might say it becomes too ripe, and in some areas the words decay and putrification are appropriate. "Inexperienced," certainly, as to how the city has dealt with an open space. "Easily deceived" is a good description in light of recent scandals, while "sickly and wan" are words that fit the bill when describing efforts to put together and to put into effect a coherent open-space policy that would make the quality of life in New York City better for everyone.

As Shakespeare wrote in *Corialanus*, "What is a city but the people?" Most people visit and live in a city for the human encounters and all that they imply — occupations, social opportunities and contacts, artistic and intellectual stimulation, and satisfaction. Many people live in cities because there is no place else to go. They are

Terry Keller is now Director of the New York Botanical Garden's Bronx Green-Up Program, which assists Bronx residents in obtaining soil, technical assistance, and horticultural training to create and maintain gardens in their communities. She is the former executive director of the Green Guerrillas Inc., a New York City nonprofit organization dedicated to making the city a better place to live through the greening of open space.

refugees, the impoverished, and the unwanted. The city is open to them with all its social agencies in place. No one I know goes to a city to breathe the clean air, to look at trees, shrubs or flowers, or to see a large piece of uninterrupted sky. Initially, these are not important. When the city dweller finally fits into or becomes acclimatized to the surroundings, however, he or she becomes aware of the lack of many necessities which ameliorate the harsh city environment. In many areas these needs are nonexistent.

The wealthy or well-off city dweller leaves the city for long weekends or vacations, because of the lack of open space and its significance in terms of privacy, insulation, feelings of spaciousness, and all kinds of psychological values that we have no way of measuring. The "not-so-well-off" court the friendship of those who have suburban or rural homes, anticipating invitations to share in the open space, the clean air, a view of unobstructed skies, and to sit among trees, shrubs, flowers, and perhaps increase one's perception of the scope of things.

As a greening agency, the Green Guerrillas works with many people who cannot leave the city, who have no friends to invite them out to country homes to get away from the terrible stress of urban living. The need to "get away" is well documented. Witness the fresh-air fund, where children from the inner cities are taken to the country for a few weeks of quality life each summer. Witness the long lines of traffic every Friday night leaving the city, and the very long lines of traffic coming back into the city every Sunday night.

We have some open spaces in New York City, but different concepts of open space are really needed. The life-style of the average New Yorker is not suited to having parks as works of art. Neighbourhoods do not need parks as ornaments, something to look at but not really use. Our city is one of different cultures with different perceptions and needs, so the open space appropriate for the people living in each community and neighbourhood must be taken into account. Someone living outside the city once asked why these people cannot use Central Park. First of all, most live too far from Central Park to use it, and subway fare for a family costs too much. Even the Black and Hispanic New Yorkers who live near the northern boundaries of

Central Park do not use it much. The park was made long before these people's needs were even begun to be considered.

People's needs and involvement in their own neighbourhood open space is what the Green Guerrillas is all about. Our organization began in 1973 with a group of neighbours on the lower east side of Manhattan. They had decided that they were tired of the disinterest in and destruction of their community. They cleaned and greened (in the best sense of that word) a vacant lot on the corner of Bowery and Houston streets, an area some of us know as Bum's Row. Today that lot is lush with plants during the growing season, and the small Metasequoia tree they planted there is now forty feet tall. The garden has meandering paths, a grape arbour, a pond, and all kinds of flowers, fruits, and vegetables. Anything that will grow in an urban environment is there. It even has a bee hive. That the garden is in an area known for its urban blight holds an important significance.

That was our first community garden, and it is called the Liz Christy Memorial Garden after the woman who gathered together that first bunch of volunteers to do something about an unsightly vacant lot and the need for a place to garden. Today, in 1987, we are a private nonprofit organization with over three hundred volunteers, some supporting and some active. The volunteers come from all walks of life, including landscape architects, designers, teachers, artists, lawyers, clerks, carpenters, retired people, and students. We work with an average of two hundred community groups each year, and these groups represent community gardens, elderly housing projects, the homeless, schools, and block associations.

We do not work alone. There are five other greening organizations in the city, yet we are unique because most of our work is done with volunteers. These volunteers, plus the fact that we are private nonprofit organization with no red tape, are our two biggest assets. The Green Guerrilla volunteers give technical assistance for starting community gardens in neighbourhoods, give workshops and hands-on lessons in urban horticulture, publish newsletters and fact sheets, and last year we gave away over $100,000 worth of plant material to community gardens. These plants and soil came from corporations such as The Rockefeller Centre. As the donors change their landscape plantings, our volunteers pick up the used plant material and take it to our holding area in the Liz Christy Memorial Garden. The various community groups then come with shopping bags, carts, cars, station wagons, and trucks to pick up plants and take them to their own gardens. These gardens have been beside a school, in the courtyard of Mother Teresa's group in the South Bronx, in a garden that is used as a means of therapy in a drug rehabilitation centre, on the rooftop of a women's prison garden, and at many of the community gardens carved out of what were once rubble-filled lots.

When we help communities in the planning stages of a community open space, we do so because we are asked. The community has to want an open space and should have a group of people prepared to work together. Our job is to present the community with a variety of green garden options. These options have in the past included play areas for children, places for a rag-tag rock group, a guitarist, or a steel band to entertain, small plots where individuals can grow vegetables, community areas for perennial and herb gardens, and grassy areas for picnics. The community decides and the community then implements the decisions once made. We have come to realize that a neighbourhood must be involved with its open space, if that space is to be used and not become a wasteland.

Open spaces in communities should be for active, not passive, events. People need open space in their immediate communities where they can meet or where they can be alone. These spaces should provide what people want and need, not what a landscape architect, employed by the city, thinks is the dream park. The space that is his dream will most likely become the nightmare of the community. In one of the boroughs of New York City, for example, there is such a park, recently built, enjoying a senior citizens' centre that is full of rhododendrons, azaleas, and romanesque architecture. When the seniors' grandchildren come to visit, they must stay off the grass and sit on the benches that line up. They cannot even face each other with a table in between for a good game of checkers or chess. What self indulgence!

Many of the gardens we have helped establish through a combination of technical assistance, providing free plants and moral and physical effort, are now endangered. The city wants to sell the land. It is as though the city has become a real estate speculator, because it is now selling off land to developers. With the city bursting at the seams, developers are snapping up all the so-called vacant land, building high rent highrises in areas where people were once able to live in affordable housing, displacing these people, and adding to the homeless population. Remember, the word is homeless, and not houseless, with all that the word homeless connotes. An apartment's neighbourhood park or garden, streets and shops, are all part of a city dweller's home. Remember the outcry over Love Canal when so many people were displaced over chemicals? In New York City it is not chemicals that are displacing people. It is greed. The city also constructs so-called low- and medium-income buildings that often turn out to cost whatever the market will bear, yet it allows for no open space. When public open space is included it is only as an afterthought, allowing the builder to construct even larger buildings.

Since community gardeners are having no luck with "City Hall," some are now banding together to work with developers, and there have been some successes. The developers in some instances find it behooves them to work with the neighbourhoods in which they tear down and build. They are not interested in people laying down in front of bulldozers and the publicity which that brings. Meanwhile, New York City is still building and we are still fighting, fighting for neighbourhood open spaces.

A Green City Program With a Bioregional Perspective: Developing the San Francisco Green City Plan
Peter Berg

> "Well, I went down to the creek and found a willow tree with low branches and climbed up into it."

A circle of bioregional workshop participants sat at the base of wave-patterned red rocks in San Francisco's Glen Canyon Park. White chalk handprints resembling Stone Age pictographs mark the rock faces, left behind by climbers who practise there. Each person in the group had been asked to go on a "vision quest" within the fifty-foot wide swath of native vegetation bordering a small creek that drains part of Twin Peeks and flows through the park. Despite the fact that several-storied buildings ring a good portion of the canyon rim close by, the creek area is still a wild place that probably hasn't changed much over the last ten thousand years. Several species of small mammals still make their homes there.

> "I sat there in a way that I couldn't see anybody else, just the other willows along the creek."

The quest had simple guidelines: be alone and don't talk to or even see anyone else for at least a half hour; think about how you are connected to the native plants and animals, watersheds, land forms,

Peter Berg is the founder and director of the Planet Drum Foundation, based in San Francisco, California. Planet Drum is an ecological education organization that is the leading proponent of the concept of bioregional planning, and is currently developing a broad-based "greening the city" program in the San Francisco Bay area.

climate, and other natural features of the northern California bioregion. A conch shell had been blown to summon everyone back.

The speaker worked as a legal secretary in the city. Now it was her turn to tell what natural insight or experiences she had just discovered. "I was there for maybe ten minutes when a very large bird landed on a branch just a few feet directly above me. It preened its wings and orange-red tail feathers right in front of the sun. Then it settled in and stayed a while before eventually flying away. It was really big so I think it must have been a red-tailed hawk."

Everyone stared at her with the mixture of incredulity and envy that should deservedly fall on someone who comes in such close contact with this avian superstar. Red-tailed hawks are high-strung hunters who rarely fail to see other animals near them, usually long before they themselves are seen. The persistence of predator birds in the city is a minor miracle in itself. That one of them revealed itself so intimately to one of the vision questers seemed much too unlikely and purposeful to be simple coincidence. Could it be an act of recognition for the group's effort to find and respect wilderness in the midst of urban pavement and exhaust fumes?

Any threat of solemnity evaporated in laughter when she asked with innocent hopefulness whether there would be another workshop like this one soon. What would have to happen to satisfy her expectations next time? Coyotes singing in Golden Gate Park?

The San Francisco Bay area is unique in so many ways that its most common characteristic is probably diversity. Differences in natural characteristics range from Pacific tide pools to redwood forests, from flat, bird-filled marshes to the abrupt rise of Mt. Diablo from where the Sierra Nevada Mountains can be seen more than a hundred miles across the Central Valley. A diversity of people matches that of the bioregion. Inhabitants generally pride themselves on being tolerant, but the truth is that if they weren't, they would probably be miserable. Italian Catholics go to school with Chinese Buddhists, surviving hippies rent apartments in the same buildings as prosperous yuppies, Latinos speak Spanish to Filipinos, and recently arrived Southeast Asians who don't speak each other's languages raise children together and build strong communities in formerly destitute downtown areas. Thousands of immigrants from foreign countries, and just as many from the rest of the United States, stream in constantly to find opportunities for both work and self-expression. Who can blame them? The Bay area is one of the most naturally endowed and enlightened life-places on the planet.

There are growing cracks in the surface of this benign picture, however, and they can eventually grow to be more devastating than anything that could emanate from the San Andreas fault. Here's the problem: No large urban area in North America is sustainable at present. How can the Bay area expect to absorb the additional two-thirds of a million people that is predicted by the beginning of the twenty-first century without loosing its liveability?

Cities aren't sustainable because they have become dependent on distant, rapidly shrinking sources for the basic essentials of food, water, energy, and materials. At the same time, they have severely damaged the health of local systems upon which any sensible notion of sustainability must ultimately depend. Water courses have become dumps for everything from petrochemicals to sewage; nearby farmland is continually lost to housing developments; soil and water tables are poisoned by seepage wastes from garbage buried in landfills; fossil fuel emissions increasingly mar the purity of the air; and the small refuges for wildlife and native vegetation that still remain are constantly reduced or threatened.

These problems are worsening at a faster rate in the San Francisco Bay area than in many other urban centres. In addition, the social benefits that make cities liveable, such as a sense of community and wide civic participation, are more typically eroded rather than strengthened as the megalopolis that surrounds the Bay continues to grow.

The situation is critical, yet there hasn't been a comprehensive movement to create a saving alternative. There isn't a single realistic plan in operation to ecologically redirect and thereby advance the quality of life for any sizeable urban area in North America. What would it take to establish a positive outcome for the seemingly overwhelming problems of cities? What features of city life should be addressed and in what ways? How would an alternative approach for the future look and feel?

First, it is necessary to understand that the nature of cities has already changed tremendously in just the last few decades. In 1950 about two-thirds of North Americans lived in cities or towns of 25,000 or more, but by 1986 the proportion had jumped to 75 percent of an overall population that had itself increased significantly. To accommodate this tidal wave of new residents, the sheer number and size of cities has grown very rapidly. Mexico City is the most dramatic example, almost doubling its population from eight to fourteen million between 1970 and 1980. Since then, it has swollen to over twenty million to become the most populous city that has ever existed. The movement of people from the countryside into the cities is one of this century's strongest demographic trends, one that promises to continue into the future. Urban dwelling, once the rarest way for people to live, is fast becoming the dominant form of human habitation on the planet.

The San Francisco Bay area's population grew from 4.6 to 5.2 million between 1970 and 1980, and is around 5.8 million at present. About 6.5 million people are expected to live in the region by the year 2000. That means that the rate of population increase in only thirty years will have been more than an astonishing 40 percent.

But while the size and number of cities is growing so drastically, there hasn't been an appropriately directed change in the way people live in them. City dwelling is still imagined as a special and privileged condition that is supported by a surrounding hinterland with rural workers to provide necessities. The fact that city living is now the norm for the vast majority of North Americans hasn't really penetrated popular awareness. The vast scale of ecological damage that is directly attributable to the ways cities currently function (for instance, roughly 40 percent of the nonagricultural pollution of San Francisco Bay is simply the result of run-off from city streets) still isn't fully recognized. The demands for resources that cities make on their own bioregions as well as on faraway locations are becoming hundreds of times greater, while means to supply them are drying up, but this urgently important issue still hasn't had an impact on the core of municipal policy making.

There needs to be a profound shift in the fundamental premises and activities of city living. Urban people have to adopt conser-

Figure 1. The Shasta bioregion.

vationist values and carry out more responsible practices in wide areas of daily life. Municipal governments need to restructure their priorities so that long-term sustainability can become a feasible goal. With such a large portion of the population removed from the land and from access to resources, ways to secure some share of the basic requirements of food, water, energy, and materials will have to be found within the confines of cities. Cities need to become "green." They must be transformed into places that are life-enhancing and regenerative.

There are dozens of sustainability-oriented groups in the Bay area who, taken together, represent a sizeable reservoir of good ideas and willing hands. Planet Drum Foundation has brought together representatives of these groups to develop proposals for an over-arching program of changes that could be supported by the general public in order to prevent further deterioration of the region and lead in the direction of greater self-reliance.

A series of "Green City" meetings, held at San Francisco's Fort Mason Center in 1986, brought together groups and individuals from specific fields of interest who were asked to contribute suggestions and visions. Over 150 representatives attended, and an equal number added recommendations to written reports of the sessions. The range of participants was usually much broader than any one of them would have predicted, and for most it was a first opportunity to meet their fellow "greeners." At the Recycling and Re-use meeting, for instance, there were not only representatives of some city and country re-cycling agencies but also a well-rounded showing from private re-use businesses, citizen groups opposed to waste, youth employment agencies, and professional scavenger companies. The Urban Wild Habitat meeting was one of the largest and included nature society members, urban gardeners, defenders of open space, native plant experts, animal tenders, teachers, environmental writers, the founder of the citizens' group that helped secure the Golden Gate National Recreation Area, and even the director of Golden Gate Park. Other meetings were held on the subjects of transportation, urban planting, renewable energy, neighbourhood character and empowerment, small business and cooperatives, sustainable planning, and celebrating life-place vitality.

Each session began with a description of the current situation from each participant's point of view. Not surprisingly, these accounts portrayed more dismal overall conditions that are usually acknowledged in political rhetoric. Renewable energy advocates complained of no significant gains of using alternatives to fossil fuels since oil resumed a low price in the late 1970s. Neighbourhood representatives related how highrises and chain stores are crowding out the last remnants of unique small businesses and block-scaled social and family life. Community gardeners spoke of loosing land to developers because city governments lacked the will to protect or ensure the acquisition of substitute space. Sustainable planning proponents detailed the failure of residents' influence on growth-dominated municipal planning processes. Transportation analysts unhappily forecast a doubling of the capacity of existing freeways and even the addition of another deck to the Golden Gate Bridge unless people began using alternatives to automobiles.

Next, the attendees were asked what alternatives were possible, at which point the outlook brightened considerably. Practical examples of many positive choices already exist in communities scattered throughout the Bay area. If all of the potential alternatives were happening at optimum levels in every city and town, the decline of the region could be halted and actually turned around.

A Green City Program for San Francisco Bay Area Cities and Towns is a full account of all the areas of sustainability that were covered in the meetings. To illustrate the way beneficial changes could occur, a "Fable," usually based in some part on an actual occurrence, is related (these are set in San Francisco but transferable to anywhere else). Pictures of how urban areas could look, and other outcomes that might result if the proposals were carried out, are presented as "in Green City: what's possible?"

The real heart of the Green City Program lies in the section headed "What can cities do to promote...?" Here the values and practices of a new kind of urban resident are matched with needed alterations in municipal policies to create a more liveable future. Transforming the outlooks of people alone won't be enough to do the job; there must also be changes in city administrations to reflect self-reliant values. Cities and towns that are serious about sustainability can carry out significant large-scale public projects (refitting all municipal building to use some form of renewable energy, for instance) while also encouraging extra-governmental changes.

The popular will that can move governments in this direction can be generated through activist groups who organize green city programs for their own communities. Invitations to join the program's planning process shouldn't be restricted to previously active veterans, but should include a wide range of interested people. These days, most individuals, citizen organizations, businesses, and labour groups are aware of urban decline and care strongly about some aspect of sustainability. Under a green city umbrella, they can begin to care about all of them.

Green city groups can develop a platform for change that is most appropriate for their particular city or town. Once a platform is made public, it will become a powerful tool for influencing boards of supervisors, town councils, elected officials, and candidates for of-

fice. (How can they explain not endorsing a green city?) Local initiatives and bond issues could be drafted so that voters would have an
opportunity to show their support and approve carrying out specific
proposals. Eventually, green city groups could link together to carry
out bioregion-wide initiatives that aren't currently possible because
of the separation of county jurisdictions.

The San Francisco Bay area has been a leader in arousing ecological
consciousness. Its residents have rallied to preserve natural features
and oppose despoliation of the earth in ways that inspire people in
the rest of North America and throughout the world. If we will now
begin to establish well-rooted green city programs, by the twenty-
first century we can create a model that will save this great Pacific
Basin life-place and show a positive direction that others can follow
to rescue their part of the planet.

REFERENCES

Brown, Lester R. and Jodi L. Jacobson. 1987."The Future of Urbanization:
Facing the Ecological and Economic Restraints." Worldwatch Paper #77.
Washington: Worldwatch Institute.

Fox, Robert W. 1984. "The World's Urban Explosion." *National Geographic*
166, no. 2.

"Projections '87." Oakland: Association of Bay Area Governments, 1987.

Appendix 1
Horticultural Services and Suppliers

This selected list is of businesses and organizations who can supply herbaceous plant and garden vegetable stock suitable to conditions found throughout Canada and parts of the United States. Each supplier should be contacted for the specific varieties of species available, their required growing conditions, and whether they are untreated or organically produced.

Abundant Life Seed Foundation, Box 772, Port Townsend, Washington 98368, USA (heirloom, medicinal and native plants of southwestern Canada).

Agrifoods, 503 Imperial Rd., Unit #1, Guelph, Ontario, N1H 6T9. (519) 837–1600 ($7.OO lawn and garden soil fertility test).

Aimers Quality Seeds & Bulbs, 81 Temperance St., Aurora, Ontario, L4G 2R1 (edible wild flower seed mixes).

Alberta Nurseries & Seeds Ltd., Box 20, Bowden, Alberta, T0M 0K0 (early maturing vegetables and flowers).

Alpine Garden Club of British Columbia, 13751–56A Avenue, Surrey, British Columbia, V3W 1J4 (native seeds distributed to members).

Annable Wholesale Nursery Ltd., 5201 Hwy. #7 E., Unionville, Ontario, L3R 1N3. (416) 477–1231 (native shrubs, trees and perennials).

Applied Bio-Nomics Ltd., P.O. Box 2637, Sidney, British Columbia, V8L 4C1 (biological control supplies).

Beach Hollow Growers, 1457 Progression Rd., Carlisle, Ontario. (416) 689–8891 (woodland and ground covers).

Becker's Seed Potatoes, R.R. 1, Trout Creek, Ontario, P0H 2L0 (seed potatoes).

Bishop Seeds Ltd., Box 338, Belleville, Ontario, K8N 5A5 (vegetable, flower and green manure seeds).

Blue Willow Farms, Hwy. #48, General Delivery, Baldwin, Ontario, L0E 1A0 (trees, shrubs, evergreens, perennials, herbs).

Canadian Wildflower Society, 35 Bauer Cres., Unionville, Ontario, L3R 4H3 (member wildflower seed exchange).

John Conon Nurseries Ltd., P.O. Box 200, Hwy. #5, Waterdown, Ontario, L0R 2N0. (416) 689–4631, 3768 (woodland and meadow plants, ferns, shrubs, trees).

Country Squire Nurseries, Steels Ave. W., R.R. 2, Brampton, Ontario. (416) 451–0778 (perennials, natives).

William Dam Seeds Ltd., P.O. Box 8400, Dundas, Ontario, L9H 6M1 (Hwy. #8, West Flamboro, Ont.).

Dominion Seed House, 115 Guelph St., Guelph, Ontario, L7G 4A2 (vegetables, flowers, herbs and seed potatoes).

Early's Farm & Garden Center, Inc., Box 3024, Saskatoon,

Saskatchewan, S7K 3S9 (northern flower and vegetable seeds).

Fish Lake Garlic Man, R.R. 2, Demorestville, Ontario, K0K 1W0 (hardy and productive garlic varieties).

Friends of the Botanic Garden, University of Alberta, Edmonton, Alberta, T6G 2E9 (area wild grass and herbaceous plant seeds).

Garden Import Inc., P.O. Box 760, Thornhill, Ontario, L3T 4A5 (woodland, ferns).

Halifax Seed Co. Inc., Box 8026, Station A, Halifax, Nova Scotia, B3K 5L8 (Atlantic Canada vegetable seeds).

Happy Herbs, Box 265, Markham, Ontario, L3P 3J7 (pesticide free wild herb seeds).

Harpers Garden Centre, 1039 Wilson Ave., Ancaster, Ontario (native perennials and seed).

Hawkswood Gardens, R.R. 1, Elmira, Ontario, N3S 2Z1 (wildflowers).

Height Garden Center, R.R. 5, Woodstock, Ontario. (519) 539–9548 (native shrubs and trees).

Heirloom Garden Project, Department of Vegetable Crops, Plant Science Building, Cornell University, Ithaca, New York 14853–0327, USA (U.S. northwest heirloom seed kits).

The Herb Farm, R.R. 4, Norton, New Brunswick, E0G 2N0 (landscaping and edible herb seeds).

Heritage Seed Program, c/o Heather Apple, R.R. 3, Uxbridge, Ontario, L0C 1K0 (exchange network for nonhybrid and heirloom varieties of vegetables, fruits, herbs, grains, ornamentals and forages).

High Altitude Gardens, Box 4238, Ketchum, Idaho 83340, USA (harsh climate herb and vegetable seeds).

Hortico Inc., 723 Robson Rd. R.R. 1, Waterdown, Ontario, L0R 2H0.

Humber Nurseries, R.R. 8, Hwy. #50, Brampton, Ontario, L6T 3Y7. (416) 794–0555 (woodland and meadow plants, native trees and shrubs).

Ed Hume Seeds Inc., Box 1450, Kent, Washington 98035, USA (cool climate vegetables).

J. Jenkins and Son Garden Supply, 789 Lawrence Ave. W., Toronto, Ontario. (416) 783–6137.

Johnny's Selected Seeds, 299 Foss Hill Rd., Albion, Maine 04910, USA (northern garden seeds).

Lindenberg Seeds Ltd., 803 Princess Ave., Brandon, Manitoba, R7A 0P5 (hardy garden seeds).

Living Prairie Museum, 2795 Ness Ave., Winnipeg, Manitoba, R3J 3S4 (tall grass prairie grass and wildflower seeds).

Midwest Wildflowers, P.O. Box 64, Rockton, Illinois, 61072, USA (seeds common to midwest U.S.).

Moore Water Gardens, Port Stanley, Ontario, N0L 2A0. (519) 782–4052 (native aquatics).

Natural Woodland Nursery Ltd., 544 Conestoga Rd. W., Waterloo, Ontario, N2L 4E2. (519) 884–1071.

Northern Star Plants and Herbs, Box 2262, Station A, London,

Ontario, N6A 4E3 (seeds of local, unusual and underutilized varieties).

Oakhill Farms, Box 27, St. Norbert, Manitoba R3V 1L5 (natives and perennials).

Oka Fleurs, 1945 Chemin d'Oda, Oka, Québec J0N 1E0. (514) 479–6963 (wildflowers and native grasses).

Ontario Seed Co. Ltd., Box 144, 330 Philip St., Waterloo, Ontario, N2J 3Z9 (general vegetable and flower seeds).

Oslach Nurseries Ltd., R.R. 1, Simcoe, Ontario. (519) 426–9533 (native perennials).

Parklane Nurseries Ltd., R.R. 1, Gormley, Ontario. (416) 887–5851.

Pine Ridge Nurseries Ltd., Brock Road North, Pickering, Ontario. (416) 683–5952 (woodland and meadow plants).

Prairie Grown Garden Seeds, Box 118, Cochin, Saskatchewan, S0M 0L0 (short season organic nonhybrid seeds).

Prairie Nursery, P.O. Box 365, Westfield, Wisconsin 53964, USA. (608) 296–3679 (NA native wildflowers and grasses).

Rawlinston Garden Seeds, 269 College Rd., Truro, Nova Scotia, B2N 2P6 (untreated garden seeds).

Rocky Mountain Seed Service, P.O. Box 215, Golden, British Columbia, V0S 1E0 (British Columbia natives).

Otto Richter and Sons Ltd., P.O. Box 26, Goodwood, Ontario, L0C 1A0. (416) 640–6677 (woodland and meadow species, herbs).

Saltspring Seeds, Box 33, Ganges, British Columbia, V0S 1E0 (west coast natives and high-protein seeds).

Frank Shenk Nurseries Ltd., Belfountain, Ontario. (519) 927–5415 (woodland, ferns).

Shades of Harmony Seeds, Box 598, Kingston, Nova Scotia, B0P 1R0 (untreated organically grown herb, vegetable and flower seeds).

Sheridan Nurseries Ltd., 700 Evans Ave, Etobicoke, Ontario. (416) 621–9111 (woodland and meadow species, ferns).

Siberia Seeds, Box 3000, Olds, Alberta, T0M 1P0 (northern variety heirloom tomato seeds).

Simple Gifts Farm Greenhouse, Oak Leaf Rd., R.R. 1, Athens, Ontario, K0E 1B0. (613) 928–2145 (woodland &meadow plants; herbaceous perennials).

Keith Somers Trees, 10 Tillson Ave., Tillsonburg, Ontario, N4G 2Z6. (519) 842–5148 (woodland and aquatics).

T-D Enterprises, 865 Milgrove Sideroad, Milgrove, Ontario, L0R 1V0. (416) 689–8718 (aquatics).

T & T Seeds Ltd., Box 1710, Winnipeg, Manitoba, R3C 3P6 (early vegetable and flower seeds).

Territorial Seeds Canada, 4592 West 2nd Ave., Vancouver, British Columbia, V6R 1K9 (Maritime northwest suitable flower, herb and vegetable seeds).

University of British Columbia Botanical Garden, 6501 N.W. Marine Dr., Vancouver, British Columbia, V6T 1W5 (seeds and live plants).

Van Dongen's Nursery, 1910 Dundas Hwy. E., Mississauga, Ontario, L4X 1L9. (416) 277–1651.

Van Dusen Gardens, 5251 Oak Street, Vancouver, British Columbia, V6M 4H1 (seeds and live plants).

Weall and Cullen Nurseries Ltd., 784 Sheppard Ave. E., Toronto, Ontario. (416) 225–7705.

Woodland Nurseries Ltd., 2151 Camilla Rd., Mississauga, Ontario, L5A 2K1. (416) 277–2961 (native trees and shrubs).

Appendix 2
Selected Introductory Bibliography

Urban Wilderness and Ecological Landscaping

General

Baines, Chris. "Conservation Comes to Town," *BBC Wildlife* 5 (June 1987): 289, 290, and 292.

—. *The Wild Side of London.* London, 1986.

Barlow, Elizabeth. "Urban Wilds," In *Urban Open Spaces*, edited by Lisa Taylor, 118–19. New York: Rizzoli International Publications, 1981.

Benjamin, Thomas, B. and David J. Gannon. "Tifft Farm Nature Preserve: Western New York's Investment for the Future." *Conservationist* (March/April 1980): 36–39.

Berg, Peter, Beryl Magilavy, and Seth Zucgerman. *A Green City Program for San Francisco Bay Area Cities and Towns.* San Francisco: Planet Drum Books, 1989.

Bradshaw, D.A., D.A. Goode, and E. Thorp, eds. *Ecology and Design in Landscape: The 24th Symposium of the British Ecological Society, Manchester 1983.* Oxford: Blackwell Scientific Publications, 1986.

Carruthers, Stuart, Jane Smart, Tom Langton, and Joyce Bellamy. *Open Space in London.* London: Greater London Council, Habitat Handbook No. 2, 1986.

Cundiff, Brad. "Let Nature do the Landscaping." *Canadian Geographic* 108 (August/September 1988): 52–57.

Davidson, Joan. *How Green is Your City? Pioneering Approaches to Environmental Action.* London: Bedford Square Press, 1988.

Desfor, Gene and Roy Merrens. "Toronto May Lose Urban Wilderness." *Alternatives* 13 (December 1985): 83–85.

Dodge, Harold, A. "Tifft Farm Nature Preserve: From Dump to Treasure." *Environmental Comment* (March 1977): 18–20.

Ecology Handbook. (Numbers One to Four). London: Greater London Ecology Unit, The County Hall, 1984.

Emery, Malcolm. *Promoting Nature in Cities and Towns: A Practical Guide*. London: The Ecological Parks Trust, 1986.

Goode, David. *Wild in London*. London: Michael Joseph, 1986.

Granger, William. *Naturalization Areas in North York*. City of North York: Parks and Recreation Department, 1985.

—. "Naturalizing City Parks." *Wildflower* 2 (Spring 1986): 40–42.

Greater Manchester Council. *A Nature Conservation Strategy for Greater Manchester*. Manchester: GMC, 1986.

Higgins, Sandra, ed. "The City Green." *A Special Issue of The Architect's Journal*, 5 February 1986.

Holland: A Tour of Created Natural Landscapes. London: London Wildlife Trust.

Hough, Michael. *City Form and Natural Process: Towards a New Urban Vernacular*. Toronto: Van Nostrand Reinhold Company, 1984.

Laurie, Ian, C, ed. *Nature in Cities: The Natural Environment in the Design and Development of Urban Green Space*. Chichester England: Wiley, 1979.

—. *Nature in Cities*. Proceedings of a Symposium Held at the University of Manchester, 29–31 March 1974.

Mostyn, Barbara, J. *Personal Benefits and Satisfactions Derived from Participation in Urban Wildlife Projects*. Shrewsbury: The Interpretive Branch of the Nature Conservancy Council, 1979.

Nash, Roderick. "The Value of Wilderness." *Environmental Review* 3 (1977): 14–25.

Nature Conservancy Council Interpretive Branch. *Nature Conservation in Urban Areas: Challenge and Opportunity*. Shrewsbury: Salop, 1979.

Nicholson-Lord, David. *The Greening of the Cities*. New York: Routledge & Kegan Paul, 1987.

Restoration and Management Notes. Madison, WI.: University of Wisconsin Press.

Ruff, Allan R. and Robert Tregay, eds. *An Ecological Approach to Urban Landscape Design*. Department of Towm and Country Planning, University of Manchester, "Occasional Paper," Number 8, 1982.

Savage, Jim. "Rolling Back the Pavement." *Probe Post* (August 1986): 10–12.

—. "Greening the City." *Probe Post* (Spring 1987): 22–25.

—. "Greening the City." *Canadian Heritage* (August-September 1987): 31–35.

Tregay, Robert. *Holland 1980: More (And Even Better) Ecological Landscapes*. Report of Study Tour to Amsterdam, Haarlem, The Hague, Delft, and Utrecht.

Whiston Spirn, Anne. *The Granite Garden: Urban Nature and Human Design*. New York: Basic Books, 1984.

Wildflower. A Journal Published by the Canadian Wildflower Society, 35 Bauer Cres., Unionville, Ontario, L3R 4H3.

Wilson, Alexander. "Toward a Culture of Diversity: Politics in the Urban Ecosystem." *Border/Lines*, no. 4 (Winter 1985–86): 38–40.

Wolfe, Theresa, L., and the Tift Farm History Committee, comps. *Tifft Farm: A History of Man and Nature.* Buffalo, N.Y.: Tifft Farm, 1984.

Woodland

Baines, Chris. *How to Make a Wildlife Garden.* London: Garden House, 57–59 Long Acre, London, UK, WC2E 9J2.

Crockett, J.U. and O.E. Allen. *Wildflower Gardening.* Alexandria, Va.: Time-Life Encyclopedia of Gardening, 1977.

Dicklemann, J. and R. Schuster. *Natural Landscaping: Designing With Native Plant Communities.* New York: McGraw-Hill, 1982.

Dorney, Robert, et al. *A Guide to Natural Woodland and Prairie Gardening.* Waterloo, Ont.: Ecoplans Ltd.

Hose, R.C. *Native Trees of Canada.* Ottawa: Canadian Forestry Service, Department of Fisheries and Forestry, 1969.

Sperka, Maria. *Growing Wildflowers.* New York: Charles Scribner and Sons, 1973.

Yonge, J.A and C. Yonge, *Collecting, Processing and Germinating Seeds of Wildplants.* Portland, Oregon: Timber Press, 1986.

Prairie

Ahrenhoerster, R. and T Wilson. *Prairie Restoration for the Beginner.* North Lake, WI.: Prairie Seed Source, 1981.

Aurand, George D. "A Backyard Prairie." *Proceedings of the Eighth North American Prairie Conference.* p. 119.

Currah, et al. *Prairie Wildflowers.* An illustrated manual of species suitable for cultivation and grassland restoration. Edmonton: Friends of the Devonian Botanic Garden, University of Alberta, 1983.

Dicklemann, J. and R. Schuster. *Natural Landscaping: Designing With Native Plant Communities.* New York: McGraw-Hill, 1982.

Dorney, Robert. et al. *A Guide to Hatural Woodland and Prairie Gardening.* Waterloo, Ont.: Ecoplans Ltd.

Lamb, Larry. "Butterflies Aren't Free: A Committment For Establishing a Prairie Garden." *Wildflower* 1, no.2 (Spring 1985).

Madison, J. *Where the Sky Began, Land of the Tallgrass Prairie.* Boston: Houghton Mifflin, 1982.

Morrison, Darrel. "Notes on the Design and Establishment of Prairie Plantings." *Prairie Landscaping: Ninth North American Prairie Landscaping Conference.* p. 55.

Nichols, S. and L. Entine. "Prairie Primer." G2736. Madison, WI.: Agricultural Bulletin Building, 1978.

Restoration and Management Notes. Madison, WI.: University of Wisconsin-Madison Arboretum.

Risser, et al. *The True Prairie Ecosystem.* Stroudsberg, Pa.: Hutchinson Ross Publishing Company, 1981.

Rock, H.W. *Prairie Propagation Handbook.* Milwaukee, Wis.: Wehr Nature Center, Whitnall Park, 1977.

Smith, J. and B. Smith. *The Prairie Garden.* Madison, Wi.: University of Wisconsin Press, 1980.

Weaver, J.E. *North American Prairie.* Lincoln, Nebraska: Johnson Publishing, 1954.

Weaver, J.E. and T.J. Fitzpatrick. *The Prairie.* 1934 Reprint. Nebraska: Prairie Plans Resource Institute of Nebraska, 1980.

Edible Landscaping

Bradley, William. "Permaculture: Re-Greening the Earth." *Regional Priorities* (October 1986).

Creasy, Rosalind. *Edible Landscaping.* San Francisco: Sierra Club Books, 1982.

—. *The Growing City: A Guide to Urban Edible Landscaping.* San Francisco: Sierra Club Books, 1982.

Gessert, Kate. *The Beautiful Food Garden.* New York: Van Nostrand, 1983.

Hall-Beyer, Bart and J. Richard. *Ecological Fruit Production in the North.* C.P. 721 Trois-Rivieres, Quebec G9A 5J3, 1983.

Kourik, Robert. *Maintaining Your Edible Landscape Naturally.* Santa Rosa, Ca.: Metamorphic Press, 1986.

White, Robert. "A Blueprint for a Self-Sustaining Foodscape." *Probe Post* (June 1982).

Groundcovers and Herbs

Bennet, J., ed. *Harrowsmith Gardener's Guide: Groundcovers.* Camden East, Ont.: Camden House, 1987.

Foley, Daniel J. *Groundcovers for Easier Gardening.* New York: Dover Publications, 1961.

Grieve, M. *A Modern Herbal* (Vols. 1 and 2). New York: Dover Publications, 1981.

Hylton, William H. *Rodale Herb Book.* Emmas, Pa.: Rodale Press, 1974.

Jeavons, John, et al. *The Backyard Homestead Mini-Farm and Garden Log Book.* Berkeley, Ca.: Ten Speed Press, 1983.

Taylor's Guide to Groundcovers. Markham, Ont.: Thomas Allen & Sons Ltd., 1986.

Urban Agriculture and Gardening

Ball, Jeff. *The Self Sufficient Suburban Gardener*. Emmas, Pa.: Rodale Press, 1983.

Bartholomew, Mel. *Square Foot Gardening*. Emmas, Pa.: Rodale Press, 1981.

Bennett, Jennifer, ed. *Northern Gardener*. Camden East, Ont.: Harrowsmith, 1982.

Carr, Anna. *Advancad Organic Gardening*. Emmas, Pa.: Rodale Press, 1982.

Dworkin, Stan and Floss Dworkin. *The Appartment Gardener*. New York: Signet, 1974.

Friends of the Trees Yearbook. c/o FOT P.O. Box 1466 Chelan, Washington 98816, USA.

Hall-Beyer, Bart and J. Richard. *Ecologiacal Fruit Production in the North*. C.P. 721 Trois-Rivieres, Quebec, G9A 5J3, 1983.

Hill, Lewis. *Cold Climate Gardening*. Emmas, Pa.: Rodale Press, 1986.

Jeavons, John. *How to Grow More Vegetables*. Berkeley, Ca.: Ten Speed Press, 1982.

Marsh, Deborah, et al. *Pest or Guest? A Guide to Alternative Pest Control in Home and Garden*. Vancouver: Vancouver Society Promoting Environmental Control, 1985.

Munroe, Glen. *The Growing City: A Guide to Urban Community Gardening in Toronto*. Toronto: OPIRG, 1986.

Newcomb, Duane. *The Postage Stamp Garden Book*. New York: Avon, 1980.

Osgood-Foster, Catherine. *Terrific Tomatoes*. Emmas Pa.: Rodale Press, 1975.

Philbrick, Helen, and Greg Philbrick. *Companion Plants*. Devin Adair, 1975.

Riotte, Louise. *Carrots Love Tomatoes*. Pownal, Vt.: Gardenway, 1985.

Rodale's Encyclopedia of Organic Growing.

Somers, Larry. *The Community Garden Book*. Burlington, Vt.: Gardens for All, 1984.

Appendix 3
Selected Organizations and Demonstration Projects

American Community Gardening Association, P.O. Box 8645, Ann Arbor, MI 48107, USA.

Boston Urban Gardeners, Sater Office Building, Suite 831, 20 Park Plaza, Boston, MA 02116, USA.

Bronx Green-Up Program, c/o The New York Botanical Garden, Bronx, New York, 10458–5126, USA.

Canadian Organic Growers, c/o Lida McMartin, 146 Elvaston Dr.

Toronto, Ontario, M4A 1N6.

Canadian Wildflower Society, c/o 35 Bauer Cres., Unionville, Ontario, L3R 4H3.

City Farmer, 801–318 Homer St., Vancouver, British Columbia, V6B 2V3.

Community Fisheries Involvement Program

Ontario Ministry of Natural Resources, Fisheries Branch, 3rd Floor, 99 Wellsley St. W., Toronto, Ontario, M7A 1W3.

Community Wildlife Involvement Program,

Ontario Ministry of Natural Resources, 10401 Dufferin St., Maple, Ontario, L0G 1E0 (funding).

Robert Starbird Dorney Ecology Garden, Faculty of Environmental Studies, University of Waterloo, Waterloo, Ontario, N2L 3G1.

Ecological Parks Trust, c/o The Linnean Society, Burlington House, Piccadily London, UK, W1C 0CQ.

Environmental Training Network for Latin America and the Carribean, Hegel 411–1, 11560 Mexico D.F., Mexico.

Friends of the Spit, P.O. Box 467, Station J, Toronto, Ontario, Canada, M4J 4Z2.

Greater London Ecology Unit, Rm. 442, The County Hall, London, UK, SEI 7PB.

International Institute for the Urban Environment, Nickersteeg 5, 2611 EK Delft, The Neatherlands.

International Tree Corps Institute USA Inc., Route 1, Black Lick Rd. Gravel Switch, KY 40328, USA (agroforestry).

Institute for Local Selfe Reliance, 2425 18th St. N.W., Washington, DC 20009, USA.

Living Prairie Museum, 2795 Ness Ave., Winnipeg, Manitoba, R3J 3S4.

London Ecology Centre, 45 Shelton St., Covent Garden, London, UK, WC2H 9HJ

Missouri Botanical Gardens, P.O. Box 299, St. Louis, MO 63166–0299, USA ($4m demonstration project).

National Institute for Urban Wildlife, 1091 Trotting Ridge Way, Columbia, Maryland 21044, USA.

Neigbourhood Open Space Coalition, 72 Reade St., New York, New York 10007, USA.

New Alchemy Institute, 237 Hatchville Rd., East Falmouth, MA 02536, USA.

The Ontario Herbalist Association, P.O. Box 253, Station J, Toronto, Ontario, M4T 4Y1.

Permaculture Institute of North America, 6488 Maxwelton Rd.,

Clinton, WA 98236, USA.

Planet Drum Foundation, P.O. Box 31251, San Francisco, Shasta Bioregion, CA 94131, USA.

Pollution Probe Foundation Ecology Park, 12 Madison Ave., Toronto,

Ontario, M5R 2S1.

Prospect Park, 95 Prospect Park West, Brooklyn, NY 11215, USA.

Social Ecology Network of Mexico, University of Xalapa, Xalapa, Mexico.

Society of Ontario Nut Growers, R.R.1, Niagara-on-the-Lake, Ontario, L0S 1J0.

Tifft Farm Nature Preserve, c/o Buffalo Museum of Science, Humboldt Parkway, Buffalo, NY 14220, USA.

Tree People, 12601 N. Mulholland Dr., Los Angeles, CA 90210, USA.

University of Wisconsin Madison Arboretum, 1207 Seminole Highway, Madison, WI 53711, USA (prairie restoration).

Urban Development Institute, 73A Mittal Tower, Nariman Point, Bombay 400 021, India.

Urban Wilderness Gardeners, Hill Cottage, 227 Kenilworth Av., Toronto, Ontario, M4I 3S7.

THE MODERN CRISIS
by Murray Bookchin

Here, the "prophet of the green revolution" exposes the under-pinnings of consumerism and contrasts the destructive reality of market economy with the potential for social and ecological sanity offered by a moral economy.

Bookchin may be the orneriest political theoriest alive. He's worth arguing with.
In These Times

Murray Bookchin stands at the pinnacle of the genre of utopian social criticism.
The Village Voice

Paperback ISBN: 0-920057-62-4	$14.95
Hardcover ISBN: 0-920057-61-6	$34.95

NO NUKES
Everyone's Guide to Nuclear Power
by Anna Gyorgy and friends

This book reveals the true costs and risks of nuclear power for consumers and workers. Gyorgy and her many helpers cover the history of "nukes" and their impact on jobs, taxes, and the community. They also introduce readers to wind, solar, geo-thermal, tidal, fossil fuel and other conservation alternatives with discussion of their political implications and economic costs.

Paperback ISBN: 0-919618-94-4	$14.95
Hardcover ISBN: 0-921689-95-2	$29.95

GREEN POLITICS
Agenda For a Free Society
Dimitrios Roussopoulos

An international survey of various Green political parties is presented, featuring their programmes and progress. The result is a stimulating book that challenges accepted ideas about how the world should be organized and suggests the possibility of a safe and more satisfying future for all of us.

Paperback ISBN: 0-921689-74-8	$15.95
Hardcover ISBN: 0-921689-75-6	$35.95

THE CITY AND RADICAL SOCIAL CHANGE
edited by Dimitrios Roussopoulos

Intriguing new essays on the role of the city and city-based movements in the evolution of society. The authors take a fresh approach to urban activism, using specific examples from Toronto, Ottawa and the active community in Montréal. They present the perspectives of those who fight to improve transport, housing and public health, and trace the development of democracy, neighbourhood control and decentralization.

For many years Dimitri Roussopoulos has been one of Canada's most distinguished political analysts of the left ...
City Magazine

A most provocative and engaging proposal.
The Kingston **Whig-Standard**

344 pages
Paperback ISBN: 0-919618-82-0   **$12.95**
Hardcover ISBN: 0-919618-83-9   **$22.95**

THE LIMITS OF THE CITY
by Murray Bookchin
2nd revised edition

"City Air makes people free." With this mediaeval adage, Bookchin begins a remarkable book on the evolution and dialectics of urbanism. Convincingly, he argues that there was once a human and progressive tradition of urban life and that this heritage has reached its "ultimate negation in the modern metropolis."

The Limits of the City *is something of a rarity: a book on real social problems informed by a political philosophy...Bookchin offers, in an admirably brief space, an historical overview of the rise of the bourgeois city. His work is based upon a viewpoint which amalgamates a critical Marxism with a Kropotkinian anarchism.*

194 pages
Paperback ISBN: 0-920057-64-0   **$14.95**
Hardcover ISBN: 0-920057-34-9   **$29.95**

BLACK ROSE BOOKS
has published the following books of related interests

Peter Kropotkin, Memoirs of a Revolutionist, introduction by George Woodcock
Peter Kropotkin, Mutual Aid, introduction by George Woodcock
Peter Kropotkin, The Great French Revolution, introduction by George Woodcock
Peter Kropotkin, The Conquest of Bread, introduction by George Woodcock
           other books by Peter Kropotkin are forthcoming in this series
Marie Fleming, The Geography of Freedom: The Odyssey of Elisée Reclus,
           introduction by George Woodcock
William R. McKercher, Freedom and Authority
Noam Chomksy, Language and Politics, edited by C.P. Otero
Noam Chomsky, Radical Priorities, edited by C.P. Otero
George Woodcock, Pierre-Joseph Proudhon, a biography
Murray Bookchin, Remaking Society
Murray Bookchin, Toward an Ecological Society
Murray Bookchin, Post-Scarcity Anarchism
Murray Bookchin, The Limits of the City
Murray Bookchin, The Modern Crisis
Edith Thomas, Louise Michel, a biography
Walter Johnson, Trade Unions and the State
John Clark, The Anarchist Moment: Reflections on Culture, Nature and Power
Sam Dolgoff, Bakunin on Anarchism
Sam Dolgoff, The Anarchist Collectives
Sam Dolgoff, The Cuban Revolution: A critical perspective
Thom Holterman, Law and Anarchism
Stephen Schecter, The Politics of Urban Liberation
Etienne de la Boétie, The Politics of Obedience
Abel Paz, Durruti, the people armed
Juan Gomez Casas, Anarchist Organisation, the history of the F.A.I.
Voline, The Unknown Revolution
Dimitrios Roussopoulos, The Anarchist Papers
Dimitrios Roussopoulos, The Anarchist Papers 2

send for a complete catalogue of books
mailed out free
BLACK ROSE BOOKS
3981 boul. St-Laurent #444
Montréal, Québec H2W 1Y5 Canada

Printed by
the workers of
Editions Marquis, Montmagny, Québec
for
Black Rose Books Ltd.